Linguistic Analysis of Biblical Hebrew

Linguistic Analysis of Biblical Hebrew

Susan Anne Groom

PATERNOSTER PRESS

First published in 2003 by Paternoster Press

Reprinted 2004

10 09 08 07 06 05 04   8 7 6 5 4 3 2

Paternoster Press is an imprint of Authentic Media,
P.O. Box 300, Carlisle, Cumbria, CA3 0QS, UK
and
P.O. Box 1047, Waynesboro, GA 30830-2047, USA

Website: www.paternoster-publishing.com

British Library Cataloguing in Publication Data
A catalogue record for this book is available from the British Library

ISBN 1-84227-164-4

Cover Design by FourNineZero
Typeset by WestKey Ltd, Falmouth, Cornwall
Printed in Great Britain by Bell & Bain Ltd, Glasgow

We will never reach a fuller understanding of the Great Mystery by analyzing our own human language more thoroughly.

B. Kedar-Kopfstein

Contents

Foreword

When I had to examine an earlier version of this book as a postgraduate thesis, I was most gratified to find that it went a long way towards filling a gap which had concerned me for several years. This was the need for a well-informed and critical, but also accessible, introduction to the use of linguistic methods, especially the more recent ones, for the study of the text of the Old Testament. I learned much from Peter Cotterell and Max Turner's *Linguistics and Biblical Interpretation* but inevitably, given the particular expertise of the authors, it was directed much more to the New Testament than to the Old, where the problems are often rather different. Many who have sought to draw responsibly on the resources of modern linguistics for the study of Biblical Hebrew (Sue Groom among them) have had reason to acknowledge their great debt to the writings of James Barr. His books *The Semantics of Biblical Language, Biblical Words for Time* and *Comparative Philology and the Text of the Old Testament* have become classics of the discipline and his numerous scholarly articles have developed and applied their principles to particular problems. I have benefited greatly from Professor Barr's incisive critique of ill-founded linguistic studies and his penetrating examination of specific issues and Hebrew words. But it was clear to me that a wider dissemination of the important contribution to scholarship which he and others had made would require a concise summary of the key arguments and some exposition in more general terms of sound linguistic method as it could be and had been applied to the study of Biblical Hebrew.

Sue Groom has risen admirably to this challenge. My first thought (a selfish one) was to ask her permission to copy her thesis for my own private use in teaching and the direction of research, but

I was delighted to find that it was going to be published as a book and so made available to a much wider readership. It is a great advantage that she has come to the task after a thorough university training in general linguistics. This made her familiar with a wide range of linguistic methods, whose more general value she had come to appreciate before she ever tackled the specific problems of Hebrew. She was thus in a position to give a genuinely scientific account of the subject, without special pleading. It also means that she is thoroughly aware of the limitations of the various methods and the care that is needed in their application to a particular language and textual corpus, especially when both derive from an ancient context which is by no means as fully known as those of the modern texts (in the widest sense) and languages on which general linguists normally work. She has in addition assembled a bibliography of nearly thirty pages, which will be an immensely useful resource in its own right.

What the book has to offer will be of value to readers of several different kinds. Those who have learned some Hebrew at university or college in the past will find here some fascinating new 'leads' to make their earlier studies more fruitful for the study of the Old Testament and its meaning for today. Even those who know no Hebrew will be able to appreciate much of the argument, because the exposition is admirably clear and the Hebrew examples are translated into English. They may well find an enthusiasm kindled for learning Hebrew, so that they can put the suggestions in this book into practice! In addition to such wider uses, I can see the book serving a very useful purpose in university and college courses and in the training of Bible translators. It combines a clear and critical account of some long-established approaches to Hebrew meanings, which are based on comparisons with other Semitic languages (such as Arabic and Ugaritic) and the use of ancient translations like the Septuagint, with a gentle introduction to newer methods such as lexical semantics and text-linguistics. Such disciplines can seem dry and unduly technical when they are presented in a very theoretical way. Here they are constantly related to examples drawn both from earlier scholarship and from the author's own researches. I can think of no more effective way of enriching the higher undergraduate and postgraduate study of Hebrew at the present time than by the careful study of this book. There is, as Sue Groom says, still a great deal of work to be done on the linguistic study of Hebrew, and it is to be earnestly hoped that her book will encourage a real growth of interest in such scholarship. I am very glad to commend it as a valuable contribution to the better understanding of the Old Testament.

Graham Davies
Professor of Old Testament Studies
Faculty of Divinity
University of Cambridge

Preface

I would like to thank my supervisors, John Goldingay, Geoffrey Khan and Margaret Barker for their patience and encouragement over the years, and also Stephen Travis at St John's College, Nottingham, for dealing so efficiently with the formalities of the Open University.

I have been very grateful for financial assistance from the Arch-deacon of Northolt's CPC Discretionary Fund and the Church of England Deaconess Trust Funds.

And last but not least, the biggest thank you of all goes to my husband Phil for his constant loving support.

Abbreviations

AB	Anchor Bible
ABH	Archaic Biblical Hebrew
AbrN	Abr-Nahrain
AbrN Sup.	Abr-Nahrain Supplement
ANE	Ancient Near Eastern
AnLing	*Anthropological Linguistics*
AOS	American Oriental Series
ArLing	*Archivum Linguisticum*
ArOr	*Archiv Orientální*
ASTI	*Annual of the Swedish Theological Institute*
BA	*Biblical Archeologist*
BASOR	*Bulletin of the American Schools of Oriental Research*
BBR	*Bulletin for Biblical Research*
BDB	Francis Brown, S.R. Driver and Charles A. Briggs, *A Hebrew and English Lexicon of the Old Testament* (Oxford: Clarendon Press, 1907)
BETL	Bibliotheca Ephemeridum Theologicarum Lovaniensium
BETS	Bulletin of the Evangelical Theological Society
BH	Biblical Hebrew
BHS	*Biblia Hebraica Stuttgartensia*
Bib	*Biblica*
BibOr	Biblica et Orientalia
BInt	Biblical Interpretation
BiOr	Bibliotheca Orientalis
BJRL	*Bulletin of the John Rylands Library*
BSac	*Bibliotheca Sacra*
BSOAS	*Bulletin of the School of Oriental and African Studies*
BTrans	*Bible Translator*
BZAW	Beihefte zur ZAW
CAD	The Assyrian Dictionary of the Oriental Institute of the University of Chicago
CahRB	Cahiers de la Revue Biblique

CB	The Computer Bible
CBQ	*Catholic Biblical Quarterly*
CBQMS	Catholic Biblical Quarterly Monograph Series
CH	Classical Hebrew
CILT	Current Issues in Linguistic Theory
CJ	*Concordia Journal*
CSL	Cambridge Studies in Linguistics
CTbL	Cambridge Textbooks in Linguistics
CTL	*Current Trends in Linguistics*
CUP	Cambridge University Press
DSS	Dead Sea Scrolls
EncBrit	Encyclopaedia Britannica
EncJud	*Encyclopaedia Judaica*
ESF	*European Scientific Foundation*
ETL	Ephemerides Theologicae Lovanienses
ExpTim	*Expository Times*
FAT	Forschungen zum Alten Testament
FilolNeo	*Filologia Neotestamentaria*
FT	*Faith Today*
GBS	Guides to Biblical Scholarship
GTJ	*Grace Theological Journal*
HAb	*Hebrew Abstracts*
HAR	*Hebrew Annual Review*
HCompL	*Hebrew Computational Linguistics*
HeyJ	*The Heythrop Journal*
HS	*Hebrew Studies*
HSM	Harvard Semitic Monographs
HTR	*Harvard Theological Review*
HUCA	*Hebrew Union College Annual*
ICO	International Congress of Orientalists
IDB	*Interpreter's Dictionary of the Bible*
IEJ	*Israel Exploration Journal*
IH	Israelian Hebrew
IJAL	*International Journal of American Linguistics*
Int	*Interpretation*
IOSCS	International Organisation for Septuagint and Cognate Studies
ITC	International Theological Commentary
JAAR	*Journal of the American Academy of Religion*
JANES	*Journal of the Ancient Near Eastern Society of Columbia University*
JAOS	*Journal of the American Oriental Society*
JBL	*Journal of Biblical Literature*
JESF	*Journal of the European Science Foundation*
JETS	*Journal of the Evangelical Theological Society*

JH	Judean Hebrew
JIES	*Journal of Indo-European Studies*
JJS	*Journal of Jewish Studies*
JLSM	Janua Linguarum Series Maior
JLSP	Janua Linguarum Series Practica
JNES	*Journal of Near Eastern Studies*
JNSL	*Journal of Northwest Semitic Languages*
JP	*Journal of Philology*
JQR	*Jewish Quarterly Review*
JSem	*Journal for Semitics*
JSOT	*Journal for the Study of the Old Testament*
JSOTS	Journal for the Study of the Old Testament Supplement Series
JSS	*Journal of Semitic Studies*
JThS	*Journal of Theological Studies*
JTT	*Journal of Translation and Textlinguistics*
Lang	*Language*
LangComm	*Language and Communication*
LBH	Late Biblical Hebrew
Ling	*Lingua*
LOS	London Oriental Series
LXX	Septuagint
MH	Mishnaic Hebrew
MSU	*Mitteilungen des Septuaginta-Unternehmens*
MT	Masoretic Text
NAWG	*Nachrichten der Akademie der Wissenschaften in Göttingen*
NICOT	New International Commentary on the Old Testament
NIDOTTE	New International Dictionary of Old Testament Theology and Exegesis
NIV	New International Version
OBO	*Orbis biblicus et orientalis*
OG	Old Greek
OL	Old Latin
OrAnt	*Oriens antiquus*
OrNS	*Orientalia NS*
OTE	*Old Testament Essays*
OTS	*Oudtestamentische Studiën*
OUP	Oxford University Press
PEQ	*Palestine Exploration Quarterly*
PIASH	Proceedings of the Israel Academy of Science and Humanities
PLO	Porta Linguarum Orientalium
Proof	*Prooftexts: A Journal of Jewish Literary History*
PWCJS	Proceedings of the World Congress of Jewish Studies

QH	Qumran Hebrew
QS	Quaderni di Semitistica
RB	*Revue biblique*
SAP	Sheffield Academic Press
SBH	Standard Biblical Hebrew
SBL	Society of Biblical Literature
SBLDS	Society of Biblical Literature Dissertation Series
SBLMS	Society of Biblical Literature Monograph Series
SBLSBS	Society of Biblical Literature: Sources for Biblical Study
SBLSCS	Society of Biblical Literature: Septuagint and Cognate Studies
SBT	Studies in Biblical Theology
ScHier	Scripta Hierosolymitana
Sem	*Semitica*
SIL	Summer Institue of Linguistics
SJOT	*Scandinavian Journal of the Old Testament*
SJT	*Scottish Journal of Theology*
SS	Studi Semitici
SSLL	Studies in Semitic Languages and Linguistics
StB	*Studia Biblica*
StTh	*Studia Theologica*
TPSoc	*Transactions of the Philological Society*
TynBul	*Tyndale Bulletin*
TZ	*Theologische Zeitschrift*
UBS	United Bible Societies
UF	*Ugarit-Forschungen*
VT	*Vetus Testamentum*
VTS	Vetus Testamentum Supplements
WCJS	*World Council for Jewish Studies*
WHJP	World History of the Jewish People
WTJ	*Westminster Theological Journal*
ZAH	*Zeitschrift für Althebräistik*
ZAW	*Zeitschrift für die alttestamentliche Wissenschaft*

Introduction

This book surveys various linguistic tools and methods used by scholars to investigate meaning in the Hebrew Bible with the aim of illustrating a comprehensive and integrated method for the investigation of meaning in Classical Hebrew. It was initially prompted by reading work by James Barr which criticizes some applications of linguistic method to Biblical Hebrew.[1]

1. Basic Hermeneutical Model

In order briefly to set the book within its wider context, the following discussion centres around this basic hermeneutical model:

AUTHOR – TEXT – READER

1.1 The reader

Reading the model from right to left, it is generally acknowledged that the reader may approach the text from any number of different perspectives and the observer's paradox is a reality, that is, the presuppositions, theology, world-view and background knowledge of the reader inevitably influence the resultant interpretation of the text. What a reader gets out of a text, to a certain extent, depends upon what that reader is looking for in the text. This is the current emphasis in biblical interpretation with reader–response criticism whereby scholars deliberately approach the text from a particular standpoint, filling in perceived gaps and constructing meaning from

---

[1] J. Barr, *The Semantics of Biblical Language* and *Comparative Philology and the Text of the Old Testament*.

their response to the text. Literary theorists such as Gadamer are primarily concerned with the reader's historical and social context.[2] That context is seen to be the determining factor in how the text will be understood. They have rejected the notion of an original or stable meaning and jettisoned concern with the text's historical context. This is a product of post-modern culture, 'the text means what it means to me' approach, whereby all interpretations are equally valid.

The Hebrew Bible can of course be read by any person as a literary text, but this reader approaches it from the perspective of faith, believing that these ancient texts remain relevant, that they have something to say about God and about life today. This inevitably influences the way that this book approaches the text. Indeed, part of the incentive for this study has been a response to how some people have been led to understand the biblical texts: if parents take the Proverb 'Discipline your son, and he will give you peace; he will bring delight to your soul' (Prov. 29:17) to be a promise from God, how do they respond when their careful discipline of that son leads to family conflict and anguish as he turns to a life of crime? Was it appropriate for those parents to have read the proverb as a personal promise in the first place? In similar vein, how legitimate is it to refer to Deuteronomy 7 (and comparable passages in the Pentateuch which encouraged Israel to destroy other nations completely) to justify Israel's treatment of the Palestinian people and ethnic cleansing in Kosovo in the 1990s? When a twentieth century scholar claims that Jael seduced Sisera (Jdgs. 4–5) and that details regarding the tent peg can be interpreted as a grim parody of the sexual act, in which the roles are reversed and Jael acts the part of the man,[3] is he merely reading today's world into a text from another age? Is that what the author subtly intended to convey to readers?

The meaning obtained from a text is indeed influenced by the questions asked of that text by the reader. Thus the same reader may ask different questions of the same text at different times and thereby gain different meanings from that text. A brief glance at the range of commentaries on any one chapter of a biblical book reveals a range of possible interpretations. The text is like a multifaceted diamond which can be viewed from any number of angles and therefore produce potentially innumerable meanings. From

---

[2] H.-G. Gadamer, *Truth and Method*.
[3] R. Alter, *The Art of Biblical Poetry*, 49.

the perspective of faith this can be highly disconcerting. Many readers who believe the Hebrew Bible to be the word of God expect that 'word' to be obvious and definitive; they are unnerved to find that it can be interpreted in various ways and provide potentially many meanings.

1.2 *The author*

Scholars have tried to limit the potential meanings of a text by asserting that the real meaning is determined by the author. Reading the basic hermeneutical model from left to right, it is claimed that the author generates the meaning. It is the author who chose the words and provided the sentence structure and who in doing so has created the text; therefore the reader should aim to uncover the meaning intended by the author.

The primacy of Authorial Intention has been vigorously defended by Hirsch who writes, 'Verbal meaning is whatever someone has willed to convey by a particular sequence of linguistic signs and which can be conveyed by means of those signs.'[4] He acknowledges that the meaning of a text is limited by linguistic possibilities, but he insists that meaning is determined by the author's actualization and specification of those possibilities. One of the difficulties with this view is that it is impossible to know the mind of the author, to know how much of that intention was subconscious or how much the choice of words and linguistic forms was shaped by unconscious desires and patterns.

In the case of biblical texts the original human author is unknown and the possible identity of the author(s) is inferred from knowledge gained primarily through the text. Talmon has written,

> Not one single verse of this ancient literature has come to us in an original manuscript, written by a biblical author or by a contemporary of his, or even by a scribe who lived immediately after the time of the author. Even the earliest manuscripts at our disposal, in Hebrew or in any translation language, are removed by hundreds of years from the date of origin of the literature recorded in them.[5]

This is no longer the case since the discovery of some early fragments of late biblical books such as Daniel at Qumran. The

---

[4] E.D. Hirsch, *Validity in Interpretation*, 31.
[5] S. Talmon, 'The Old Testament Text', 161–2.

majority of biblical texts nevertheless have a history of redaction and transmission, so when interpreters claim to have discovered the author's intention, they need to be able to specify which author. Is it 'the original author', a particular redactor like the Deuteronomist, the person or group responsible for the text as it existed at a certain point in time, the Masoretes for instance, those responsible for a particular translation or version of the text like Jerome, or the team which produced the NIV?

Certainly an author brings the text to birth, *someone* made those first marks on the skin, stone or parchment, but thereafter the text exists as an autonomous reality, it becomes an adult in its own right. Once the language has been recorded and subsequently transmitted then it takes on a life of its own; its transmission and interpretation are beyond the author's control. It is debatable whether Ezekiel would have intended his record of his vision of the valley of dried bones to be understood in the way in which many Christians have read it in the light of the resurrection of Christ. As Schökel points out, Ezekiel was a man of his time and culture who was preoccupied with the repatriation of his people and was unlikely to have believed in the resurrection of the dead.[6] Therein lies the distinction between the sense and significance of a text. The sense can be thought of as the linguistically determined meaning, whereas the significance is the importance of that meaning for a reader or readers. As Juhl observes, it is perfectly plausible to suggest that what is inexhaustible about a particular text, which may be understood differently in different ages, is not its meaning but rather its significance.[7]

Some scholars prefer to make a distinction between exegesis, which is the discovery of the sense of a text, and interpretation, which is the explanation of the significance of that text. This distinction is frequently made in the field of homiletics. However, bearing in mind the observer's paradox, this distinction, like the discovery of authorial intention, is an ideal rather than an achievable objective which can be known to have been achieved. The reader is continually making decisions during the process of reading and understanding, decisions which may or may not be conscious but nevertheless influence even the sense attributed to the text.

As Hirsch acknowledges, it is the reader who is in the position to set goals for validity of interpretation and these goals are ultimately

---

[6] L. Alonso Schökel, *A Manual of Hermeneutics*, 35.
[7] P.D. Juhl, *Interpretation*, 31–41.

determined by value preferences.[8] The author can limit the potential meaning through the choice of language but when the text is read the author has no control over the mind of the reader and therefore cannot insist that the text be interpreted in one way rather than another. From the perspective of faith authorial intention remains an appropriate goal for interpretation because it encourages readers to immerse themselves in the language and world from which the texts emerged, to grapple with their linguistic and pragmatic context, to engage with the horizon of the biblical world. As Goldingay notes, the impossibility of total understanding does not negate the worth of attempting whatever degree of understanding will turn out to be possible.[9]

Modern linguistics highlights the fact that the meaning of any word without cotext and context is highly ambiguous. Words are polysemous: the English word 'field' can refer to agricultural land, the influence of a magnet or an electric current, an area of human activity or knowledge, a group of words related in meaning, research conducted away from the laboratory or library, horses in a race, or the players in the non-batting side in a game of cricket. 'Cotext' is defined as the relevant linguistic context (sentences, paragraphs, etc.) within which a word occurs. The surrounding cotext places constraints on the interpretation of an individual word. If the sentence previous to that in which 'field' occurs contains the word 'wheat' then 'field' is understood to refer to agricultural land; if an earlier paragraph discussed the odds-on favourite then it is presumed that 'field' refers to racehorses. Context similarly places constraints on interpretation. 'Context' is defined as the extra-linguistic factors (social, historical, etc.) which influence the production and interpretation of a text. The word 'field' will be understood differently when read in the report of a race from Ascot than when read in a physics paper.

A word has no meaning of itself; it consists of an arbitrary string of sounds or marks: words mean in relation to each other and to the world. Meaning arises from the interplay between language and life. The author both provides the linguistic cotext and lives within the pragmatic context; therefore any knowledge of the author's historical and cultural background can only assist in the process of gaining meaning from the text. After all, no text is produced from within a vacuum, for there is always an author as well as a reader.

---

[8] Hirsch, *Validity*, 24.
[9] J. Goldingay, *Models for Interpretation of Scripture*, 50.

1.3 *The text*

The above sections have looked at either end of the basic hermeneutical model, that is from the perspective, or horizon, of the reader and from the perspective, or horizon, of the author. In attempting to comprehend a Biblical Hebrew text, the student is looking at a different culture in a distant century recorded in a foreign language, and the task for that student is to draw the two horizons as close together as possible along the hermeneutical spiral, without ever knowing if the exact meaning intended by the original author of the text has been identified. The field of hermeneutics is vast and this introduction merely serves to raise one or two important issues which provide the overall context for this piece of work. It has already been mentioned that in the case of biblical texts much of what can be known about the author is actually inferred from the text itself.

It is the text which is at the centre of the model and with which this book is primarily concerned. Texts are encoded in language and the linguistic form of the texts and the limitations on meaning that such encoding enforces are therefore at the heart of this study. The majority of it concentrates on surveying the various linguistic tools and methods which have been applied to Biblical Hebrew. Each theory is described in detail, with an examination of its presuppositions, an analysis of the meaning that it can elucidate, and some suggestions on how it could perhaps be more appropriately employed in the future.

The whole thesis is conducted on the basis of two premises:

1.   A word primarily gains its meaning from within its own language. The text therefore provides the most important clues to meaning.
2.   Words mean in relation to the world and language is used for communication: therefore pragmatic (extra-linguistic) context is also highly significant.

2. Linguistic Theories and Classical Hebrew Data

There are two key ways in which Hebrew texts and linguistic theories can be brought together: these – using terminology from computer programming – are *top-down* and *bottom-up* processing. The top-down approach takes a particular theory, such as the existence of semantic fields within the lexicon, and then searches for words which comprise particular fields within the Hebrew data. The bottom-up approach starts with the Hebrew material and conducts a comprehensive survey of all available data to see whether any semantic fields become evident. Many applications of linguistic theories to Biblical Hebrew have been top-down. Scholars have appropriated useful linguistic tools and techniques, which have (usually) been developed from detailed study of modern European languages, and applied them to Classical Hebrew data. This, however, has been without always taking sufficiently careful consideration of the origin and presuppositions of linguistic theories on the one hand, and the nature of the Classical Hebrew corpus on the other. Computer programmers have concluded that algorithms need to combine top-down and bottom-up processing: they need to have as much information as possible available about both theory and data and at each stage of application to be driven by both.

One problem repeatedly encountered in discussions of Hebrew and linguistics is the lack of agreement in the definition of terminology both within biblical studies and within the discipline of linguistics itself. Careful definition of technical terms is therefore a priority in this book. The nature of the Hebrew data and the foundations of each linguistic theory furthermore are examined in considerable detail (with examples provided in the language(s) on which the theories were developed). Such detail provides the necessary background information both for evaluating whether the application of a theory to Biblical Hebrew is appropriate and for discerning whether scholars working in the field have understood and taken into account the premises and principles of the theory. These considerations are vital because biblical scholars tend to resort to linguistic methods when there is a difficulty in understanding the Hebrew text and they do not always have all the relevant data available for appropriate use of the method.

The first three chapters survey key preliminary issues which need to be taken into consideration when investigating meaning in Classical Hebrew. This commences with a definition of 'Classical Hebrew' and a review of the data available to be included within that corpus (Chapter 1). This chapter seeks to ascertain how informative each different type of material including inscriptions, Dead Sea Scrolls and Mishnaic Hebrew can be to a reader of biblical texts. This is followed in Chapter 2 by a detailed look at the nature of the Biblical Hebrew material itself including the implications of the

Masoretic Text and its history of transmission for the investigation of meaning. There is no one text of the Bible: scholars need to indicate which text they are referring to when discussing the meaning of 'the' biblical text. Each text of course has been produced by different people (authors and redactors). Although the Masoretes have produced a reasonably standard text, the language encoded in that text is not monochrome. When comparing biblical texts in order to clarify the meaning of a word or phrase, scholars also need to be aware of the material discussed in Chapter 3 which looks at the synchronic and diachronic variation apparent within the language of the biblical texts.

One fundamental feature of Hebrew as a Semitic language is the (usually) tri-radical 'root' and the debate about the link between the form and meaning of a root. This is the most important component in any study of lexical semantics in Classical Hebrew because the traditional method of comparative philology has been applied to Semitic languages as if it is based precisely on a correlation between form and meaning in the root. This presupposition has lead to the dismaying tendency to assume that identical forms across languages carry identical meanings within their own language. Chapter 4 therefore includes detailed description of the comparative method with a thorough examination of its linguistic foundations. This is followed by a summary of key factors to be remembered when relying on comparative philology to discover the meaning of Hebrew words. The third section of the chapter provides a brief overview of James Barr's criticisms of the application of linguistic method to biblical texts. The final part lists questions to be answered when proposing new meanings for Hebrew forms based on the practice of comparative philology.

There is a tremendous wealth of material available to assist scholars in extracting as much meaning as possible from a Classical Hebrew text. Not only are there texts encoded in related Semitic languages, but there also exist translations of parts of the Hebrew Bible into languages such as Greek, Aramaic and Latin. Chapter 5 considers the contribution of the versions to the investigation of meaning in the Hebrew Bible. The various translations provide information on how the Hebrew texts were understood, or not (as the case may be), by certain people at particular points in time. Naturally, it must be remembered that the interpretation provided by translators has been influenced by their motives, theology, world-view and linguistic ability. It is vitally important to be aware of the translation techniques employed within each text examined.

This is particularly so when the versions are used as justification for the emendation of the Masoretic Text. The chapter includes an overview of the Greek text of the book of Judges and a more detailed analysis of some of its deviations from the Masoretic Text. It concludes with cautions on using the versions for the study of meaning in Classical Hebrew.

The thesis then moves on to modern linguistic methods. Structural linguistics, stemming initially from the work of Ferdinand de Saussure, views each language as a system of signs.[10] Due to continuing confusion over terminology in this area, the theory is discussed in considerable detail in Chapter 6. Suffice to say at this point that the meaning of a sign is considered to be defined by its relations to other signs within the same system. This principle underlies lexical semantics which concentrates on investigating the meaning of a word by working out which other words it relates to within its own system. As this theory has gained ascendancy in biblical studies, so comparative philology and use of the versions, which rely on other languages to shed light on the meaning of Hebrew words, have decreased in popularity. But more recently cognitive scientists in particular have questioned the validity of linguistic systems. Linguistic categorization is not so clear cut in life: pragmatic context has to be taken into consideration when investigating lexical semantics. Nevertheless, in the last twenty years there has been an increasing number of studies of semantic fields within Classical Hebrew and the fruit of such work has been included in more recent dictionaries and databases.[11] A detailed survey of such material and an analysis of its contribution to the investigation of meaning in Classical Hebrew provide the concluding sections of the chapter.

Clearly biblical texts contain a variety of literature: poetry, apocalyptic, legal and narrative material. Readers benefit therefore from familiarity with the whole of the Hebrew Bible, that is the wider cotext, when attempting to gain meaning from any one part of it. Such familiarity should bring an awareness of how language is used in each genre, of how the various types of literature encode meaning in their choice of both words and linguistic structure. Such awareness should also raise questions about the significance of the author's choice of one particular form rather than another propositionally equivalent

---

[10] F. de Saussure, *Course in General Linguistics*.

[11] Notably, D.J.A. Clines (ed.), *The Dictionary of Classical Hebrew*, vols. 1–4, and ESF Database reported in T. Muraoka (ed.), *Semantics of Ancient Hebrew*.

one. Text linguistics or discourse analysis studies the structure of texts longer than a sentence and Tagmemics is one theory which has been applied to Biblical Hebrew texts. Chapter 7 therefore includes a detailed description of the basic theories of text linguistics, along with definitions of key terminology and a survey of the results of some applications to Biblical Hebrew. It also includes a text linguistic analysis of Judges 4 and an evaluation of the usefulness of such applications in the investigation of meaning. It must be acknowledged at this stage that information gained through the application of modern linguistic methods may or may not have been in the consciousness of those who produced the biblical texts.

This comprehensive review of various linguistic theories and methods which have been applied to the Hebrew Bible in order to obtain greater understanding of these important texts concludes with the illustration of an integrated method for the investigation of meaning in Classical Hebrew. Each method surveyed approaches the text from a different perspective and therefore shines light on different facets of its meaning, whether that be the meaning encoded by the Masoretes, that understood by the translators of the Septuagint, or that derived through modern linguistic methods. It is desirable to combine every available method to gain access to as many levels of meaning as possible.

It must be recognized, however, that there is a limit to the comprehension of a text. It is possible to construct a complete linguistic analysis at every level of the text, but still not quite to understand what it means. That situation may arise due to a lack of knowledge about the topic under discussion, or the precise referents indicated by particular nouns or phrases, or to unfamiliarity with the appropriate connotations for a particular linguistic form, or the inability to recognize a metaphor. It should be remembered that to understand a text is to apprehend both its propositional content and its illocutionary force, the sense and the significance of the communicative act.

Once all the current linguistic theories have been appropriately applied to the Classical Hebrew text, bearing in mind all the available pragmatic knowledge, then the limit of comprehension has been achieved. But as archaeological excavations unearth more artefacts, inscriptions and even texts from the biblical period, and as linguistic theories are refined and applied again to the available Classical Hebrew corpus, and more is understood of the cognate languages, then further elucidation of the meaning of a particular text may be possible. The work continues!

Part One

Preliminary Issues

1

The Data

1. The Corpus of Classical Hebrew

1.1 Definitions

A first task for any study of meaning in Classical Hebrew (CH) is to define the corpus under investigation and thereby clarify what is meant by CH. In defining a corpus pragmatic decisions are made regarding which material should be included therein and which excluded. This is not to deny that the excluded material may still provide important information about the meaning of words within the corpus.

Historically, study has concentrated on Biblical Hebrew (BH), i.e. the Old Testament or Hebrew Bible, because such study was conducted primarily from within the community of faith and prior to this century there was very little extra-biblical evidence of the Hebrew language from biblical times. Even today many who use the term CH are in practice only talking about BH, or even a subdivision of BH.

The confusion over terminology is well exemplified by The European Science Foundation Network which in 1991 was approved for the study of 'The Semantics of Classical Hebrew'. At a meeting of the subcommittee it was agreed that 'Ancient Hebrew' would be used instead of CH because for some people the latter meant only the central stage of BH and the aims of the project were much wider.[1] The stated policy of the network is to include the language of the Hebrew Bible, ancient Hebrew inscriptions, Ben Sira and the Hebrew Qumran texts. The language of the Mishnah may be incorporated at a later date.[2]

---

[1] G.I. Davies, in correspondence, 1.2.1996.
[2] J. Hoftijzer, 'The History of the Data-base Project', 80.

Rendsburg in his work on diglossia refers to 'Ancient Hebrew' within which he includes extra-biblical material. He then employs the term CH to refer to BH.[3] Van der Merwe prefers the term 'Old Hebrew' which he uses interchangeably with 'Old Hebrew Text' and 'Old Testament Text', thus 'Old Hebrew' as used by van der Merwe appears to refer to BH. Yet his article surveys lexica which include data from extra-biblical sources.[4] Other scholars use the term 'BH' and extend its reference to include extra-biblical material. As Lemaire has already observed, the time is ripe for a consensus on terminology and particularly on the definition of the term CH.[5]

This study recommends that the label 'BH' be retained for discussion of all the language contained within the Hebrew Bible. As regards the subdivisions of BH, the terms 'Archaic Biblical Hebrew' (ABH) and 'Late Biblical Hebrew' (LBH) appear to be in general usage (although their precise referents are still debated). It is suggested that 'Standard Biblical Hebrew' (SBH), as used by Young and Rendsburg, be employed to refer to the majority of BH prose from which material labelled 'Archaic' and 'Late' are said to differ.[6] The term CH is then reserved to describe the Hebrew language within a specific time period, which includes extra-biblical material alongside the biblical data. CH can thus be characterized as 'a language phase from the past with a limited corpus'.[7] The introduction of the further term 'Ancient Hebrew' only serves to confuse matters.

The vital question about the definition of CH concerns identification of the cut-off point. Which date appears to be most appropriate? The answer to this question should determine precisely which material is included within the corpus of CH. In the opinion of J.H. Hospers, 'this corpus not only consists of the Hebrew of the Old Testament, but also the old Palestinian epigraphic material written in that same language, and the Hebrew Qumran texts'.[8] James Barr is likewise careful to define his corpus for Hebrew Lexicography: 'I take it we are thinking of a dictionary of Classical Hebrew or

---

3 G.A. Rendsburg, *Diglossia in Ancient Hebrew*.
4 C.H.J. van der Merwe, 'Recent Trends in the Linguistic Description of Old Hebrew', 217–41.
5 A. Lemaire, 'Réponse à J.H. Hospers', 124.
6 Cf. Chapter 3, section 2.
7 J.H. Hospers, 'Polysemy and Homonymy', 120.
8 Hospers, 'Polysemy', 120.

Biblical Hebrew and biblical-type Hebrew: that is, basically it would register the Hebrew of the Bible, of inscriptions of biblical times, of Ben Sira of course, and of such Dead Sea Scrolls as are more or less in a Late Biblical stage of the language.'[9] *The Dictionary of Classical Hebrew* takes CH to mean 'all kinds of Hebrew from the period prior to about 200 CE, that is, earlier than the language of the Mishnah'.[10] This dictionary therefore includes the texts of the Hebrew Bible, Ben Sira, the Qumran manuscripts, inscriptions and other occasional texts. Muraoka in his review of this work points out that there is a growing consensus, especially among Israeli scholars, that there are vital links between BH and Mishnaic Hebrew (MH), at least in the Tannaitic phase when a form of Hebrew was still being spoken.[11] Therefore this thesis recommends that the term CH be used to refer to all Hebrew prior to 200 CE including the language of the Tannaim. The following sections take a more detailed look at the materials included within such a corpus.

1.2 Biblical Hebrew

Traditionally lexica such as BDB and grammars such as Gesenius have taken BH as their corpus.[12] For both Jews and Christians the Hebrew Bible is a recognized canon of Holy Scripture and there is no doubt that as such these texts provide a conveniently restricted corpus of Hebrew. However, this restriction is not random, but 'a restriction to a purposively selected body of literature, a canon of books considered more or less complete'.[13] The choice of this selection was not primarily concerned with the language evidenced by these texts or even the precise form of the texts. It was concerned with their subject matter. The religious leaders of the community determined that the linguistic corpus of BH be restricted to these particular texts.

---

[9] J. Barr, 'Hebrew Lexicography: Informal Thoughts', 138.
[10] Clines, *Dictionary*, vol. 1, 14.
[11] T. Muraoka, 'A New Dictionary of Classical Hebrew', 89.
[12] F. Brown, S.R. Driver and C.A. Briggs (eds.), *A Hebrew and English Lexicon of the Old Testament*; L.H. Koehler and W. Baumgartner (eds.), *Lexicon in Veteris Testamenti Libros*; W.L. Holladay (ed.), *A Concise Hebrew and Aramaic Lexicon of the Old Testament*; E. Kautzsch, *Gesenius' Hebrew Grammar*; P. Joüon and T. Muraoka, *A Grammar of Biblical Hebrew*.
[13] J. Barr, 'Scope and Problems in the Semantics of Classical Hebrew', 5.

One advantage of canonization has been that the corpus of BH has been extensively studied both linguistically and exegetically throughout the centuries. There is an enormous tradition of inter-pretation. But any study of BH has to bear in mind that these texts have been preserved because of their religious significance rather than because of the language in which they are encoded. The actual text has also been highly regarded so it has been preserved with relatively little variation from the standard Masoretic Text (MT).[14] This leads many scholars today to confine their semantic analysis to the MT. Sawyer in *Semantics in Biblical Research* decided that 'the final form of the text as preserved in Masoretic tradition and transmitted to us in the Codex Leningradensis should be the literary corpus in which the terms to be discussed occur'.[15] He then correctly observes that the subject for semantic analysis based on this text is how the masoretes themselves understood the text.[16] Rendsburg likewise continues to maintain that 'as things now stand, the Masoretic Text remains the best source from which to analyse the ancient Hebrew language'.[17]

The relatively small number of contemporary Hebrew inscrip-tions and extra-biblical material has further justified the traditional concentration on the Hebrew Bible as the corpus for semantic analysis. This fact is exemplified by the realization that 'a rather small corpus of inscriptions like the Lachish ostraca is the most extensive single corpus of extra-biblical Hebrew that we have from the period in which the Old Testament was written'.[18] Clines notes that the non-biblical texts referred to in *The Dictionary of Classical Hebrew* are in extent about 15 per cent of the size of the Hebrew Bible.[19] Until the epigraphic discoveries of the twentieth century and particularly the discovery of the Dead Sea Scrolls at Qumran the biblical texts were practically the only available data for the investi-gation of CH. But that is now no longer the case and, as Muraoka has pointed out, to restrict semantic study to BH today hardly makes sense.[20]

---

[14] Cf. Chapter 2.

[15] J.F.A. Sawyer, *Semantics in Biblical Research*, 11.

[16] Sawyer, *Semantics*, 11.

[17] Rendsburg, *Diglossia*, 32.

[18] W.C. van Wyck, 'The Present State of Old Testament Lexicography', 88.

[19] Clines, *Dictionary*, 14.

[20] Muraoka, 'New Dictionary', 88.

The restriction of linguistic study to BH means that the rider 'this is true of the corpus, but we cannot say whether it is true of the language' must qualify all statements about the language. A well-known example of this is the familiar verb בָּרָא 'create', which is used only of divine creativity in the Hebrew Bible. This may not necessarily be true of CH. Semantic investigation of such a limited corpus has been difficult and for the most part tentative. The apparent paucity of lexemes in certain semantic fields may be due to the nature of the restricted corpus rather than the lack of a word in CH. There is for instance no lexeme for 'hour' in BH (although there is in the Aramaic of Daniel); there are five words for 'lion' which are difficult to distinguish semantically, but none for 'cat'.[21] Linguists would expect to find Hebrew lexemes for these phenomena.

Edward Ullendorff in *Is Biblical Hebrew a Language?* concluded that 'Biblical Hebrew is clearly no more than a linguistic fragment. To be sure, a very important and indeed far-reaching fragment, but scarcely a fully integrated language which in this form, with these phonological features, and these morphological aspects, and stylistic and syntactical resources, could ever have been spoken and have satisfied the needs of its speakers.'[22] He could not envisage Hebrew as it is found in the Bible serving as the language of everyday life in the Israelite community. This is hardly surprising considering that the biblical texts were collected and transmitted because they were considered to be Holy Scripture: they were never proposed as a record of the language as it was spoken among the people during biblical times. But this does raise the point that there had to be more to CH, particularly in the area of vocabulary, than is attested in the Hebrew Bible. Ullendorff points to the potential contribution from the language of the inscriptions and particularly the vocabulary of the Mishnah, which he believes records an older oral tradition.[23]

It must be concluded that the BH corpus contains evidence of only a subset of the CH language. This corpus nevertheless remains a rather large subset of the currently available data. It is furthermore a literary creation which was deliberately collected, vocalized and copied by scribes over the centuries, thus resulting in a coherent and convenient linguistic entity. The religious significance of the Hebrew Bible has ensured a long tradition of interpretation and the

---

[21] Examples from Barr, 'Scope', 6.
[22] E. Ullendorff, *Is Biblical Hebrew a Language?*, 16–17.
[23] Ullendorff, *Language?*, 16.

biblical texts therefore provide a very convenient corpus for study in their own right. But, as Muraoka writes, 'Even if one's principle concern is with the Hebrew Bible, one cannot possibly turn a blind eye to contemporary literary remains in basically the same language.'[24] The ideal corpus for the linguistic investigation of CH therefore needs to have a broader base than just the biblical texts.

1.3 Inscriptions

The relatively small number of contemporary extra-biblical inscriptions exhibits several lexical and grammatical features not attested in BH. These were almost certainly features of CH. Ullendorff notes that the Gezer Calendar, which is only seven lines long, produces one major new grammatical variation in the nominal ending ו-, and several lexical idiosyncrasies. He also observes that the Mesha Inscription, Siloah Inscription and Lachish Letters all contain lexical items unattested in BH.[25] However, Sarfatti is surprised at the small number of words and roots found in the inscriptions which were not already known from BH.[26]

Most currently available Hebrew inscriptions date from after the United Monarchy: the earliest Hebrew inscription thus far discovered, the Gezer Calendar, is from the tenth century BCE and the Mesha Inscription from the ninth century BCE. This could be owing to accidents of discovery rather than to any linguistic or historical factors. Rendsburg acknowledges that the relatively small corpus of Iron Age Inscriptions from Eretz Israel has increased knowledge of CH. He follows Albright in pointing out that by and large their language is identical to BH.[27] Sarfatti has even commented that 'Passages from the Lachish Letters could be interpolated into the Book of Jeremiah with no noticeable difference.'[28]

The Hebrew inscriptions contemporary with the biblical period are obviously written in the same language as the Hebrew Bible. There are, however, as noted above, some differences in both morphology and lexicography. To explain these features Knauf has suggested that BH was never spoken as a language, but that it was

---

[24] Muraoka, *Semantics*, x.
[25] Ullendorff, *Language?*, 8–9.
[26] G.B. Sarfatti, 'Hebrew Inscriptions of the First Temple Period', 76.
[27] Rendsburg, *Diglossia*, 32; W.F. Albright, 'The Gezer Calendar', 25; W.F. Albright, 'A Re-examination of the Lachish Letters', 20.
[28] Sarfatti, 'Hebrew Inscriptions', 58.

an artificial literary construct devised by later redactors – a product of the canonization process. He perceives new linguistic evidence from the inscriptions as revealing the great linguistic diversity in pre-exilic Hebrew: 'Nicht nur ist Biblisch-Hebräisch keine Sprache, auch eine "althebräische" Sprache hat es nach derzeitigem Erkenntnisstand nicht gegeben. Was es gegeben hat, war eine judäische Sprache des 8. bis 6. Jh. v. Chr. mit lokalen und schichtspezifischen Dialekten, und waren wenigstens zwei israelitische Sprachen.'[29] Knauf views the Gezer Calendar as an example of the official Israelite language, and the Samaria Ostraca and Deir 'Alla as evidence of local dialects.

Young proposes that the differences between BH and the Hebrew of the inscriptions are due to differences in genre – biblical texts being written in a literary style, while inscriptions are recorded in an official administrative language. He also recognizes the existence of at least a northern dialect and evidence of diachronic variation within the biblical texts.[30] According to Young, the Gezer Calendar displays ABH connections; the Samaria Ostraca are examples of the administrative style of the northern dialect; and the Mesha Inscription is written in the style of a war narrative which is closely related to BH prose. He agrees with Knauf that Deir 'Alla is a peripheral local dialect.[31]

These suggestions about synchronic and diachronic variation within the biblical and extra-biblical parts of the corpus must be borne in mind. Care should also be taken not to place excessive weight on single instances of linguistic features which could result from inaccurate knowledge of the language recorded or errors in its transmission.

One further important factor to be taken into consideration in any linguistic description of the inscriptions is the consonantal nature of the script.[32] Unlike the MT there is no history of scribal study and interpretation. Investigation into meaning in CH therefore has to take into account the differences between pointed biblical text and consonantal inscriptions.

Contemporary inscriptions remain important to the semantic study of CH because they provide both further instances of BH

---

[29] E.A. Knauf, 'War Biblisch-Hebräisch eine Sprache?', 22. Translation towards the end of this book; see p. 175.
[30] Cf. Chapter 3, section 2.
[31] I. Young, *Diversity in Pre-exilic Hebrew*, 203–4.
[32] Cf. A. Sáenz-Badillos, *A History of the Hebrew Language*, 62–8.

lexical items and new lexemes. Linguistic context provides important clues to the meaning of a word; therefore any example of a word being used in a new context assists in the comprehension of its possible semantic range and collocational relations. The inclusion of such epigraphic material in the corpus for CH is therefore to be welcomed.

1.4 Dead Sea Scrolls

The discovery of the Dead Sea Scrolls (DSS) in 1947 was heralded as providing the missing link between BH and Palestinian or Mishnaic Hebrew (MH). Until then the only extant texts from the period were fragments of Ben Sira and the Damascus Documents from the Genizah. Traditionally BH was thought to have died out as a spoken language in the last centuries BCE, while MH was viewed as the literary evidence of continuing vernacular Hebrew.[33] Thus there were two main phases of early Hebrew: BH and its successor MH. Other contemporary varieties of Hebrew were regarded as mixtures of these two types.

The term DSS is used here in the broadest possible sense to refer to the Hebrew material discovered in the Judaean desert. This has been dated from the Second Temple Period (approximately 200 BCE to 70 CE), which falls neatly between Biblical and MH. It has generally been assumed that the Qumran Hebrew (QH) of the DSS was a literary continuation of LBH such as is found in the books of Chronicles.

The DSS consist of both biblical and non-biblical material, with most of the biblical texts being essentially identical with the MT. The scrolls employ *plene* (full) spelling but not vowel pointing. This can leave scholars dependent upon the MT for their interpretation as new texts are read as if they were pointed identically to the MT. But *plene* orthography with vowel letters sometimes reflects a different pronunciation to that of the MT. The DSS have a short history of transmission and their place and date of composition is better known than that of the MT,[34] therefore they provide valuable information about the Hebrew language of the Second Temple Period.

---

[33] E.Y. Kutscher, 'Hebrew Language', 16:1584.
[34] E. Qimron, 'Observations on the History of Early Hebrew (1000 BCE–200 CE) in the Light of the Dead Sea Documents', 353.

The complete scroll of Isaiah has received the most detailed linguistic attention,[35] which tends to take the form of direct comparison with BH. QH is not, however, homogeneous. Morag distinguishes three types of texts: the majority which he labels 'General Qumran Hebrew', the Copper Scroll, and texts showing a close affinity to MH. He concludes that while General QH does have some features which constitute a continuation of LBH, it also possesses a number of grammatical traits which are not related to BH. These, suggests Morag, represent the continuation of old dialectal variation.[36]

The lexicon of the DSS primarily consists of BH words. It also includes MH items and otherwise unknown Hebrew lexemes, along with loanwords from Aramaic and Persian. Qimron maintains that whilst the lexicography of the DSS is influenced by the Hebrew Bible, morphology differs from that of both BH and MH. He notes that QH uses pronouns and pronominal suffixes which differ markedly from those of any other type of Hebrew. QH cannot therefore have been merely a mixture of two major phases of Hebrew. It is, Qimron maintains, independent in character and furthermore contains features which must have evolved in a spoken language.[37]

In recent decades many scholars have called for inclusion of post-biblical Hebrew, particularly QH, in the corpus for study of CH lexicography. In response to this call, some dictionaries have extended their coverage of Hebrew. According to Wyk, the third edition of Baumgartner's lexicon adds material from oriental and Samaritan textual traditions, in addition to the Hebrew text of Ben Sira, the DSS, the Mishnah and Midrash.[38] Barr, on the basis of his experience as editor of the Oxford Hebrew Lexicon, asserts that the corpus taken as the basis for the dictionary includes Qumran materials,[39] so does *The Dictionary of Classical Hebrew*.[40]

The DSS provide many instances of BH lexical items in new linguistic contexts. They also contain evidence of lexemes unattested

---

[35] E.Y. Kutscher, *The Language and Linguistic Background of the Isaiah Scroll*.

[36] S. Morag, 'Qumran Hebrew', 148–64; cf. Sáenz-Badillos, *History*, 130–1.

[37] Qimron, 'Observations', 354; cf. E. Qimron, *The Hebrew of the Dead Sea Scrolls*.

[38] Wyk, 'Lexicography', 90.

[39] Barr, 'Hebrew Lexicography: Informal Thoughts', 138.

[40] Clines, 'The Dictionary of Classical Hebrew', 73–80.

within the biblical texts, which may well have existed within spoken Hebrew of the biblical period. QH furthermore displays a much larger lexicon than BH. Bearing in mind both the synchronic and diachronic variation within this lexicon, the extra linguistic data provided by the DSS remains valuable to the study of meaning in CH and it will be particularly so once a thorough investigation of all the material has been completed.

When the complete data from the DSS is added to that of the biblical texts, the Hebrew represented by that corpus covers a period of over a thousand years. This fails to provide a synchronic sample of the language. It inevitably contains instances of semantic change. Lemaire emphasizes this point: 'On peut accepter d'y inclure les textes hébreux de Qumrân et donc une extension jusqu'au début de l'époque romaine mais, alors, l'hébreux classique devient une langue utilisée pendant un bon millénaire et, dans ce cas, une approche purement synchronique paraît irréaliste et fallacieuse.'[41]

Responding to this problem, Lieberman suggests that this corpus be split into two sections: Early Hebrew which would end with the fall of Judah at the beginning of the sixth century BCE; and 'Judean' or 'post-exilic' Hebrew which would be based on texts from the Babylonian exile to 200 CE when Hebrew ceased to be a spoken language.[42] This approach puts the later biblical books, the DSS and the Mishnah together, thus emphasizing the continuity of the language and at the same time reflecting the historical experiences of Hebrew speakers.

Lieberman's suggestion challenges the traditional view that the biblical texts be treated as a particularly coherent corpus. As mentioned above, however, it is the orthography of the Hebrew Bible which is consistent rather than the language it transcribes. There have recently been several detailed studies of diachronic variation within BH: Young concentrated on pre-exilic Hebrew including both biblical and extra-biblical materials in his corpus.[43] Sáenz-Badillos in *A History of the Hebrew Language* divides his subject matter into 'Pre-exilic Hebrew' and 'Hebrew in the period of the Second Temple', with a separate chapter looking at 'Biblical Hebrew in its various traditions'.[44] Other scholars have concentrated on

---

[41] Lemaire, 'Résponse', 125. Translation towards the end of this book; see p. 175.
[42] S.J. Lieberman, 'Response', 25.
[43] Young, *Diversity*.
[44] Sáenz-Badillos, *History*, vii.

detailed study of LBH.[45] Lieberman's division thus proves to be useful and is to be borne in mind in the study of meaning within CH. But to limit the corpus to either pre-exilic or post-exilic Hebrew at this stage severely restricts the available data. Therefore this book proposes that the DSS be included within the single CH corpus along with BH and the inscriptions.

1.5 Mishnaic Hebrew

Traditionally MH was seen as an artificial revival of written Hebrew, coloured by heavy Aramaic influence. The claim of some that on the contrary MH gave the impression of a living language was upheld by the discovery of the Bar Kochba letters written in 131–4 CE in good MH. As Rabin comments, 'A private document like this would hardly be styled in a language of "pious scholarship".'[46] It is now generally accepted that MH existed as a spoken language long before the destruction of the Second Temple and continued to be spoken until 200 CE.

The sizeable body of documentation in existence demonstrates that in most of its linguistic phenomena MH contains both aspects of BH and elements of Hebrew not attested in the biblical texts. It also contains evidence of Aramaic influence, however, Segal has maintained that as far as grammar is concerned, MH is absolutely independent of Aramaic: it is in fact identical in the main with BH. Where it differs from the latter, differences can generally be traced back to an older stage of the Hebrew language, out of which new forms have developed in a natural and systematic manner. He did not doubt that Aramaic exercised a profound and far-reaching influence upon MH, but argued that this influence was confined to vocabulary and hardly extended to the grammar at all.[47] His position is now recognized to be exaggerated, and some have since argued that MH was a mixed language, or 'langue mélangée'.[48]

The differences from BH are clear.[49] The MH lexicon shares about half of its vocabulary with BH including words for parts of

---

[45] R. Polzin, *Late Biblical Hebrew*.
[46] C. Rabin, 'Hebrew', 318.
[47] M.H. Segal, 'Mishnaic Hebrew and its Relation to Biblical Hebrew and Aramaic', *JQR*, 734.
[48] J. Fellman, 'The Linguistic Status of Mishnaic Hebrew', 22.
[49] Sáenz-Badillos, *History*, 172–3.

the body which would be expected to remain reasonably constant in any language, although even some of these have changed. The Hebrew element of MH vocabulary does include BH words whose meaning has remained the same, BH words which have taken on a different form, and some that retained the BH form but changed in meaning. MH also contains loanwords borrowed from Persian, Akkadian, Greek, Latin and Aramaic.[50]

Kutscher has distinguished two main types of MH: mhe[1] and mhe[2] corresponding to the Hebrew of the Tannaitic and Amoraic periods respectively. The Tannaim includes the Mishnah itself dating back to the time when MH was still spoken. The language of the Amoraim contains far more evidence of Aramaic influence and was written in the period 300–500 CE when MH was no longer a spoken language in Palestine. The mhe[2] material is therefore excluded from the study of MH.[51] The corpus of MH is more or less restricted to the Mishnah but this material has not been without its problems – there are very few early manuscripts, texts generally date from the first half of the second millennium CE and in more recent manuscripts vocalization has usually been adjusted to Tiberian norms.[52] However, discoveries in the early decades of this century have found manuscripts with a much more reliable vocalization.

In order for data from MH to contribute fully to the investigation of meaning in CH there needs to be further systematic study of the MH corpus. Although Baumgartner enlisted the help of Kutscher in preparing the third edition of his lexicon, the resultant effect on the dictionary remains slight.[53] The Dictionary Project of the Hebrew Language Academy in Jerusalem is preparing a comprehensive study of MH lexicography, and Sarfatti has produced a good guide to how the use of a BH word in MH and Mishnaic Literature can offer an important contribution to understanding that word in BH.[54]

To summarize, MH was a living language which developed naturally and systematically out of earlier Hebrew. It is further-more the linguistic medium through which biblical meanings were

---

[50] E.Y. Kutscher, 'Hebrew Language', 16:1603; cf. Sáenz-Badillos, *History*, 199–201.

[51] Kutscher, 'Hebrew Language', 16:1591.

[52] Sáenz-Badillos, *History*, 174–5.

[53] Reported in Barr, 'Lexicography', 138.

[54] G.B. Sarfatti, 'Mishnaic Vocabulary and Mishnaic Literature as Tools for the Study of Biblical Semantics', 36–7.

historically transmitted. To exclude MH from CH, particularly in view of its evident links with both LBH and QH, is to draw an artificial linguistic boundary. Ben-Hayyim, in his periodization of the Hebrew language, considers as one period the span of time from the beginning of biblical literature to the end of the Tannaitic literature when Hebrew was a spoken as well as a written language.[55] It is therefore the end of spoken MH in 200 CE which provides the obvious historical and linguistic cut-off point for the corpus of CH.

1.6 *Proposal of a corpus for the study of Classical Hebrew*

In the light of the above survey of data from BH, inscriptions, DSS and MH, it is hereby proposed that CH refer to the Hebrew language up until the cessation of spoken Hebrew in 200 CE. This period provides a wide and varied range of textual and epigraphic material for the study of meaning. The currently available data includes biblical texts, contemporary Hebrew inscriptions, the DSS, Ben Sira, the Bar Kochba letters and the Mishnah.

Obviously this data does not comprise a homogeneous synchronic sample of the language. This section of the thesis has deliberately taken the bottom-up approach to the investigation of meaning in CH in order to allow the broad sweep of available data to reveal subdivisions of the corpus. It is hoped that careful linguistic investigation of CH will enable scholars to clarify the synchronic and diachronic variation within the data and to propose a more refined corpus for future study.

Whilst the later Hebrew material excluded from this corpus may nevertheless be an important source of information about the subsequent development and interpretation of CH items, the systematic study of Medieval Hebrew began only a few decades ago; its relationship to CH is complicated and such analysis falls beyond the scope of this book.

---

[55] Reported in Sarfatti, 'Vocabulary', 35.

2

The Masoretic Text

1. The Development of the Masoretic Text

When talking about the meaning of the Hebrew Bible, or the Hebrew text of Judges, or the Hebrew rendition of a particular verse, scholars seem to believe they have precisely defined the text to which they refer. Commentaries tend to use the *Biblia Hebraica Stuttgartensia* (*BHS*) as their source material but even that is a critical edition of the text, based on one manuscript (Leningrad Codex B19ᵃ), but with variant readings from both Hebrew texts and texts in other ancient languages incorporated into an abundant critical apparatus.

The Hebrew manuscripts on which printed editions of the Bible are based date from the Middle Ages and derive from the Masoretes of Tiberias. The MT has a long history which can be roughly divided into three stages: a Pre- (or Proto-) Masoretic period; the activity of the Masoretes; and the period of stabilization of the MT. Thus the Bible has passed through several stages in acquiring its present written form. Epigraphic evidence from Hebrew orthography indicates that before the ninth century BCE Hebrew was written in a purely consonantal script based on the Phoenician alphabet of twenty-two letters. Subsequently, a system of final *matres lectionis* (vowel letters) similar to that found in Aramaic inscriptions was introduced. Henceforth, all final vowels were indicated in the orthography. Then during the Middle Ages the vowel-pointing and accents of the present MT were added.[1]

The consonantal text appears to have been fairly consistent since the beginning of the second century CE. Texts from

---

[1] F.M. Cross and D.N. Freedman, *Early Hebrew Orthography*, 56–7; F.I. Andersen and A.D. Forbes, *Spelling in the Hebrew Bible*, 31.

Murabba'at show that by 132–5 CE there existed a single authoritative text. The consonantal framework of the MT is even attested in texts from the Judean Desert dating from the third century BCE,[2] although there is no evidence of Hebrew texts before this time. The broad profile of orthographic practices fixed in the Proto-Masoretic text have been dated to approximately 500–300 BCE. This coincided roughly with the canonization of the Pentateuch and the Prophets. The emergence of this concept of a canon of sacred literature no doubt was the main factor motivating concern for the exact preservation of the text.[3] There is a gap in textual evidence between 200 CE and 900 CE because none of the BH manuscript evidence can be dated prior to the ninth century CE.[4] The vast majority of manuscripts originate from the medieval period. There is nevertheless a remarkable consistency between the hundreds of medieval manuscripts, and between medieval manuscripts and consonantal texts from the second century CE.

There is also evidence of non-Masoretic-type base texts. The biblical material discovered at Qumran was centuries older than that previously found and although the majority of texts follow the Masoretic type, they also provide evidence for a wider variety of text types. Some Qumran texts appear to be related to the Samaritan Pentateuch and others to the reconstructed *Vorlage* of the Septuagint. It has therefore been concluded that by the beginning of the Common Era there were several texts.

Various theories have been proposed about the history of the biblical text. In the nineteenth century Paul de Lagarde assumed an analogous development of Hebrew and Greek texts, whereby one might be able to go back to the archetype in each case. The *Urtext*, the one original text, was thought to be attainable along eclectic lines from existent manuscripts. Variations from the *Urtext* were considered to have derived from the transmission process.[5] Lagarde's sharpest critic was Paul Kahle whose studies of various biblical manuscripts from the Cairo Genizah led him to believe that there existed *Vulgärtexte*, texts which were copied less precisely, if not carelessly, with simplified readings to facilitate use by the

---

[2] E. Tov, *Textual Criticism of the Hebrew Bible*, 27.

[3] G. Khan, 'The Masoretic Hebrew Bible and Its Background', 16; cf. Talmon, 'Text', 166.

[4] M.H. Goshen-Gottstein, 'The Development of the Hebrew Text of the Bible', 209–11.

[5] M.J. Mulder, 'The Transmission of the Biblical Text', 100.

people in general.[6] Albright, and then Cross, recognized the plurality of text-types prior to the first century CE but claimed that this derived from one prototype in existence in the fifth century BCE. Discoveries at Qumran and study of the Pentateuch led Cross to distinguish three text-types: Palestinian, Egyptian and Babylonian.[7] But the decision as to which form a particular text belongs is often subjective, and in Qumran texts two different forms existed alongside one another thus confounding the primarily geographical basis of textual grouping.

Talmon insists that extant text-types must be viewed as remains of yet more variegated transmission rather than witnesses to solely three archetypes. He emphasizes the social aspects of preservation of literature and suggests that the variety discovered at Qumran was due to a collection of people from diverse localities, witnesses to living faith communities. He also points out that variation between texts is relatively restricted with major divergences which intrinsically affect sense being extremely rare.[8] Tov insists that these data do not attest to just three groups of textual witnesses but rather to a textual multiplicity.[9] Barthélemy has further argued that differences are not merely due to different text-forms but also to different redactional traditions.[10] Thus, although the MT provides the standard biblical text today, it rose to prominence from among a variety of consonantal text types most probably in the last part of the first century CE. That is not to say that the MT won a victory but that most religious groups did not exist after the destruction of the Second Temple. The sole group to possess influence was the Pharisees so the only texts to be expected after 70 CE are Proto-Masoretic.[11]

It has already been pointed out that nearly a millennium separates the Masoretes of Tiberias from spoken Hebrew, hence the validity of their vocalization has been questioned. Paul Kahle regarded the Masoretes' work as the creation of an artificial language different from spoken language: 'The Tiberian Masoretes created a correct

---

[6] P. Kahle, *The Cairo Genizah*.

[7] F.M. Cross, 'The Evolution of a Theory of Local Texts', 306–20.

[8] S. Talmon, 'The Textual Study of the Bible', 323–6.

[9] Tov, *Textual Criticism*, 161.

[10] Mulder, 'Transmission', 103.

[11] E. Tov, 'Hebrew Biblical Manuscripts from the Judean Desert', 36; cf. B. Albrektson, 'Reflections on the Emergence of a Standard Text of the Hebrew Bible', 49–50.

Hebrew text which they indicated by a consistent system of signs added to the consonantal text, thereby regulating in every detail the pronunciation and recitation of the text of the Bible.'[12]

More recently, however, a growing number of scholars has seen the MT as authentic tradition with a long history behind it. During the period of the Tannaim there were several crises which contributed towards the establishment of a *textus receptus* (received text): the fall of Jerusalem in 70 CE, the rise of heretics and Christianity and the persecution of Jews.[13] As Sáenz-Badillos reminds his readers, the Soferim were professional scribes. In the era of the Amoraim, the *halakah* (Hebrew literally 'the way' is the vast body of Jewish law laid down in the Torah and by subsequent generations of rabbis.) provided precise guidelines on how the text should be read and recorded, and pauses and accents were introduced without touching the consonantal text.[14] Morag insists that 'as a source of historical information, the vocalisation should be accorded serious consideration'.[15]

A distinction needs to be made between the existence of vocalization and its written marking. The vocal systems and traditional readings were fixed and transmitted orally many centuries before it was necessary to embody them in graphic notation. The Tiberian pointing system grew up from about the sixth century BCE. The Masoretes did not invent the vocalization. What they did invent was a series of increasingly subtle systems for the marking of a reading tradition which was already in use. Barr concludes, the Masoretes were 'in essence phonetic conservators rather than interpretative innovators'.[16]

2. The Choice of Text for Semantic Study

Theoretically there is a choice of three texts for study of BH: the original text written by author, the canonical shape of the text, and

---

[12] Kahle, *Genizah*, 185.

[13] F.E. Deist, *Witnesses to the Old Testament*, 19.

[14] Sáenz-Badillos, *History*, 77; M. Fishbane, *Biblical Interpretation in Ancient Israel*, 24–5.

[15] S. Morag, 'On the Historical Validity of the Vocalization of the Hebrew Bible', 315.

[16] J. Barr, 'The Nature of Linguistic Evidence in the Text of the Bible', 40; cf. *Comparative Philology*, 195–6.

the oldest recoverable text. Textual critics have tended to search for 'the original text': the *Urtext*. Deist points out that search for authorial intention was replaced by search for the original text, then when historical-critical research showed that one could hardly speak of authographia it was replaced by search for the final, canonical reading of every book, because that is deemed inspired and authoritative.[17] But, as Orlinsky succinctly writes, 'There never was, and there never can be, a single fixed masoretic text of the Bible! It is utter futility and pursuit of a mirage to go seeking to recover what never was!'[18]

There has also been a tendency to see the MT as consisting of simply two layers: consonantal text and vocalization. The existence of a purely consonantal Hebrew text remains, however, hypothetical and unattested. Barr prefers therefore to make a distinction between 'base text' and 'pointing' with 'base text' including *matres lectionis* because 'something like 20 per cent of vowels are so marked, and conversely perhaps 20 per cent of the "consonants" written stand in fact for vowels'. The pointing also includes consonantal information: the dagesh (dot in a word) in gemination and the distinction between שׂ and שׁ.[19]

Barr's distinction between base text and pointing is useful when considering the practice of textual emendation of unfamiliar Hebrew words. Some philologists have regarded the vocalization of the MT as less important and less historically accurate than 'the original consonantal text'. Such an attitude has led to a very high regard for consonants coupled with relatively free emendation of vowels in unrecognized lexical items.[20] But the MT cannot legitimately be subdivided into consonantal text and vocalisation. These two aspects are intimately interrelated and have been transmitted as one down the centuries. The current form of the text is due to the most recent revision of the received tradition. Thus, as Payne points out, now to view the consonants alone 'as an almost infallible guide to the original text is nothing but a prejudice'.[21]

Tov reminds his readers, 'Given that the MT is only one among a large number of textual witnesses, one should relate to the biblical text as a large abstract entity rather than placing the MT at the

---

[17] Deist, *Witnesses*, 4–5.
[18] Orlinsky, 'The Masoretic Text', xviii.
[19] Barr, 'Text', 36–7; cf. Khan, 'Masoretic Hebrew Bible', 7.
[20] L. Grabbe, *Comparative Philology and the Text of Job*, 159.
[21] D.F. Payne, 'Old Testament Textual Criticism', 102.

centre of one's approach to it.'[22] He argues that study should be focused on the oldest recoverable text, the text which was regarded as 'sacred scripture' during the period in which the canon came into being. This period lasted from approximately the fourth to the first century BCE.[23] Tov 'does not refer to the most ancient form or earliest literary strand of a biblical book nor to the earliest attested textual form, but rather to the copy (or textual tradition) that contained the finished literary product and which stood at the beginning of the process of transmission'.[24] But, as Deist points out, in practice that means using the MT as the base text and, if it seems corrupt, trying to reconstruct from available evidence the oldest/ best reading in such *instances*.[25] Tov admits that had he used a more practical approach, he should not have aimed at an original text which is far removed and which can never be realized.[26] Mulder mentions the Hebrew Old Testament Project in which a form of textual criticism based on the history of interpretation is applied.[27] This may well produce a feasible text for semantic study.

Meanwhile, however, the MT remains the obvious choice for semantic study. It is the only complete Hebrew Bible text; it has a long history of interpretation; it is the best attested textual tradition, and it is recorded in a remarkably consistent orthography. As Hurvitz explains:

> This procedure is not followed out of an axiomatic belief in the supremacy of the MT, nor does it imply that it has reached us in exactly the same form in which it left the hands of the ancient writers ... However, at the same time it seems to us that a linguistic study whose central purpose is to seek facts and avoid conjectures, should base itself on *actual* texts – difficult though they may be – rather than depend on *reconstructed* texts. These latter are indeed free of difficulties and easy to work with; but we can never be absolutely certain that they ever existed in reality.[28]

---

[22] Tov, *Textual Criticism*, 352.
[23] E. Tov, 'The Original Shape of the Biblical Text'.
[24] Tov, *Textual Criticism*, 171.
[25] Deist, *Witnesses*, 199.
[26] Tov, *Textual Criticism*, 180.
[27] Mulder, 'Transmission', 99, n. 43.
[28] A. Hurvitz, *Linguistic Study of the Relationship between the Priestly Source and the Book of Ezekiel*, 19.

This choice implies that the meaning sought from the text is the meaning of the text at the time its form was fixed in Jewish tradition. In practice the *BHS* text which witnesses to the MT provides data for this study and therefore meaning derived from this text is read through the lens of the compilers of the *BHS*.

3. Reading the Masoretic Text

The division of biblical texts into sections is an ancient one as are some of the orthographic irregularities such as the dots over more than a dozen words, isolated letters which in manuscripts developed into the inverted *nun*, a few suspended letters and some letters which were written smaller or larger than usual.[29] There is also evidence for the antiquity of the accents, the tradition of reading with stresses and pauses.

The purpose of the Masorah, whether it be oral or written, was without doubt the precise preservation of the holy text. R. Ishmael wrote to the scribe R. Meir, 'Be careful in your work, for your work is the work of the heaven; lest by your omitting one letter or adding one letter the whole world be destroyed.'[30] The MT does nevertheless preserve variation. The spelling of many words is not uniform: even the name 'David' is spelt both *defective* דָּוִד and *plene* דָּוִיד. There is furthermore a variation in spelling consistency both within a single book and across books, with the Pentateuch being more uniform in orthography than any other part of the Bible. The noun *tol°dot* 'the generations of' provides an example of inconsistent spelling within a single book. This noun appears in the construct plural form without suffix in Genesis in the following forms: תֹּלְדֹת (25:12); תּוֹלְדֹת (5:1; 6:9; 10:1; 11:10, 27; 25:19); תֹּלְדוֹת (36:1, 9; 37:2); תּוֹלְדוֹת (2:4).[31] The four different spellings of *tol°dot* do not entail different pronunciations and therefore variation would not be audible. On the other hand, variation in the consonants of a word would be likely to make a difference in both sound and meaning: if אַחַד 'one' (construct form) was written instead of אַחַר 'after', then the difference would be noticed when the text was read aloud. Variation in the use of *matres lectionis* does not necessarily

---

[29] A. Dotan, 'Masorah', 16:1406–9; I. Yeivin, *Introduction to the Tiberian Masorah*, 44–9.

[30] Quoted in Dotan, 'Masorah', 16:1413.

[31] J. Barr, *The Variable Spellings of the Hebrew Bible*, 1–2.

represent semantic differences. The *BHS* as it is printed retains such variation in its spelling and this should be remembered when investigating meaning in BH.

The Masoretes were responsible for indicating the division of paragraphs; the accent signs indicating the musical cantillation of the text and position of the main stress in a word; they wrote notes on the text in margins and added treatises to some manuscripts.[32] The result of their work, the Masorah, is commonly divided into *Masorah Parva* and *Masorah Magna*. In essence the *Masorah Magna* complements the *Masorah Parva*, being a more detailed explanation and expansion of the latter.

The most important notes for reading the text are those concerning the *kethib* and *qere*. These demonstrate that the Masoretes themselves were aware of variations within the material they worked on. The consonants of one word were written (*kethib*) in the text proper, but together with the vowels of another word or form of the same root. The consonants of the other form were written in the margin. The vowels in the text and the consonants in the margin were to be read together to form the *qere*.[33] The consensus of opinion has been that the *qere* represents a correction of the *kethib*. Orlinsky's close investigation of all instances of *kethib–qere* in the MT, however, does not accord with this view. He suggests that virtually all *kethib–qere* readings are actually textual variants of the kind scribes might bring in unintentionally.[34]

The overall picture according to Gordis is rather more complicated. He notes that there are a number of passages in which the *kethib* in one instance serves as the *qere* in another. There are also instances where the *kethib* occurs without the *qere*, passages where the same word occurs several times, some marked by a *qere* and others not, sometimes *qere* with regard to a *kethib* which causes no difficulty and instances where the *qere* creates a *hapax legomenon* and the *kethib* is the normal form.[35] Such observations led him to conclude that there were several stages in the development of *qere*. The first stage marks the *qere* as a warning to the reader, for instance to avoid blasphemy, or to ensure 'clean speech'. The next level attempted to deal with the problem of reading the Hebrew text

[32] Khan, 'Masoretic Hebrew Bible', 2.
[33] H.M. Orlinsky, 'The Origin of the Kethib–Qere System', 184–5.
[34] Orlinsky, 'Origin', 188; cf. Orlinsky, 'Masoretic Text', xxv–xxvi; Tov, *Textual Criticism*, 58–63.
[35] R. Gordis, *The Biblical Text in the Making*.

without vowels. A word written *defective* in the text, was written *plene* in the margin. Subsequently the system of annotations in the margin was used to record variant readings of certain manuscripts. Gordis points out that lack of uniformity in orthography provides further evidence that the Masoretes were not concerned with correction or improvement of the text, but rather its preservation in the form it had reached them.[36]

Barr questions the whole idea of *kethib–qere* being concerned with correction or textual collation. He argues that *kethib–qere* are to do with reading the text. He observes first that difference between the *kethib* and *qere* is very seldom a difference purely of vocalization of identical consonantal skeleton, rather a *kethib–qere* always involves a difference in *consonantal* writing, even a small one. Secondly, the mere difference between *plene* and *defective* spelling of words is not normally the subject of *kethib–qere* variation. He emphasizes that in the vast majority of cases the difference between *kethib* and *qere* is a difference of *one* element only in the consonantal text, that is, the alteration or transposition of a single letter.[37] Thus the *kethib–qere* system is interested in words that have only minimal difference in form, whether they make a big semantic difference or not. In Judges 4:11 for instance, the *kethib* בְּצַעֲנַ֫יִם is to be read *qere* בְּצַעֲנַנִּים as in Joshua 19:33, giving both a different syntax and meaning.[38]

Dotan distinguishes four main types of *qere*: euphemisms dating back to when Hebrew was a spoken language and strong language was changed to euphemisms; the correction of forms, where archaic forms or grammatically exceptional forms are substituted by a standard one; the correction of errors, which were likely to be of various types such as metathesis, substitution of letters, the omission or addition of letters, changes in the division of the words or even the substitution of whole words; and changes in writing because of *matres lectionis*. He also comments on the *qere perpetuum* which were not noted but rather handed down orally from generation to generation. These include the name of God, the tetragrammaton, which is pronounced differently from the way it is written.[39] Other notes in the *Masorah Parva* point out forms which may cause the reader or copyist to err. They are concerned

---

[36] Gordis, *Biblical Text*, xxviii.
[37] J. Barr, 'A New Look at Kethibh–Qere', 24–5.
[38] Cf. Chapter 5, section 2.4.
[39] Dotan, 'Masorah', 16:1421, cf. Yeivin, *Introduction*, 56–60.

with the precise lettering of the text and are descriptive rather than directive, recording for instance the number of times a particular word is spelt *defective* rather than *plene*.[40] It is in this respect that the greatest number of mutual discrepancies between the various manuscripts exist.

The accent signs marked above and below words in the MT indicate the music of biblical chant, the interrelationship of words in the text and the position of stress, which can be crucial for determining meaning.[41] Disjunctive accents mark the last word of a clause or phrase, indicating a pause or break in the sense. Conjunctive accents are marked on words between disjunctives, showing that they form part of the phrase ending at the next disjunctive. According to Wickes's 'Law of Continuous Dichotomy', the division of a verse is always into two, and dichotomy continues time after time until there remain in each small unit only one word or two joined by a conjunctive accent.[42] The accentuation system is purely relational: it marks only constituent breaks and provides no labels for them. This purely binary system may seem simplified when compared with phrase structure trees of modern syntax, but such a system proves to be ideal for computer analysis of sentence structure.

The accents can be crucial to meaning for they indicate how a verse should be interpreted: in Deuteronomy 26:5 the disjunctive accent on the first word of the clause אֲרַמִּי אֹבֵד אָבִי indicates that it is syntactically separated from the following word and so should be interpreted as subject and predicate rather than noun and attributive adjective. The sense is therefore 'An Aramean was seeking to destroy my father' and not 'My father was an Aramean about to perish'.[43]

The marking of paragraphs by the Masoretes divided text according to content. The *parasha petuha* (open paragraph, indicated by פ) started on a new line, leaving the preceding line partly or wholly blank, and marked a major division in content. The *parasha setumah* (closed paragraph, indicated by ס) began part way through a line after a space of nine letters, and marked a subdivision of the *petuha*.[44] פ appears at the end of Judges 4, although its predecessor is

---

[40] Yeivin, *Introduction*, 64–5.
[41] Yeivin, *Introduction*, 158.
[42] M. Aronoff, 'Orthography and Linguistic Theory', 34; cf. Yeivin, *Introduction*, 172; Dotan, 'Masorah', 16:1454–5.
[43] Cf. Khan, 'Masoretic Hebrew Bible', 22.
[44] Cf. Dotan, 'Masorah', 16:1407; Tov, *Textual Criticism*, 50–1.

after 3:11 before Ehud is introduced as the deliverer of Israel. ס appears at the beginning of chapter 4, after verse 3 and after verse 12. These divide the content of the chapter into the Israelites' initial cry to God, the introduction of key characters Deborah, Barak and Heber, and defeat of the enemy.[45]

A familiarity with the various types of notation in the MT assists the reader in seeing how the Masoretes understood the structure of the text on which they worked. But, as Yeivin points out, the function of the Masorah, which describes the text in order to preserve the tradition, is not that of grammar, which describes the language. By its very nature the Masorah does nevertheless contain much grammatical information.[46]

4. Textual Transmission

The MT has been transmitted by scribes over centuries. The process of copying often resulted in unintentional 'errors', but also granted opportunity for intentional alteration of the text. Talmon points out that in ancient Hebrew literature no hard-and-fast lines can be drawn between authors' conventions of style and tradents' and copyists' rules of reproduction and transmission. Rather than viewing the professional scribe as merely a slavish copyist of the material he handled, Talmon suggests he should be considered a minor partner in the creative literary process.[47] An example of scribal change for theological reasons is replacement of the name בעל in theophoric names to בשת 'shame' at a later date when the original text with בעל was clearly considered theologically undesirable. Thus in Chronicles the original form is often retained whilst in parallel passages in Samuel it has been changed.[48] The *tiqqune sopherim*, according to rabbinic tradition, are places where scribes changed the original text in order to avoid expressions which might seem disrespectful to God.[49] But as McCarthy points out the

---

[45] Cf. Chapter 7, section 2.7.

[46] Yeivin, *Introduction*, 153.

[47] Talmon, 'Textual Study', 381.

[48] Khan, 'Masoretic Hebrew Bible', 17; cf. C. McCarthy, *The Tiqqune Sopherim and Other Theological Corrections in the Masoretic Text of the Old Testament*, 214–15; Fishbane, *Biblical Interpretation in Ancient Israel*, 66–7.

[49] Yeivin, *Introduction*, 49.

majority of cases are not genuine emendations and not even genuine euphemisms. She concludes that this tradition belongs more to Midrash than to Masorah but is useful because it draws attention to the fact that there were genuine scribal emendations.[50]

Simple mechanical errors may be due to mistakes in reading or writing. The most frequent cause of such errors is confusion of similar letters. In Hebrew square script the following might be confused: ב and כ, ד and ר, ה and ח, י and ו. In Old Hebrew script י might be confused with ה. In Isaiah 9:8 the MT reads וְיָדְעוּ הָעָם כֻּלּוֹ 'But all the people *knew*' whereas 1QIsaᵃ reads וירעו העם כלו 'But all the people *shouted*'. Adjacent letters might be transposed. A letter or word may be omitted, particularly where it is repeated (haplography). In Isaiah 26:3–4 the MT reads כִּי בְךָ בָּטוּחַ בִּטְחוּ בַיה' 'for in You it trusts. Trust in the LORD …' whereas 1QIsaᵃ reads כי בכה בטחו בה' 'for in You. Trust in the LORD …' A single occurrence may be accidentally repeated (dittography) as in Isaiah 30:30 where the MT reads וְהִשְׁמִיעַ ה' 'then the LORD shall make heard', whereas 1QIsaᵃ reads השמיע השמיע ה' 'then the LORD shall make heard shall make heard'. Where two words have similar endings the scribe may start with the first item and miss the intervening text to continue with the ending of the second word (homoioteleuton). Errors were also made with respect to word divisions.

All of these possible alterations to the text have to be considered when a word or form is unrecognized or does not make sense in its current context. The linguistic cotext always provides vital clues about the expected lexical item. When an appropriate word is not evident, but the orthography of the extant word is similar to that of the expected item, then the possible presence of a simple scribal error should be investigated. As the above examples illustrate, the comparison of 1QIsaᵃ with the MT of Isaiah has confirmed the existence of many such errors.[51]

---

[50] McCarthy, *Tiqqune Sopherim*, 246.
[51] Cf. Tov, *Textual Criticism*, ch. 4.

3

The Nature of Biblical Hebrew

It has been observed that BH contains traces of both synchronic and diachronic variation.

1. Diglossia

One proposed linguistic distinction is that between the prestige literary language and the vernacular. According to this view, the continuum of LBH and QH is considered to be an artificial literary creation, whilst the vernacular is found in speech, records, letters, documents and the Mishnah.[1] Some scholars have gone as far as retrojecting this phenomenon into pre-exilic Hebrew.[2] Such co-existence of two varieties of the same language is called diglossia, a term Ferguson introduced:

> Diglossia is a relatively stable language situation in which, in addition to the primary dialects of the language (which may include a standard or regional standards), there is a very divergent, highly codified (often grammatically more complex) superposed variety, the vehicle of a large and respected body of written literature, either of an earlier period or in another speech community, which is learned largely by formal education and is used for most written and formal spoken purposes but is not used by any sector of the community for ordinary conversation.[3]

Ferguson identifies several important characteristics of diglossia including specialization of function for High and Low varieties of

---

[1] Lieberman, 'Response', 26.
[2] Rendsburg, *Diglossia*; Young, *Diversity*, 74–5.
[3] C.A. Ferguson, 'Diglossia', 336.

the language: political speeches and poetry are written in the High variety, whilst personal letters and folk literature appear in the Low variety. There are always extensive differences between the grammatical structures of High and Low varieties.[4] Rendsburg has identified twelve grammatical points which he claims are character-istic of ancient spoken Hebrew (Low) but not of ancient written Hebrew (High).[5] He collected examples of divergences from BH grammatical norm which appear within biblical texts yet anticipate standard usages in MH. These usages are explained as colloquial-isms of spoken MH which have penetrated the written High compositions of the Bible.[6]

Rendsburg concludes that colloquialisms are less likely to appear in poetry or cultic language, although they are more freely employed in prose. He also observes that more colloquialisms are present in later biblical material and books which may be of north-ern origin.[7] The standard explanation for occurrence of these unusual grammatical features in BH has been that they are evidence of later composition, but Rendsburg's study shows that the situation is not that simple. He does not, however, prove that these unusual features are typical of MH and that MH was there-fore spoken in biblical times.[8] Young approaches the subject of diglossia in pre-exilic Hebrew from the perspective of the origins of BH. He argues that Israel had adopted a super-tribal literary prestige language on entering Canaan which remained relatively static whilst spoken dialects diverged. Thus, he claims, there was diglossia at the very beginning of Israelite history.[9] His hypoth-esis is more difficult to verify because of the relative paucity of appropriate linguistic data.

One further striking feature of diglossia is the existence of many paired lexical items, one High and one Low, referring to fairly common concepts frequently used in both High and Low varieties of the language. The range of meaning of the two items is roughly the same, and use of one or the other immediately stamps the utter-ance or text as High or Low.[10] Rendsburg, however, assumes that

---

[4] Ferguson, 'Diglossia', 333.
[5] Rendsburg, *Diglossia*, 151–2.
[6] G.A. Rendsburg, 'The Strata of Biblical Hebrew', 84.
[7] Rendsburg, *Diglossia*, 157–70.
[8] Cf. Young, *Diversity*, 76–7.
[9] Young, *Diversity*, 87–91.
[10] Ferguson, 'Diglossia', 334.

vocabulary differences are not always that great between written and spoken versions of a language.[11] Therefore he does not consider lexical data. Young likewise makes no comparison between the vocabulary of the High and Low varieties. If it is assumed that MH is a continuation of an earlier low variety of Hebrew then there needs to be a detailed study of MH lexicography and for the results to be compared to BH lexicography.

According to Ferguson, diglossia is likely to come about when the following three conditions hold: (1) there is a sizeable body of literature in the language, and this literature embodies some of the fundamental values of the community; (2) literacy is limited to a small elite within the community; (3) a period of several centuries passes from the establishment of (1) to (2).[12] These conditions held for Hebrew in the Second Temple Period, resulting in the recognized diglossia between BH and MH. Diglossia typically persists for at least several centuries.[13] The existence of diglossia in Hebrew was curtailed by destruction of the temple in 70 CE and exile of the intelligentsia. Although this may have acted as a catalyst in the preservation of the literature, it meant the dispersion of those who had intimate knowledge of BH. This gap made way for the rise of MH to become the standard written variety.

Discussions about literary language, the existence of an Official Hebrew style and diglossia all impinge on lexical semantics as the meaning of a word is dependent upon both its pragmatic and linguistic context. Genre can dictate how a text is to be interpreted. It puts certain expectations on the possible semantic range and connotations of a word. In the Official Hebrew style of the inscriptions, a more expository form of language, words would be expected to adhere to their literal sense and usual denotation, rather than being stretched in meaning by employment in metaphor. The proposed existence of diglossia within the CH corpus calls for more detailed linguistic investigation of the two main literary collections and for further comparison of the lexica of literary and colloquial varieties of the language. Such study is inevitably restricted to a certain extent by the relatively limited amount of data providing evidence of colloquial Hebrew during the biblical period.

---

[11] Rendsburg, *Diglossia*, 26–7.
[12] Ferguson, 'Diglossia', 338.
[13] Ferguson, 'Diglossia', 332.

2. Diachronic Variation

The corpus for CH outlined above (Chapter 1, section 6) covers a large span of time. Language changes over time but it does not evolve at a constant rate: vocabulary is more subject to change than grammar. A lexicon may gain new items, lose old ones, borrow a few from its neighbours, alter the connotations of a particular word, and change the shape of its semantic fields. Language change is influenced by developments in society such as new inventions and linguistic contacts.

There has been a tendency to divide the history of the Hebrew language into chronological time slots according to the available collections of literature. The Bible, Mishnah and Dead Sea Scrolls provide convenient linguistic corpora, but they are collections of literature, rather than language data from specific historical periods. Traditionally BH has been judged the precursor of MH and other data were fitted into this basic time frame. However, with the proposal that these two varieties of Hebrew comprise an instance of diglossia, the situation should be reviewed.

Scholars have recognized diachronic variation within BH. Traditionally this has led to the distinction between pre-exilic and post-exilic Hebrew. More recently, however, Kutscher and others have preferred to distinguish three historical phases: Archaic Biblical Hebrew (ABH), Standard Biblical Hebrew (SBH), and Late Biblical Hebrew (LBH) respectively.[14] In recent decades there have been several detailed studies which attempt to isolate ABH and LBH isoglosses and thereby identify a corpus for each phase of the language.

There is not as yet a definitive corpus of ABH. Texts such as the Song of Deborah (Jdgs. 5), Song of the Sea (Ex. 15) and some psalms tend to be labelled 'early'.[15] But, there are no agreed criteria for explaining why a particular text is ABH. The general method appears to treat the majority of biblical texts as the corpus of SBH. The scholar then seeks collections of texts which share a number of linguistic features differing from the norm. This group of texts are then labelled 'early' by virtue of extra-linguistic factors. Henceforth they are deemed to constitute evidence of ABH.

Robertson sought to discover whether any biblical poetry could be dated from the thirteenth to the tenth century BCE.[16] His method

---

[14] E.Y. Kutscher, *A History of the Hebrew Language*, 12.
[15] Sáenz-Badillos, *History*, 56–7.
[16] D.A. Robertson, *Linguistic Evidence in Dating Early Hebrew Poetry*, ix.

was to reconstruct the nature of early poetry by a correlation of rare grammatical features of biblical poetry as a whole with Ugaritic poetry and the Amarna glosses.[17] He then compared the reconstructed early poetry with the biblical standard. Robertson discovered that Exodus 15, Deuteronomy 32 and Job resemble early poetry, but only Exodus 15 shows a consistent use of archaic linguistic elements. All other texts which are assumed to be ABH show a mixture of elements of ABH and SBH, thus suggesting the influence of archaizing tendencies.[18] The only linguistic distinction that Robertson could draw between ABH and SBH was the clustering of archaic elements in ABH. For, as Robertson himself points out, a single rare form is not necessarily an old one.[19]

The Song of Deborah (Jdgs. 5) is still referred to as one of the oldest parts of the Bible dating from the twelfth or thirteenth century BCE.[20] It exhibits many ABH features: in verse 7 the form שַׁקַּמְתִּי illustrates both the archaic relative pronoun ־שֶׁ (Akkadian *ša*) and the second feminine singular suffix ־תִי. This poem uses ־שֶׁ to the exclusion of the SBH form אֲשֶׁר.[21] The demonstrative pronoun זֶה (possibly equivalent to Ugaritic and Arabic *ḏū*) occurs in verse 5 in the phrase זֶה סִינַי 'the one of Sinai'.[22] Verse 10 illustrates the Aramaic plural ending in מִדִּין and תִּשְׁלַחְנָה in verse 26 illustrates the *nun energicum* of Arabic.[23]

Robertson's study concentrated on grammatical and morphological features. Little work appears to have been done on the lexicography of ABH. Young remarks that it contains *hapax legomena* and that some common words seem to have significantly different meaning in their ABH context.[24] He does not, however, provide any examples. Kutscher lists some poetic lexical items which can be paired with SBH counterparts. He notes that many of them share roots with Canaanite and Ugaritic.[25] ABH vocabulary in Judges 5 includes מחץ 'to strike, smite' (v. 26; SBH הכה but see section 3), רֹזְנִים 'princes' (SBH שַׂר) and אזן (v. 3; but in parallelism

[17] Robertson, *Linguistic Evidence*, 5.
[18] Robertson, *Linguistic Evidence*, 135.
[19] Robertson, *Linguistic Evidence*, 4.
[20] Sáenz-Badillos, *History*, 35.
[21] Except for possibly v. 27; cf. R.G. Boling, *Judges*, 115.
[22] Cf. Joüon and Muraoka, *Grammar*, vol. 2, 533.
[23] Cf. Joüon and Muraoka, *Grammar*, vol. 1, 173.
[24] Young, *Diversity*, 129.
[25] Kutscher, *History*, 80.

with SBH שׁמע). SBH גדול 'great' occurs twice where ABH כָּבִיר might be expected.

Young concludes that, 'ABH is a style of Hebrew (poetry) which exhibits a markedly freer employment of archaic and dialectal forms than is the case in SBH'.[26] This raises the question whether it is possible to identify an ABH reflecting an earlier stage of Hebrew than SBH, or whether ABH features are evidence of a different poetic style.[27]

Moving to post-exilic or LBH, the core of this corpus is more easily defined. Texts which are indisputably late are the books of Chronicles, Ezra–Nehemiah, Esther and Daniel.[28] Polzin adds Ben Sira for his study of LBH.[29] One problem with respect to this corpus is that the books of Chronicles provide two-thirds of the available data, thus there is a danger that LBH is basically the Hebrew of the Chronicler. The corpus can be expanded by including the post-exilic works Ezekiel, Haggai and Zechariah and even the DSS, although inclusion of the last needs to be combined with consideration of their unique characteristics. Rooker includes the DSS and MH as part of the LBH corpus in his investigation of the language of Ezekiel.[30]

There appear to be two basic and contradictory approaches to the study of LBH: Hurvitz insists that parallel passages in the Bible are the most important aids for diachronic research and he also believes that lexicographical differences are good indicators in distinguishing pre-exilic from post-exilic Hebrew.[31] Polzin refuses to use synoptic texts in the belief that he can thereby get back to the language of the Chronicler, and he maintains that grammatical–syntactical distinctions provide more objective criteria than lexicographical features.[32] Rooker looks at both grammatical and lexical features. He defines two linguistic principles for dating BH texts: linguistic contrast or opposition, and linguistic distribution.[33]

---

[26] Young, *Diversity*, 123.
[27] Cf. Sáenz-Badillos, *History*, 61–2.
[28] Young, *Diversity*, 82; cf. Sáenz-Badillos, *History*, 114–15.
[29] Polzin, *Late*.
[30] M. Rooker, *Biblical Hebrew in Transition*.
[31] A. Hurvitz, 'Linguistic Criteria for Dating Problematic Biblical Texts', 74–9.
[32] Polzin, *Late*.
[33] Rooker, *Transition*, 55.

Polzin distinguished nineteen features of LBH, thirteen of which are not attributable to Aramaic influence. He concluded that there is a diachronic contrast between P and not-P. Hurvitz also concluded that P is totally independent of exilic and post-exilic writings and the special priestly terminology which is characteristic of them. He places P chronologically before Ezekiel and the later books of Chronicles.[34] Rooker discovered twenty late grammatical features and seventeen late lexical features in the book of Ezekiel. However, these do not appear to the exclusion of contrasted earlier features. All of the early grammatical features also appear in the book of Ezekiel, as do eleven early lexical features. Thus, given the fact that Ezekiel contains many late biblical features, but not to the extent of other LBH books, Rooker concludes that Ezekiel is better understood as a transitional work.[35] Despite their differing methodology all three scholars have agreed on the relative dating of the material concerned.

Kutscher notes that quite a few words which are common in MH first appear in LBH. Not all of the innovations, however, are evidenced in MH. He also observes that some SBH verbs have undergone a change in meaning in LBH.[36] Thus there is evidence of diachronic variation in word meaning within BH, particularly with respect to dating relative to the exile.

The identification of lexemes and expressions identified as 'Aramaisms' has traditionally been considered evidence of the late date of a text. This conclusion has been enforced by increased similarity between MH and Aramaic. However, it has also been observed that many features of ABH resemble Aramaic. Thus the equation Aramaism = evidence of lateness is no longer valid. Rather, as Hurvitz suggests, an Aramaism in BH may be used as a criterion of lateness only when it is evaluated in the light of other linguistic phenomenon associated with that text,[37] hence Polzin's distinction between those features of LBH considered to be due to Aramaic influence and those which were not. Young, however, points out that Hebrew and Aramaic share too many isoglosses at

---

[34] A. Hurvitz, 'The Evidence of Language in Dating the Priestly Code', 47; cf. Hurvitz, *Linguistic Study*; G.A. Rendsburg, 'Late Biblical Hebrew and the Date of "P"'.

[35] Rooker, *Transition*, 182–4.

[36] Kutscher, *History*, 82–5.

[37] A. Hurvitz, 'The Chronological Significance of "Aramaisms" in Biblical Hebrew', 240.

various levels to be readily distinguishable. He therefore concludes that Aramaisms do not contribute to the dating of a late text because they are Aramaisms; rather it is because they occur in linguistic opposition to a SBH item that they can be evidence of LBH.[38] It must not be forgotten that Aramaic would also have been changing during the CH period.

Gervitz notes that linguistic features which have been considered characteristic of LBH are being increasingly identified in early documents of northern origin. He concludes therefore that such linguistic features are merely free variants.[39] Gordon had earlier proposed that such northernisms had reached the post-exilic authors in Babylonia and Persia via northern Israelite tribes who had been in exile since the eighth century BCE in the Assyrian Empire. These exiled tribes must have retained their identity and so survived to join Judean exiles in Neo-Babylonian times. Thus, Gordon views the sharp break between pre-exilic and post-exilic prose to be due largely to the impact of northern Israelite exiles.[40] Young, however, tackles the issue from another angle. He suggests that it was establishment of the centralized monarchy which caused the change of emphasis in SBH leading to avoidance of earlier Aramaisms and dialectal variations.[41] It was the exile which subsequently put an end to the linguistic stability of SBH.

This survey of diachronic variation, particularly within BH, has demonstrated that words may change in meaning over time. It has also indicated some of the difficulties encountered in attempting to identify early or late linguistic variants. The linguistic distinctions between pre-exilic and post-exilic Hebrew appear to be more clearly defined than those between ABH and SBH. This raises the question whether ABH features are retained from a particular poetic style or a northern dialect. The reader also needs to be aware of the interplay between Hebrew and Aramaic throughout the CH corpus.

---

[38] Young, *Diversity*, 63.

[39] S. Gervitz, 'Of Syntax and Style in the "Late Biblical Hebrew"–"Old Canaanite" Connection', 25–9.

[40] C.H. Gordon, 'Northern Israelite Influence on Post-exilic Hebrew', 85–8.

[41] Young, *Diversity*, 87–8.

3. Dialectal Variation

Most scholars assume that the majority of the Hebrew Bible was written in Judah. There are, however, portions which are plainly non-Judean in origin. These include stories in Judges dealing with northern heroes (including the Song of Deborah), material in Kings describing the history of the northern kingdom of Israel, the work of the prophet Hosea and certain psalms. It has been noticed that this group of texts contains a concentration of atypical Hebrew grammatical features. The clustering of these linguistic features is taken to characterize the northern dialect. The methodology for identifying northern dialect is therefore as follows: non-linguistic factors suggest a text may be northern; it shares several atypical Hebrew linguistic features with other texts considered to be northern; it is possible to posit an opposition and distinction between each of these features in the northern dialect and its equivalent in SBH; the concentration of these features in a particular text then becomes diagnostic for the northern dialect.

Rendsburg notes that many of these northern features can be found in other Canaanite dialects such as Phoenician, Ammonite and Moabite, and/or in Aramaic.[42] It appears that there was a northern dialect of Hebrew, Israelian Hebrew (IH), separate from the Judean standard (JH), which shared isoglosses with neighbouring languages. Both geographic and social factors influence linguistic convergence and diversity. As a general rule, dialects on either side of a range of mountains for instance will diverge, whilst neighbouring dialects whose speakers have frequent friendly contact will converge as they share increasing numbers of isoglosses. As Rabin observes, 'the geographical separation of Judah and its non-participation in the political events affecting the North must have led to a certain amount of linguistic separation'.[43]

The first indication of possible dialectal differences between the tribes is the famous שִׁבֹּלֶת – סִבֹּלֶת story of Judges 12:1–6. The sibilants ס and שׁ often appear to be confused in the Hebrew Bible and the majority of examples of their interchange derive from northern texts.[44] It is usually claimed that the Samaria Ostraca provide additional features of the northern dialect, namely,

[42] G.A. Rendsburg, 'Morphological Evidence for Regional Dialects in Ancient Hebrew', 68.

[43] C. Rabin, 'The Emergence of Classical Hebrew', 71.

[44] Young, *Diversity*, 188–9.

contraction of the dipthong [ay] into [e:] as represented in the word
יִן for the usual יַיִן 'wine', a feature also present in Phoenician.[45]
Young, however, questions the validity of this assertion.[46] The
Samaria Ostraca provide only a limited number of words and
phrases and there is a lack of other inscriptional material from the
northern part of the country.

Rendsburg identifies a number of morphological features of
BH which he considers characteristic of Israelian but not Judean
Hebrew. These include occurrence of the interrogative pronoun
meh before non-laryngeal consonants and use of feminine singular
nominal endings -*at* (in the absolute state) and -*ot*. One example is
the phrase חַכְמוֹת שָׂרוֹתֶיהָ 'the wisest of her ladies' in Judges 5:29.[47]
Another feature, the reduplicatory plural of nouns based on
geminate stems, is exemplified in verses 14, 15 (בַּעֲמָמֶיךָ and חִקְקֵי).
Rendsburg also lists several lexical items characteristic of IH.[48]
Judges 5 includes the verb הלם 'to strike' (vv. 22, 26) and noun
הַלְמוּת (v. 26) which are found in Phoenician and Ugaritic. Young
also notes in verse 26 the Aramaizing dialectal form מָחֲקָה alongside
SBH מָחֲצָה. Many of these features are evident in neighbouring
languages. Rendsburg maintains that IH must still be reckoned as
Hebrew, albeit a regional dialect thereof, sharing many isoglosses
with Phoenician and Aramaic.[49]

In a more detailed study of IH in the Psalms, Rendsburg
concludes that thirty-six poems in the book of Psalms contain
linguistic evidence pointing very clearly to northern provenance.[50]
In this survey Rendsburg examined both morphological and lexical
features, identifying many more linguistic features which may
indicate the northern dialect. He takes the clustering of several
northern features to identify northern origin and suggests that these
psalms were most probably composed prior to 721 BCE.[51]

It appears that most of the material labelled IH and most of the
material labelled ABH is poetry. There is furthermore no systematic
description of either the northern dialect or ABH. The identification

---

[45] E.g. Sarfatti, 'Hebrew Inscriptions', 81.

[46] Young, *Diversity*, 166–7.

[47] Rendsburg, 'Morphological Evidence', 79.

[48] Rendsburg, 'Morphological Evidence', 71–85.

[49] Rendsburg, 'Morphological Evidence', 87.

[50] G.A. Rendsburg, *Linguistic Evidence for the Northern Origin of Selected Psalms*.

[51] Rendsburg, *Linguistic Evidence*, 104.

of both has relied on the linguistic criteria of opposition and distinction and the clustering of features. The relative paucity of features and their lack of opposition to SBH raises serious doubts as to the proven existence of IH and ABH. Passages such as the Song of Deborah are frequently described as archaic or, as Knauf writes, 'ein ursprünglich israelitischer Text',[52] and yet Young, among others, insists that it is of northern origin. There is simply not enough linguistic data available to make distinctions within BH.[53]

4. Dialect Geography

The existence of shared linguistic features between Hebrew and Phoenician or Aramaic demonstrates the continuity between dialects and languages. Each linguistic feature has its own distinct area of distribution, the boundaries of which form an isogloss. Isoglosses are not walls, they are more like sieves. There is a considerable overlapping of dialectal features across neighbouring languages in border regions, although the standard form of each language may be quite distinct. It is the collection or bundle of isoglosses which will differentiate the standard varieties.

There are two basic models for describing relationships between languages: trees and waves. The tree model aims to show derivational history, the splits between languages over time. A language family is represented by a node in the tree. The parent language is the trunk and daughter dialects over a period of time diverge and bifurcate as they each adopt different isoglosses. The family-tree model shows time depth but it does not display the linguistic features which define nodes. It also tends to bunch languages together and not allow for diffusion. The diversity of the Semitic languages makes it difficult to represent them in a single tree diagram. Blau illustrates the more recent preference for classification of West Semitic languages according to the wave hypothesis. He classifies Ugaritic, Canaanite (which includes Hebrew and Phoenician) and Aramaic as North-West Semitic, with Ugaritic being closer to Canaanite than Aramaic.[54]

---

[52] 'An original Israelite text' (my trans.). See Knauf, 'Biblisch-Hebräisch', 18.
[53] D.C. Fredericks, 'A North Israelite Dialect in the Hebrew Bible?', 8.
[54] J. Blau, 'Hebrew and North-West Semitic', 40; cf. J. Huehnergard, 'Remarks on the Classification of the Northwest Semitic Languages'.

The wave hypothesis, proposed by Johannes Schmidt in 1872, allows for diffusion but does not show chronological relations between languages. It is based on observation that linguistic changes spread over an area like a wave, each one spreading over a different area and producing an isogloss. The wave model shows isogloss lines between items, and bundles of isoglosses define sub-groups of languages. It displays the distance between languages synchronically rather than diachronically. There have been attempts to combine both models to give more detailed historical and synchronic linguistic information.[55]

Harris, following the first model, surveyed linguistic changes from proto-Semitic to daughter languages: Phoenician, Hebrew, Moabite and Ugaritic. He looked for examples of convergence and divergence. Convergence was defined as independent identical changes within the daughter languages. Divergence was due to a change which spread over only part of the area.[56] Harris concluded that from 1800 to 1365 BCE the whole area developed similarly. Subsequently, dialect boundaries began to appear, and from 800 to 200 BCE distinctive languages developed.[57] Divergent changes were more common in later times and convergent ones less so, possibly because the gradual piling up of isoglosses made it more difficult for changes to spread.

Harris distinguished two dialects of Hebrew: North Palestine and Jerusalem. The Jerusalem standard resisted several early general Canaanite changes, whilst the North Palestine dialect accepted certain general Canaanite and Phoenician changes.[58] Harris believed that the origins of most changes were Phoenician seaports from where isoglosses moved inland.[59]

Garr's dialect geography of Syria–Palestine covered all areas west and north of the Syrian desert in which a North-West Semitic dialect was spoken.[60] He based his study on all extant texts including inscriptions, but excluding various isoglosses: retentions deriving from the common stock of linguistic features; analogical formations resulting from internal structural pressures; and parallel, independent developments. Garr emphasized the importance of the

---

[55] F.C. Southworth, 'Family-tree Diagrams', 557–8.

[56] Z.S. Harris, *The Development of the Canaanite Dialects*, 91.

[57] Harris, *Canaanite Dialects*, 96.

[58] Harris, *Canaanite Dialects*, 98.

[59] Harris, *Canaanite Dialects*, 99.

[60] W.R. Garr, *Dialect Geography of Syria-Palestine*, 7.

history of an outcome in linguistic classification: a feature must not be borrowed but must represent a native linguistic development.

Garr concentrated on isolating sets of shared linguistic innovations. He believed that the greater the number of shared linguistic innovations, the greater the likelihood of a common linguistic development.[61] Syntax was considered to be an unreliable tool because a syntactic feature may reflect a well-attested innovation and not demonstrate any particular shared history. Garr decided that phonological features would be easiest to evaluate in classifying North-West Semitic dialects. Morphological features were equally important.[62]

Garr adheres to the second model of language change, viewing dialects lying along a continuum with Standard Phoenician and Old Aramaic representing the extremes of the chain. He did not distinguish dialects within Hebrew and in fact considered the position of Hebrew to be unclear. He suggested it could have been a minor linguistic centre, a slight break in the chain.[63] This would cohere with Jerusalem being a political and cultural centre during the period of centralized monarchy.

Kaufman shares Garr's presupposition that he is dealing with a dialect continuum created by the diffusion of numerous waves of linguistic change. He also agrees that linguistic features are only significant for classification if they are shared innovations.[64] Kaufman surveyed some of the major methodological approaches to the problem of language classification and the assignment of border dialects. The first test to be applied is mutual intelligibility, which is usually only applied to spoken languages, although there are some hints about mutual intelligibility within the biblical texts (2 Kgs. 18). For two languages or dialects to be mutually intelligible their basic vocabularies and fundamental grammatical structures must coincide.[65] The second task is to assemble a list of isoglosses distinguishing between the dialects in question. Not all isoglosses are equally significant. As Kaufman observes, 'An isogloss that cuts boldly across a large area is more significant than a petty, peripheral line, while a bundle of isoglosses evidences a larger historical

---

[61] Garr, *Dialect Geography*, 215–16.

[62] Garr, *Dialect Geography*, 216–17.

[63] Garr, *Dialect Geography*, 229–30.

[64] S.A. Kaufman, 'The Classification of the North West Semitic Dialects of the Biblical Period and Some Implications Thereof', 46–7.

[65] Kaufman, 'Classification', 44.

process and offers a more suitable basis of classification.'[66] Whereas Garr concentrated on phonological and morphological features, Kaufman is content to use both grammatical and lexical information for dialect differentiation. However, he asserts that if lexically based conclusions contradict the evidence of grammar, then the evidence of grammar must prevail. But if they complement each other, then lexical evidence has every right to be adduced as corroborative evidence.[67]

The traditional models of language change represented by tree and wave respectively do not entirely account for the position with respect to North-West Semitic dialects. Possibly a more appropriate model of dialect geography for Hebrew and its neighbours would be a Venn diagram. The background would represent the super-tribal prestige language used for commerce and official communications. Each spoken dialect would then have its own circle which would overlap with each of those neighbouring dialects with whom it shared isoglosses. The Venn diagram would represent a synchronic time slot and therefore need updating for different periods within the history of CH as it demonstrated the relative interplay between languages.

The study of dialect geography demonstrates how languages and dialects overlap. The fact that there is no discrete boundary between two dialects helps to explain the difficulty in delineating IH. It also raises important questions for lexicography because lexical items may function identically in different dialects with the same semantic range, or they may diverge in meaning. An awareness of these factors is fundamental to the study of meaning.

BH is not homogeneous and the existence of more than one variety, whether due to diglossia, archaic poetry, later prose or a northern dialect, causes conundrums for the study of semantics. In principle there needs to be a standard coherent method for identifying words and morphological variants as belonging to a particular subset of the language. The linguistic principles of opposition and distribution appear to offer a suitable foundation for such work. Yet these struggle with the limited data available.

---

[66] Kaufman, 'Classification', 46.
[67] Kaufman, 'Classification', 48.

Review of Part One

The first three chapters have surveyed key preliminary issues concerning the data available for investigating meaning in the Hebrew Bible. Chapter 1 acknowledged that the biblical texts witness to a small subset of CH. For the purposes of this study CH is defined as Hebrew prior to the cessation of the spoken language in 200 CE. The available pool of linguistic data therefore derives from a wide variety of material which includes inscriptions, Dead Sea Scrolls and the Mishnah.

Chapter 2 recognized that the source text for study of the Hebrew Bible is produced by the Masoretes of Tiberias; therefore both an understanding of their context and a familiarity with their work is essential. It is necessary to recognize that the meaning encoded in the MT is that which was understood at the time the text was fixed in Jewish tradition. This text furthermore has a long history of transmission and interpretation which inevitably influences its reading today.

Chapter 3 noted that the investigation of BH alone demonstrates both synchronic and diachronic variation along with dialectal variants and loanwords. Languages are living organisms; they are constantly changing and adapting to the requirements of their speakers. Knowledge of the context within which the texts were produced is therefore an important aid to their interpretation. An awareness of all these factors is vital to comprehension of the Hebrew Bible.

Part Two

Form and Meaning

4

Comparative Philology

1. Introduction

When encountering difficult words in biblical texts, scholars sometimes look to other Semitic languages for similar forms to illuminate
the meaning of the awkward Hebrew word. Such behaviour is
subsumed under the method of comparative philology which, in
its modern form, was developed on the older Indo-European
languages in the nineteenth century. This chapter undertakes a
detailed investigation of the linguistic presuppositions and principles of this method, followed by a brief overview of Barr's concerns
about applications of linguistic method to biblical texts. The final
section suggests important guidelines for applying comparative
philology to biblical texts.

1.1 Hebrew as a Semitic language

Hebrew is a member of the family of Semitic languages, traditionally classified as part of the larger grouping called Hamito-Semitic.
This label is misleading because it implies incorrectly that 'Hamitic'
is an entity which can be contrasted with Semitic. At the suggestion
of Greenberg in 1952 the family was renamed Afro-Asiatic.[1] It
includes Egyptian, Berber, Cushite, Chadic and Semitic.[2] The division of the Semitic family into two branches, East (Akkadian,
Babylonian, Assyrian) and West is well established. There are, however, two common classifications of the West Semitic branch. The
first distinguishes South Semitic (South Arabian, Arabic, Ethiopic)

---

[1] J.H. Greenberg, 'The Afro-Asiatic (Hamito-Semitic) present', 1–9.
[2] W.P. Lehmann, *Historical Linguistics*, 38; C. Rabin, 'Semitic Languages',
14:1149.

from North-West (Aramaic, Canaanite).[3] The second distinguishes South Semitic (Ethiopic, South Arabian) from Central Semitic (Aramaic, Canaanite, Arabic).[4] The two classifications differ with respect to their placing of Arabic. There is also discussion about whether Canaanite includes the ancient languages Moabite, Ugaritic, Amorite and Eblaite along with Hebrew and Phoenician.[5]

Two important factors in the classification of West Semitic languages are the vast difference in dating of the available materials and the extreme shortage of data in some languages. Scholars must question whether an ancient language such as Ugaritic can be measured by the same criteria as BH, and whether the single inscription in Moabite provides enough information for that language to be classified with any certainty.[6]

The Semitic languages originate from western Asia – the areas of Mesopotamia, Syria–Palestine, Arabia – and Ethiopia. They are characterized by a large number of common elements in phonology, morphology, lexicography and syntax. The preservation of these elements over a period of time suggests a common ancestor, designated 'Proto-Semitic'. As Moscati points out, 'By Proto-Semitic we refer to the *ensemble* of elements which an examination of the historically documented Semitic languages leads us to regard as common property of the Semitic group in its most ancient phase ... It must not be forgotten that "Proto-Semitic" is merely a linguistic convention or postulate.'[7]

Semitic languages share two linguistic characteristics: the almost invariably triradical root or word-stem; and the relationship between consonants of that root and the superimposed vowel pattern. The traditional view is that the consonants carry primary semantic distinctions (at least in the verb and its nominal derivatives), whilst the vowels act as modifiers indicating grammatical function and secondary semantic features: 'The meaning of a root inheres exclusively in the consonants of the root; the vowels, along

---

[3] Rabin, 'Semitic Languages', 1149–56; Sáenz-Badillos, *History*, 3–4.

[4] R. Hetzron, 'Semitic Languages'; cf. Huehnergard, 'Remarks', 283; R.M. Voigt, 'The Classification of Central Semitic', 15.

[5] P.R. Bennett, *Comparative Semitic Linguistics*, 21; cf. Sáenz-Badillos, *History*, 9–16.

[6] M. Sekine, 'The Subdivisions of the North-West Semitic Languages', 205–21.

[7] S. Moscati (ed.), *An Introduction to the Comparative Grammar of the Semitic Languages*, 15.

with consonantal repetitions or lengthenings and certain consonantal affixes, serve only to modify this root meaning through
the formation of various nominal and verbal stems and their
inflection.'[8]

The Hebrew root שָׁמַר, basically meaning 'to guard, watch', has
forms אֶשְׁמֹר 'I shall watch', מִשְׁמָר 'watch', שׁוֹמֵר 'watchman' and
שָׁמוּר 'guarded'.[9] A similar Indo-European example is the English
strong verb 'to sing' with forms 'he sang', 'song', 'singer' and
'sung'. Both display variations within a paradigm. In Germanic
languages, however, a change of vowel can result in an entirely
unconnected lexeme and hence a completely different meaning, for
example, *lieben, loben, leben* in German, or 'live', 'love', 'leave' in
English. As Ullendorff pointed out, the picture is not as simple as
once assumed.[10] Semitic languages cannot be classified simply on
the basis of root and vowel pattern, nor on the basis of triliterality.
He nevertheless asserts that concurrence of most of the principal
data in morphology and a general homogeneity of the phonological structures affirm genetic connections between the Semitic
languages as a whole.[11]

1.2 *The root and meaning*

There is ongoing debate about how semantically significant the root
is in Hebrew lexemes. Barr defines 'the root fallacy' as the belief
that 'the "root meaning" can confidently be taken to be part of
the actual semantic value of any word or form which can be
assigned to an identifiable root; and likewise that any word may
be taken to give some kind of suggestion of other words formed
from the same root'.[12]

Seow suggests the Semitic root 'defines a word inasmuch as it
gives the basic semantic field within which words with that root
fall'.[13] This does not allow for polysemy, homonymy and poetic
licence. Waltke and O'Connor similarly define 'root' as 'a sequence

---

[8]   G. Bergsträsser, *Introduction to the Semitic Languages*, 5.

[9]   Kutscher, *History*, 5.

[10]   E. Ullendorff, 'What Is a Semitic Language?'.

[11]   Ullendorff, 'Semitic Language?', 73. For discussion of the structure of
      Semitic cf. Hetzron, 'Semitic Languages', 657–63; Moscati, *Comparative
      Grammar*; W.S. LaSor, 'Proto-Semitic', 189–205.

[12]   Barr, *Semantics*, 100.

[13]   C.L. Seow, *A Grammar of Biblical Hebrew*, 21.

of consonants associated with a meaning or group of meanings ... The root is an abstraction, based on the semantic field of the words as they are used.'[14] According to Barr, the root exists as a morpheme, 'commonly and characteristically discontinuous',[15] which combines with a pattern (vocalic or consonantal like the נ prefix of the *niphal*) to form actual Hebrew words. The common type of Semitic root like ל–ח–מ does not appear independently but only in words in combination with a pattern. As Barr notes, the relation between such a root and the formed word לֶחֶם is not historical but generative.[16] He acknowledges that the root may have had a semantic influence, but only in a diachronic prehistoric sense: in actual Hebrew usage it was insignificant as an indicator of meaning in any of the lexemes found.[17]

Roots may be defined formally, but they cannot necessarily be defined semantically. There is a qualitative difference between those lexical items which are formed from a root via specific rules like שמר and those which do not follow such paradigms. The root may be semantically significant in a synchronic sense, according to Barr, only where the root morpheme is active and productive, usually as a basic verb or noun in the Hebrew of the biblical period.[18] By this he means that semantic links between two lexical items sharing the same consonantal root must be obvious. Where there is no semantic continuity then the term 'root' loses its significance. Perception of semantic similarity depends on the individual investigating meaning.

In Hebrew orthography, particularly in unpointed texts, root consonants are usually written (except when certain phonological rules apply). In a passage of any length cotext and context assist the reader in vocalizing the text in a way which makes sense, for the same sequence of consonants will not always convey the same meaning: אב may indicate 'father', 'ghost' or 'bud' according to the appropriate vowel pattern. The notion of a common consonantal root is therefore inappropriate for such nouns.

---

[14] B. Waltke and M. O'Connor, *An Introduction to Biblical Hebrew Syntax*, 83.

[15] J. Barr, 'Three Interrelated Factors in the Semantic Study of Ancient Hebrew', 37.

[16] J. Barr, 'Etymology and the Old Testament', 13.

[17] Barr, 'Three Interrelated Factors', 35.

[18] Barr, 'Three Interrelated Factors', 35.

It is debatable how conscious Hebrew speakers of ancient Israel were of the root in the meaning of a word.[19] The writers of the Hebrew Bible often explained names by means of 'popular etymology', but they worked in terms of assonance and association of ideas rather than by appealing to derivations from a root.[20] The place name Beersheba, for example, is given two different etymologies in one verse (Gen. 21:31). Concentration on roots is a relatively recent phenomenon, most probably deriving from studying the vocalization of biblical texts. It was not until the Middle Ages that Jewish grammarians worked out the principles of the triradical Hebrew root.[21] Students today are taught particularly BH with an emphasis on being able to identify the root of a word. Many standard Hebrew dictionaries are organized according to consonantal roots.[22] Thus, in order to look up the majority of lexical items, one must first identify the root: students need to know that מוֹשָׁב and חוֹשָׁב derive from יָשַׁב. The *Dictionary of Classical Hebrew* claims to be arranged on a strictly alphabetical principle with the 'root' forms of verbs being used as headwords.[23]

To summarize, scholars working in Hebrew still rely on the semantic significance of the root in lexical meaning. However, the same root does not always carry the same semantic significance. There is no automatic one-to-one correlation between root and meaning. Homophonous roots do exist. Individual words and their relationship to their own root will determine whether that particular root is semantically significant for those lexical items within which it appears. Those working in the field of lexical semantics therefore must be cautious about relying on root-meanings in their study of CH.

2. Comparative Philology

2.1 *Language change*

Comparative Philology relies on the recognition that languages are in constant flux: they are dynamic systems and language change is a

---

[19] J.F.A. Sawyer, 'Root-Meanings in Hebrew', 37.
[20] Barr, 'Three Interrelated Factors', 43.
[21] Barr, *Comparative Philology*, 60–1.
[22] *BDB*; Koehler-Baumgartner.
[23] Clines, *Dictionary*, 1:15.

function of language use. In observation, no speech community is ever quite uniform: there are different accents, dialects and even idiolects. Such variation leads to change over time as particular variants gain prestige and spread to the detriment of alternatives.

2.1.1 Sound change

Sound change is basically of two sorts: it can be merely a change in pronunciation with no effect on the sound system like the variation between different speakers of the same dialect; or it can be a structural phonemic change, which effects the number or distribution of phonemes. These structural changes in the phonology of a language are vitally important to comparative philology.

Structural changes are triggered only when instances of phonetic change have piled up to result in a change in the sound system. Various types of structural change are:

1.   Complete loss of a phoneme (infrequent).
2.   Partial merger of two phonemes.
3.   Partial loss of a phoneme (subtype of number 2).
4.   Complete merger of two phonemes (frequent).
5.   Split of a phoneme into two or more distinct phonemes (usually due to a merger).
6.   Excrescence (which does not really arise out of nothing because it occurs within a phonetically specified environment).[24]

Although the Neogrammarian position of absolute (100 per cent) regularity in sound change is untenable and has usually been recognized as such by the majority of practitioners, the method nevertheless relies on such regularity and in practice operates as if all sound change was absolutely regular. The observed regularity can be coded in rules. These rules have a definite form: for example, sound **a** becomes sound **b** in environment **c**, is written: $a \rightarrow b \, / \, c$, where the elements **a**, **b** and **c** are often decomposed into relevant distinctive features.

A key aim of historical linguistics is to establish the relative chronology of particular sound changes. The synchronic order of application of relevant phonological rules is taken to reflect chronological changes in the language. The resultant ordering of rules, however, is a hypothesis of what happened historically, not an account of fact. All language change leaves some variation behind

---

[24]   R. Anttila, *Historical and Comparative Linguistics*, 69–70.

which stays indefinitely. These 'relics' cannot be accounted for by rules; only innovations can be easily described by rules. This may explain the difficulty in providing a coherent and comprehensive picture of ABH or IH where the only evidence for such varieties is based on exceptions to the standard.

The significance of sound change for lexical semantics lies in the observation that language functions as an organic whole where everything depends on everything else: 'Speech sounds do not exist for the sake of speech sounds but as carriers for semantic units, embodied as linguistic signs, which are handled according to the grammatical rules of the language.'[25] Grammatical conditioning can affect sound changes and sometimes a sound change may be governed by different syntactic positions. The various levels of a language are intimately interrelated and all aspects of the whole need to be taken into consideration when investigating the meaning of a particular word or phrase.

2.1.2 Analogy

Whereas sound change usually involves change only in form, analogy involves change in meaning. Predominantly conditioned by morphology, analogy is a relation of similarity: language has a general iconic tendency whereby semantic sameness is reflected by formal sameness. Unfamiliar forms tend to change to conform with more familiar ones. This can be noted in *folk etymology* where loanwords are adapted to more familiar native patterns.

There is a complex relationship between sound change and analogy. Sturtevant noted the paradox that sound change is regular and causes irregularity, whereas analogy is irregular and causes regularity.[26] A regular change in the sound system of a language may result in irregularities in its morphology, whereas changes in morphology due to analogy will not necessarily occur in every possible instance; thus the change is irregular. This irregularity of analogical levelling means it is virtually impossible to encode such change in rules. The observed regularity of sound change, however, is merely the *result* of change, for whilst *in progress* such change is not noticeably regular. The Proto-Semitic first and second person singular endings in the verbal suffix-conjugation (*-ku*, *-ta*, *-ti*) and their development in Arabic (-*tu*, -*ta*, -*ti*) or Ethiopic (-*ku*, -*ka*,

---

[25] Anttila, *Historical*, 77.
[26] Cf. Anttila, *Historical*, 94.

-*ki*) illustrate analogical extension of the elements *t* and *k* respectively.[27] The process of analogy completes the picture of regularity once morphology has been sufficiently eroded by sound change. Language change is therefore a complex process of sound change and analogy.

2.1.3 *Semantic change*

Sound change, analogy and semantic change represent a whole. It is not possible to formulate general rules of semantic change because meaning is intimately connected with culture and historical events. Semantic changes can, however, be classified *quantitatively* according to the range of a word's meaning: change may be an example of semantic extension or restriction. As the semantic range of one lexical item changes, so will its relations with other items in its semantic fields.

There are three principal categories of semantic change: shift, metaphoric and metonymic. In shift there are relatively small movements in the sense of the word-extension: 'manuscript' moves from referring to a handwritten document to an original document of any kind; or restriction: 'meat' moves from a general reference to food to a specific reference to flesh. Any form may become the basis for metaphorical extension: 'spine' being applied to the back of a book, or 'leaf' to the flap of a table. Metonymy arises between words already related by contiguity in the same semantic sphere: 'door' is used for the doorway, whereas 'gate', originally referring to the gap, becomes the means of closing the gap.[28]

2.1.4 *Borrowing*

The meaning of word **a** may change over time because of the borrowing or adoption of word **b** from another language. Borrowed item **b** changes relations within the semantic fields to which both words belong. There are always more meanings than words in a language; thus speakers may borrow words from other languages to fill perceived gaps in their native lexicon, particularly for new tools and artefacts which originate with speakers of language **B**. The word בַּרְזֶל 'iron' is not native to Hebrew.[29] Another motive for borrowing

---

[27] Moscati, *Comparative Grammar*, 139.

[28] P. Cotterell, 'Linguistics, Meaning, Semantics, and Discourse Analysis', 153.

[29] Cf. Kutscher, *History*, 47.

is prestige. During the first millennium BCE, Aramaic was the official language of the vast Persian empire, the language of diplomacy and international trade of the Near East – Hebrew adopted various elements from it.[30] Borrowing is usually the result of cultural contact, but words can be borrowed from one language into a lingua franca and then deposited into another language without lending and receiving peoples having any contact. When investigating meaning in biblical texts it is important therefore to note both cultural contacts of Hebrew speakers and prestige languages used during the period under investigation.

It may be possible to identify the direction of borrowing by comparing sound correspondences between two languages: if one can predict language **B** sound given language **A** sound, but not vice versa, then **A** is the original language. Knowledge of different sound changes in Semitic languages enables identification of non-Hebrew roots that exhibit sound changes alien to Hebrew. It is also possible to identify loanwords by means of morphological and grammatical criteria: a word is a loan in the language where it cannot be analysed. Nouns of an unusual formation or words whose root is absent from Hebrew except for the lexical item in question may therefore be loans. The borrowing of vocabulary is complete when foreign words are adopted into native morphological and syntactic patterns. As noted above, the entry of a new word into the lexicon will cause change in the pre-existing semantic relationships. It is possible to derive certain indications about the geographical position of a language family in relation to other families by plotting the corresponding borrowings. Borrowing from the same language at different times can also provide evidence of phono-logical change.[31]

2.1.5 Symmetry

Languages as systems strive towards symmetry with the clear rule of 'one meaning, one form'. As Anttila explains, 'A maximally effi-cient system avoids polysemy (forms with many [related] meanings, especially if these occur in the same semantic sphere) and homo-phony, two (unrelated) meanings getting the same form.'[32] Either of these one-to-many correlations between form and meaning are easily tolerated, however, if they have to do with different parts of

---

[30] Cf. Kutscher, *History*, 46–53; Sáenz-Badillos, *History*, 115–27.
[31] Cf. Hurvitz, 'Chronological Significance'.
[32] Anttila, *Historical*, 181.

speech or different semantic spheres. Redundancy nevertheless is preserved in language by avoidance of homophony in paradigms (analogic resistance to sound change) and therapeutic removal of homophony (by analogy, borrowing, or grammatically conditioned sound change). There is change furthermore towards maximal differentiation in phonology through the processes of assimilation and dissimilation as observed within the Semitic languages.[33]

2.2 The Comparative Method

The Comparative Method begins by identifying words (usually nouns) in the relevant languages which both sound similar and have related meanings. Phonological correspondences between the sound systems of source languages are then abstracted. The method observes the phonetic/phonemic conditioning of variants in each case and initially requires a good semantic matching of original forms. If resultant sets of correspondences are regular (they recur) then they are assumed to indicate a historical connection and not chance similarity. The source languages are regarded as related, daughters of a common ancestor or parent language, the 'proto-language', and the reconstructed proto-language provides a basis from which extant languages can be described historically as the result of consistent development.

2.2.1 Linguistic resemblances
The proposed historical connection may, however, be due to inheritance or borrowing: extensive borrowing easily creates regular sets of correspondences between source and target languages. One way to guard against effects of borrowing is to start the method with vocabulary items that come from semantic spheres not usually borrowed from, that is, basic non-cultural vocabulary such as body parts, natural objects, animals, plants, pronouns, lower numerals. The Swadesh list provides a useful starting point.[34]

Some languages resemble each other to a degree that can only be explained in terms of historical connections, but other resemblances between languages bear no significance whatsoever: 'Only strictness in the application of sound correspondences prevents the

---

[33] Cf. Moscati, *Comparative Grammar*, 56–63.

[34] M. Swadesh, 'Towards Greater Accuracy in Lexicostatic Dating', 121–2; cf. Bennett, *Semitic Linguistics*, 40; C. Rabin, 'Lexicostatistics and the Internal Divisions of Semitic'.

student from quick and easy conclusions based on semantic identity or similarity.'[35]

2.2.2 Family relations

In Comparative Linguistics 'related' is a technical term, like the equivalent 'cognate'. When languages are said to be related, they are declared to be later forms of a single earlier form, that is, they are historically connected. Cognate languages are those recognized to relate to one another consistently in phonemic, morphemic and semantic structures. Languages connected by such sets of correspondences form a language family. Evidence or proof of such relationship is based on fulfilment of two fundamental criteria: multiple agreement in basic and unborrowable vocabulary with *sound correspondences*; and considerable and frequent agreement in grammatical forms (prefixes, endings and auxiliaries) with *sound correspondences*.

The operation of the comparative method rests on two factors: arbitrariness of the linguistic sign and regularity of phonetic change. If two or more languages show a regular correspondence between themselves in items where meanings are the same or similar, that is, if there are diagrammatic relations between different languages, this means there must be only one underlying colligation of sound and meaning (link-up of the linguistic sign). Differences in attested sound segments therefore depend on regular phonetic change, which has changed the sounds of the original linguistic sign (often the meaning has also changed). The comparative method cannot handle innovations that involve irregular phonetic change.

The regularity of sound change is due to the fact that all sound units mean the same, that is, 'otherness': sounds are diacritical marks that keep morphemes separate; they have no meaning of their own. Many sound changes are irreversible, so giving an indication of direction and enabling the reconstruction of earlier forms. Sound change, however, is not always completely regular, hence the need for abundant linguistic data. In a good case there are hundreds or even thousands of matching words across the source languages giving a solid basis of material which can tolerate a certain amount of indeterminacy. In using comparative philology scholars refer to a list of such basic correspondences which have been built up

---

[35] Barr, *Comparative Philology*, 85; J. Barr, 'The Ancient Semitic Languages', 48.

wherever possible with plentiful examples of words which do not present immediate semantic uncertainties.

Bergsträsser identified some common Semitic vocabulary which includes words for close kinship relations, animals, parts of the body and lower numerals.[36] A more recent compilation of such material has been undertaken by LaSor.[37] Goshen-Gottstein, however, is cautious about relying on lexical similarities between the Semitic languages to carry the weight of a Proto-Semitic hypothesis. He argues that the lexicon can only retain a subsidiary role, with the major points of Comparative Semitics relying on laws of phonology and morphology.[38] He appears to have overlooked reliance on sound correspondences in the identification of common lexical items. However, his point remains valid – all aspects of the source languages have to be compared to identify family relationships.

2.2.3 *Proto-language*
Elements of daughter languages are compared to reconstruct earlier forms, which are not themselves directly evidenced. Reconstruction of an ancestor like Proto-Semitic will not be complete, as only those features which are observed in at least one Semitic language can be identified. Such reconstructed elements are abstractions and therefore hypothetical, so usually marked by an asterisk. A reconstructed form is 'a formula that tells us which identities or systematic correspondences of phonemes appear in a set of related languages'.[39] Bergsträsser notes, 'Proto-Semitic is not the name of a unified language that is clearly delimited temporally and spacially; it is a cover term for everything that we can infer to have temporally preceded the emergence of the individual Semitic languages.'[40]

A fundamental principle of the comparative method is that it is both simplest and most plausible to assume one conditioned change in the proto-language, rather than two or three identical changes in exactly the same environment. The method assumes that the parent community possessed a completely uniform language and that the community split suddenly and sharply into two or more daughter languages which lost all contact with each other. Each branch or

---

[36] Bergsträsser, *Semitic Languages*, 209–23.
[37] LaSor, 'Proto-Semitic', 189–205.
[38] M.H. Goshen-Gottstein, 'The Present State of Comparative Semitic Linguistics', 564–9.
[39] Bloomfield, *Language*, 302.
[40] Bergsträsser, *Semitic Languages*, 2.

language is then presumed to bear independent witness to the forms of its parent, and observed correspondences among these daughter languages are expected to reveal features of the parent. Dialectal differences in the parent language are reflected as irreconcilable differences in daughter languages. A well-known axiom is that the comparative method is powerless if two or more languages have undergone the same change after splitting, a process called 'drift'. The results of the method are always highly tentative and abstract.

Anttila comments, 'The method is very powerful and very use-ful, but not omnipotent.'[41] Synchronic variation may impose far-reaching effects on reconstructions when not all variants are included in the sets of correspondences and newly discovered material forces continual revision of tentative results. Any recon-struction is valid only for the languages used and there is never any certainty of exact historical unity. As Murtonen observes, more recent discoveries of previously unknown languages such as Ugaritic, Ya'udi and Eblaite have forced reconsideration of the subclassification of Semitic languages.[42]

2.2.4 *Written data*

It does not matter whether the comparative method is applied to orthographic or phonetic units. Despite the lack of exact one-to-one correspondence between spoken and written language, writing does mirror speech and therefore provides clear evidence of linguistic change in gross outline.[43] The difference between orthographic and phonetic units matters only for the correctness of the results, because sometimes orthography obscures phonetic distinctions which must be known in order to secure correct results.

In texts without definite phonetic information, comparative philology concentrates on the correspondences between written signs. Changes observed in these signs are recognized as being changes in the sounds they represent rather than changes in the way a sound is recorded. As Bloomfield points out, 'The comparative method tells us, in principle, nothing about the acoustic shape of reconstructed forms; it identifies the phonemes in reconstructed forms merely as recurrent units.'[44] The acoustic character of such

---

[41] Anttila, *Historical*, 243; cf. E. Pulgram, 'The Nature and Use of Proto-Languages', 18–37.
[42] A. Murtonen, 'On Proto-Semitic Reconstructions', 1121.
[43] Anttila, *Historical*, 34–5.
[44] Bloomfield, *Language*, 309.

phonemes can only be guessed at; the symbols by which they are represented are merely labels for correspondences.

2.2.5 *Internal reconstruction*

The results obtained from the comparative method can be tested through Internal Reconstruction. This method is never 'historical', because whatever can be captured on the basis of one language is synchronically present in that language. All that results is a higher level of abstraction, that is morpho-phonemes.

Assuming that at some stage there was a single shape for each noun stem, Bennett reconstructed the following table of Hebrew nominal paradigms:[45]

	Absolute	The man's	My	Base form
slave	ʿebed	ʿebed hāʾiš	ʿabdī	*ʿabd
gold	zāhāb	zhab hāʾiš	zhābī	*zahab
carpet	marbad	marbad hāʾiš	marbaddī	*marbadd
blood	dām	dam hāʾiš	dāmī	*dam
lord	rab	rab hāʾiš	rabbī	*rabb

He then deduced five linguistic rules:

(a) in antepenultimate open syllables, *a was eliminated: *zahab-ī > *zhabī;

(b) in open syllables and singly closed syllables bearing phrase stress, *a became ā: *zahab > zāhāb;

(c) before word boundary, original geminate consonants were simplified: *rabb > rab;

(d) before word boundary, a consonant cluster was broken up by insertion of e: *ʿabd > *ʿabed;

(e) in words of shape CaCeC, *a became e: *ʿabed > ʿebed.

The rules can be ordered: c has to follow b because the alternative predicts *rabb > *rab > **rāb; and the results verified by comparative evidence: Arabic has forms which match the assumed Hebrew forms.

There is widespread agreement among linguists that internal reconstruction should be undertaken before application of the comparative method because this eliminates the effect of most recent changes. The danger, however, is that internal reconstruction

---

[45] Bennett, *Semitic Linguistics*, 50.

antedates the split-off point which is the goal of the comparative method, thus obscuring the relevant data. The methods do not in themselves observe an inherent order of application; rather the particular state of the languages under investigation and the task at hand are allowed to determine which method should be called upon.

Both methods use identical mechanisms: they handle sound units in connection with meaning; conditioning is stated; and they give ultimate units from which there is a one-way mapping relation to the units they started from.

The methods are inductive because they start with the hypothesis that certain facts can be explained from a common origin. They base themselves on the regularity of sound change either to classify languages or to reconstruct earlier stages of languages. The sound rules themselves are formed by means of abduction. Abduction is a reasoned guess about how an observed fact may have come about and becomes an 'explanation'. The comparative method is built on a framework of item and arrangement as phonemes are classified according to the principles of contrast and minimal pairs. There is always indeterminacy because material fed into the method must be pre-screened and the output post-edited and linguists, being human, disagree.

2.2.6 Etymology

In *philology* language is studied in order to understand the people who produced it in a particular historical and cultural environment. Philology has mainly been directed to literary documents produced by past cultures. The Neogrammarian emphasis on language as a system has led to concentration on the study of language apart from its pragmatic context. In investigating semantics, however, it is essential to know about the culture being referred to – words have meanings in relation to the world as well as to each other. One particular branch of philology is *etymology*, the scientifically controlled study of the history of words. Etymology is crucial to both the comparative method and internal reconstruction. It can likewise concentrate on either the origin of a word or its history.

Linguists tend to rely on intuition, but words deriving from different sources may become psychologically linked, and words deriving from the same source may be completely separated in a speaker's consciousness. Both occurrences are due to analogy. Anttila recommends some principles of investigation for etymology with constant attention being paid to the three aspects of

phonetics (sound correspondences), morphology (word formation) and semantics. Phonetics and semantics correlate strongly
with the comparative method, and morphology with internal
reconstruction. His principles are:

1.   If the apparent connection between two words contains pho-
     netic difficulties, look elsewhere for a more economic solution.
2.   Etymology has to satisfy the well-known rules of word-
     formation; if there are clashes, look elsewhere for a solution.
3.   If in an apparent connection an unusual semantic development
     must be assumed, then go back to 1 and 2.
4.   If the word is guaranteed for the proto-language, its (alleged)
     absence in any daughter language requires explanation.
5.   Test results against a dialect map. If a word is guaranteed for
     the proto-language, then adjacent dialects should demonstrate
     the greatest similarity.[46]

2.3 Summary

The above overview of linguistic presuppositions and principles of
comparative philology is vitally important because scholars' use of
this method tends to be problem driven and does not always take
into account the full picture. Key factors to be remembered are:

1   The fundamental significance of sound correspondences and
     the requirement for sets of regular correspondences between
     languages to be identified from plentiful data.
2   That Proto-Semitic is merely a system of dialect-free phonemes
     abstracted from observed regular sound change in the daughter
     languages. Its forms may have existed at any time prior to the
     languages from which it was abstracted.
3   The assumption that the parent language is uniform and there-
     fore all information about possible variation and complexity
     within it is lost.
4   The reconstructed units are symbols; they may or may not
     have phonetic reality.
5   The results of the method are only as good as available linguistic
     data: new information may lead to radical alterations in the
     reconstructed language system.

---

[46] Anttila, *Historical*, 331–2; cf. Grabbe, *Comparative Philology*, 133–4;
     Chapter 3, section 4.

3. James Barr's Critique of Linguistic Method in Biblical Interpretation

When Barr's books *The Semantics of Biblical Language* and *Comparative Philology and the Text of the Old Testament* were published in the 1960s they caused a commotion. Since then scholars have often referred to his work without always taking note of the points which he raised. This section therefore briefly reviews some of Barr's key concerns about the application of linguistic method to biblical interpretation.

3.1 Confusions

Barr notes confusion between the synchronic application of morphological rules of word-formation and evidence for historical changes in word-formation. 'Logicism' indicates the approach whereby the mental process of explanation, instead of a historical study of the language, is used to explain why the form is what it is.[47] It is possible, given the absolute form of a Hebrew noun, to form the construct according to certain rules. But this process is not the historical one through which the construct was formed; therefore the explanation cannot be historical.

In a similar vein, 'etymologizing' is giving excess weight to the origin of a word as against its semantic value.[48] 'Etymology is not, and does not profess to be, a guide to the semantic value of words in their current usage, and such value has to be determined from the current usage and not from the derivation.'[49] It is perfectly valid to trace the etymology of a word; the danger lies in the semantic authority given to that history. Semantic statements should be based on contemporary social linguistic consciousness.

Barr defines a word 'as a semantic marker, indicating an essential difference from another word and having the ability to mark that differentia in any one of a number of contexts; not becoming intrinsically infected by any particular one of these contexts, and having its sense as a marker sustained and determined not by metaphysical or theological usage but by a general social milieu, in which the language has its life'.[50] This echoes Semantic Field Theory which

---

[47] Barr, *Semantics*, 93.
[48] Barr, *Semantics*, 103.
[49] Barr, *Semantics*, 107.
[50] Barr, *Semantics*, 188.

considers a concept to be covered by a range of words, and the choice of word **a** rather than word **b** in a particular context C1 reveals the sense of word **a** on that occasion t12. The use of the same word a in a different context C2 does not incorporate its sense from t12 and t1 ... t11 inclusive. When the meaning of word **a** is considered to be a sum of senses of all its previous occurrences then this is 'illegitimate totality transfer'.[51]

An object may be signified by word **a** or word **b**. This does not entail that **a** is synonymous with **b**. Different words carry different information, often about the speaker as much as about the referent. The mistake of supposing that words **a** and **b** convey the same meaning is 'illegitimate identity transfer'.[52] An essential part of lexicography is observation of the oppositions between words, the points at which they become contrasted, where it is possible to discover why one word has been used rather than another, and where they may differ in connotation or overtone.

3.2 *Applications*

Barr recognizes that the CH corpus is small, containing many rare words, and the only way of reaching the meaning of some words has been through comparative etymological research. His major concern is that where a difficulty in the Hebrew text has been identified, almost anything in a cognate language anywhere may be appealed to for help.

Comparative philology, particularly as applied to Semitic languages, has tended to concentrate on forms to the disregard of meanings. There is intrinsic emphasis on forms because they are empirically attested in a way that meanings are not – written evidence may reveal when a particular form was in use but it cannot demonstrate when that form had a certain meaning. It is tempting to identify the meaning of a word by quoting the meaning of corresponding forms in cognate languages. As Barr emphasizes, the meaning of a word is its meaning in its own language, not its corresponding lexical items in cognate languages.[53]

If a Hebrew word normally thought to have a particular meaning is identified as another word through reference to a cognate language, then ideally the researcher would know all cognate

---

[51] Barr, *Semantics*, 218.
[52] Barr, *Semantics*, 218.
[53] Barr, *Comparative Philology*, 90.

languages. This is an unrealistic expectation and is rarely, if ever, realized. The short cut consists of dictionaries and a table of phonological correspondences between relevant languages. But, as Barr points out, there is danger in excessive reliance on a dictionary, especially if that dictionary has been influenced by etymological emphasis.[54] Such a dictionary may state the 'basic' meaning of a lexical item in addition to its meaning in the current context. This is often abstracted from the variety of contexts within which that word, or even its triradical root, has been found. Meanings given may not be real linguistic information but a product of the lexicographical process itself. This can happen through etymologizing, through telescoping of past etymological decisions, and through the collection, and representation as different existing senses, of the suggestions made by different scholars.[55] The English of a dictionary may also be ambiguous.

A comprehensive linguistic knowledge of Semitic languages alongside familiarity with their regular phonological correspondences and critical use of available linguistic tools (dictionaries and comparative grammars) are necessary qualifications for the philologist.

Philological treatments tend to increase the number of homonyms in Hebrew. Barr distinguishes four kinds:

1. Products of phoneme mergers traceable through reference to other Semitic languages. Two lexemes through sound changes have converged, and now produce identical forms. In another Semitic language the sound changes have produced a different outcome: the two words are still readily identifiable: Proto-Semitic phonemes /ʻ/ and /gh/, identifiable in Arabic, merged in Hebrew to become /ʻ/ giving ענה 'sing' and ענה 'answer'.[56]

2. In complete homonyms all forms in the paradigm of a word are identical. These can only be identified when the usual meaning is entirely inappropriate to its current context. In partial homonymy, where only some forms overlap, the appropriate meaning can be identified through grammatical and semantic context.

---

[54] Barr, *Comparative Philology*, 115–16; cf. J. Kaltner, *The Use of Arabic in Biblical Hebrew Lexicography*, 98–100.

[55] Barr, *Comparative Philology*, 118.

[56] Barr, *Comparative Philology*, 127; cf. 'Three Interrelated Factors', 39; Muraoka, 'Response', 46–7.

3.   Two roots may be identical without producing homonyms in actual forms. Although traditional dictionaries list words according to roots – *BDB* has סלל I 'to lift up, cast up' and סלל II with the form סַל 'basket'[57] – these forms do not occur together in texts. Barr comments, 'The problem of understanding how homonyms functioned as discriminatory communicative signals depends on sound rather than on writing, and depends on the whole word concerned and not on the abstraction we call the "root".'[58]

4.   Problems with homonyms are particularly noticeable in verbs. If verbs are homonymous in their sequence of root consonants, they will necessarily be homonymous in their entirety. Sometimes, however, a distinction of *binyanim* prevents verbs of identical roots from being homonymous: two Hebrew verb forms חלה mean 'to be weak, sick' and 'to appease'. The latter is only attested in the *piel*, the former is rare in *piel*.[59] Philologists should remember that the CH corpus is limited and it can only be said that certain forms are not attested, rather than that they did not exist.

Barr is concerned that philological treatments have generally emphasized search for a cognate root rather than particular word-formations in which lexical items are found.[60] If a corresponding root can be found with an appropriate meaning then it is assumed the corresponding form existed in Hebrew. Such philological treatments tend to be atomistic in nature and do not always consider wider implications of the discovery of another homonym and potential problems for communicative efficiency.

Barr remains cautious about the collection of corresponding lexical items in Semitic languages.[61] Whereas glottochronology depends on a small core of vocabulary remaining static over a long period of time, philological treatments tend to assume all vocabulary remains static; yet even basic vocabulary does change eventually.

Barr summarizes the importance of these observations in three points:

---

[57] *BDB*, 699–700.
[58] Barr, *Comparative Philology*, 131.
[59] Cf. Barr, *Comparative Philology*, 132.
[60] Barr, *Comparative Philology*, 133.
[61] Barr, *Comparative Philology*, 157–8.

1. Traditional comparative philology has tended to concentrate on the individual word and has failed to give equal place to its function in relation to other words.
2. The consideration of groups of words within a semantic field may help us understand why a particular word which appears in cognate languages does not appear in the language being studied.
3. Given a form in one Semitic language it is possible to predict the form in another language, but it is more difficult to predict the meaning because both are dependent on their interrelations with other words.[62]

3.3 Criteria for philological treatments

Barr provides a useful list of twelve points that should normally be considered when a philological treatment is suggested:

1. How far does the word lie within the normal phonological correspondences with a cognate word considered for its elucidation?
2. Is the meaning of the cognate word a real word, stated with accurate precision, and known to go back to a time when a Hebrew cognate with a semantically related meaning could have existed?
3. Has there been a critical examination of the semantic connections presumed in the identification?
4. The philologist must be aware that words may be adoptions from non-Semitic languages.
5. There needs to be a recognition of the possibility of textual error.
6. If a new identification produces a new homonym, then its statistical relationship to other homonyms must be considered.
7. If the new identification produces a new or near synonym, then some regard should be taken for the change of balance this causes in the lexical stock.
8. Scholars should consider the statistical probabilities that a word from this Semitic language is likely to produce a cognate.
9. If the identification relies on versional evidence, then particular relevant considerations need to be taken into account.[63]
10. There needs to be an investigation of post-biblical usage.

---

[62] Barr, *Comparative Philology*, 172–3.
[63] Cf. Barr, *Comparative Philology*, chapter 10.

11. If the new identification involves abandoning the Masoretic vocalization, then there should be a consideration of how that vocalization came about.
12. A new proposal should always be weighed against the more traditional or accepted reading.[64]

Barr concludes:

> The basic assumption, that study of the relations between the Semitic languages may further the understanding of the Hebrew Bible, is incontrovertible. The trouble has not lain in comparative scholarship, but in poor judgment in its application, and in failure to see and to follow out some of the general linguistic questions which are already implied in the primary use of the comparative method.[65]

3.4 *Related issues*

Among Barr's subsequent publications those concerning Hebrew lexicography and etymology are most relevant to the application of comparative philology to BH texts.

3.4.1 *Dictionaries of Biblical Hebrew*

In writing about method and purpose in compilation of BH diction--aries,[66] Barr makes a distinction between the semantics of a language and biblical theology. He then identifies a crucial distinction between 'the language as a system or a stock (e.g. the grammar or the lexicon of Hebrew) and the body of spoken or literary complexes which are created by the use of this system and this stock (e.g. the OT)'.[67]

Concerning classification, Barr favours investigation of vocabulary according to a language's own semantic fields, paradigmatic analysis, thinking it more appropriate to restrict discussion of syntagmatic relations to commentaries.[68] Barr emphasizes concern

---

[64] Barr, *Comparative Philology*, 288–90; cf. C. Cohen, 'The "Held Method" for Comparative Semitic Philology'; J.A. Emerton, 'Comparative Semitic Philology and Hebrew Lexicography'.

[65] Barr, *Comparative Philology*, 304.

[66] J. Barr, 'Semantics and Biblical Theology'; cf. J. Barr 'Hebrew Lexicography', 103–126.

[67] Barr, 'Semantics', 13.

[68] Barr, 'Semantics', 15; cf. 'Hebrew Lexicography', 122; 'Hebrew Lexicography: Informal Thoughts', 144–5.

with meanings within BH – English equivalents are not meanings of Hebrew words but glosses: 'approximate English labels sufficient to enable one to identify which word it is, which of several senses is referred to, which of several Hebrew homonyms is intended, and so on'.[69] The dictionary in general provides 'a rough classification of typical references and contexts'.[70]

Barr surveys some criteria to classify meanings in Hebrew dictionaries:

(i)   according to etymology;
(ii) by reference to chronology within Hebrew;
(iii) priority given to 'direct' sense over metaphorical senses, even when rarely attested;
(iv) classification dominated by statistical proportions;
(v)   suggested by componential analysis.[71]

He notes that these criteria have been eclectically combined, a process which he accepts as appropriate 'in a situation where complete and adequate information about word usage is seldom expected'.[72] He expresses concern that future Hebrew dictionaries will have to develop criteria for deciding between those suggestions made on the basis of cognate languages which are probable and those which are far-fetched.

Barr considers the ordering of different types of material within each entry: he objects to the traditional positioning of comparative-etymological material at the beginning of articles before any indication of meaning, yet believes that incorporation of such material within Hebrew dictionaries may still be justified in certain instances.[73] Barr warns against expectation that comparative work will clarify problem words because 'the typical Semitic root, formally defined, does not lead us back to a conceptual unity but rather to a variety of unconnected semantic possibilities which can be listed but cannot be explained through derivation from one another or from a putative common ancestor'.[74]

---

[69] Barr, 'Semantics', 16.
[70] Barr, 'Hebrew Lexicography', 120.
[71] Barr, 'Hebrew Lexicography', 121; cf. Barr, 'Scope', 4.
[72] Barr, 'Hebrew Lexicography', 121.
[73] J. Barr, 'Limitations of Etymology as a Lexicographical Instrument in Biblical Hebrew', 43–59.
[74] Barr, 'Limitations', 61.

As editor of the *Oxford Hebrew Lexicon*, Barr decided that entries should be ordered alphabetically according to words rather than roots. In a more recent article he provides a detailed discussion of advantages and disadvantages of ordering a Hebrew dictionary according to roots or lexemes.[75]

3.4.2 *Etymology*
Barr distinguishes six different types of operation within etymology:

A. Reconstruction of form and sense in so-called proto-language. Practical implications are distinction between homonyms resulting from phoneme merger and recovery of non-linguistic history, such as information about the geographical area where speakers lived.[76]

B. Tracing of forms and meanings within observable historical development.[77]

C. Identification of loan words. It is important to distinguish between borrowing of a form with its meaning, or merely adoption of the form.[78]

D. Analysis of words into component morphemes, not a historical process.[79]

E. Use of a cognate language to discover the meaning of a Hebrew word: depends on reconstruction of a prehistoric state of the language and is concerned almost entirely with *gross* semantic differences.[80]

F. Simple comparison of institutions with cognate names, not etymology at all: 'decisions about the degree of similarity of institutions are dependent on the comparison of the things themselves and are neither proved nor disproved by the community of the terms used'.[81]

According to Barr, *A–D* are 'real cases' of etymology, *E* is an application, sometimes of *C* but more often of *A*, and *F* is not a real case but often found in association with etymology. He observes, 'the

---

[75] Barr, 'Three Interrelated Factors', 33–6.
[76] Barr, 'Etymology', 4–7.
[77] Barr, 'Etymology', 7–9.
[78] Barr, 'Etymology', 9–11.
[79] Barr, 'Etymology', 11–15.
[80] Barr, 'Etymology', 15–16.
[81] Barr, 'Etymology', 17.

term etymology is a loose designation for a somewhat ill-assorted bundle of different linguistic operations'.[82] Barr points to the importance of etymology for identification of unusual words in Hebrew by reference to type *E*. However, this does not mean he is content to endorse application of all types of etymology to BH – the aim of the individual investigation is the determining factor.

3.5 Barr's contribution to Hebrew semantics

Barr raises awareness of modern linguistic method within the community of BH scholars. He urges philologists to be more careful in their treatments of problem texts. He calls philologists to note their own motives and mental processes in investigating Hebrew and to become better acquainted with the Semitic languages and their phonological correspondences. He cautions against undue reliance on the root in the meaning of lexical items and also against excessive emphasis on a word's origin versus its semantic value in its current context. He reminds scholars that discovery of a cognate form does not entail recovery of the meaning of a Hebrew word. Yet Barr continues to uphold the validity of both comparative philology and etymology. He encourages scholars to be more rigorous in their method, to consider the wider linguistic and pragmatic consequences of their suggestions and to remember that philological results are always tentative, never final.

4. Comparative Philology and Meaning in Biblical Hebrew

Comparative philology is but one linguistic method available to the scholar investigating the meaning of a Hebrew word and, contrary to the impression given by the traditional ordering within dictionary entries, it should never be the first method employed. Following the premise that a word primarily gains its meaning from within its own language, investigation begins with the text itself. Once all possible information about the word has been gleaned from the immediate text, then the search continues with the wider cotext of the Hebrew Bible, then it broadens to include the CH corpus, and later Hebrew.

---

[82] Barr, 'Etymology', 18.

Only when all the available Hebrew material fails to elucidate the meaning of a word should cognate languages be investigated. The obvious category of candidates for the application of comparative philology is *hapax legomena*, where *hapax legomenon* is defined as any word other than a proper noun which is the only exemplification of its root within the Hebrew sections of the received text.[83] Greenspahn notes that application of such criteria yields 289 *hapax legomena*.[84] When dealing with a *hapax legomenon* it must be remembered that even it has a Hebrew context and that although it may occur only once in BH, it may be attested elsewhere in the CH corpus. As with any other word, this should be investigated prior to the application of comparative philology.

Data input to comparative philology is therefore usually a Hebrew word which does not make sense in its current cotext and context. There is no obvious reason to question the text, only its meaning. The researcher should have access to the recognized regular phonological correspondences between the Semitic languages and dictionary data. It is preferable that a specialist in that language writes a dictionary of a particular language, rather than a Hebraist writing for biblical scholars. When referring to dictionary entries the researcher must beware of illegitimate totality transfer and 'core' meanings abstracted from a variety of occurrences. It is important to check whether the corresponding form appeared rather than just the root and to note when it appeared with a particular meaning and in what context.

Anttila's principles for investigation and Barr's criteria for philological treatments have already been mentioned. These suggestions are to complement them. When a cognate is identified, then as far as possible the following questions should be answered:

1. Does it comply with normal phonological correspondences between the source language and Hebrew? If not, then try again.
2. How closely related is the source to Hebrew? Is it Canaanite? West Semitic?
3. Which other languages does the form occur in? What does it mean in them?

---

[83] F.E. Greenspahn, *Hapax Legomena in Biblical Hebrew*, 29; cf. H.R. Cohen, *Biblical Hapax Legomena in the Light of Akkadian and Ugaritic*, 7; Y. Hoffman, *A Blemished Perfection*, 180–1.

[84] Greenspahn, *Hapax Legomena*, 46.

4. What place does each item have in its source language's lexicon?
5. What is known of its use in its source language?
6. How does its use compare to the current Hebrew context?
7. What is the relative dating of occurrence of each form to Hebrew? Was it feasible for that form and meaning to exist in Hebrew at that time?
8. How does the suggestion affect the structure of the Hebrew lexicon?
9. Does it produce a homonym? How does this affect communicative efficiency?
10. Does the discovery fit better than the usual sense elsewhere in BH texts?
11. Has Hebrew borrowed this item? From which language? When? Why?
12. How does the reconstruction compare to previous suggestions?

Any reconstruction derived via comparative philology is an abstraction from available data and there is no certainty that that particular link-up of form and meaning existed in Hebrew, or that the author of the text under investigation knew it. The meaning obtained through such linguistic enquiry is inevitably a product of the philological process and ultimately that which seems most reasonable to the reader.

5

Versions

1. Introduction

The versions are early translations of the Hebrew Bible into Greek, Aramaic, Latin and other languages. In textual treatments they are typically taken to be separate witnesses to 'the original text'. When the MT is difficult then versions are used as sources from which another Hebrew text can be reconstructed. In philological treatments versions witness to a different understanding of the same Hebrew text. However, it is not always possible to distinguish between these types of treatment. Discussion in this chapter focuses on the Septuagint, the version most frequently referred to for elucidating the Hebrew text, with examples taken from Judges 4.

The fundamental factor for consideration is that versions are translations. The basic hermeneutical model described in the Introduction,

AUTHOR – TEXT – READER,

becomes more complicated when dealing with translation. In this situation the model is

AUTHOR – TEXT1 – TRANSLATOR – TEXT2 – READER,

where TRANSLATOR is READER of TEXT1 and AUTHOR of TEXT2. Whereas the author encodes the text, the translator recodes the text from one language into another. As a reader the translator may have approached the source text from any number of different perspectives which will have influenced the resultant interpretation of that text. That interpretation combined with the translator's competence in both source and target languages and the translator's intention as an author all affect the final form of the target text.

Modern scholars read versions (TEXT2) to increase their under-standing of the MT (not necessarily identical to TEXT1). In effect, they seek to reverse the process of translation and reconstruct the *Vorlage* (TEXT1). But they are extremely unlikely to uncover 1:1 mapping between two texts. The original translators provide the key to the process; hence the need to learn as much as possible about them, their intentions and their techniques. Tov insists the translator's intention determines the meanings of words in the Septuagint (LXX),[1] but Muraoka notes that even when scholars claim to be absolutely certain about the identity of the MT and the translated *Vorlage* it may not always be possible to agree on how the translator understood the Hebrew text and what he intended by his translation.[2] As with authorial intention, the translator's intention is a useful goal but not necessarily an achievable one.

2. The Septuagint

2.1 The data

The Septuagint is the ancient Jewish translation of the Hebrew Bible into Greek. According to a letter of Aristeas, the Pentateuch was translated in Alexandria by seventy-two Jewish scholars (hence the name 'LXX') during the third century BCE. Other books of the Hebrew Bible were variously translated into Greek by many different hands at other times. Today 'Septuagint' denotes both translations of the Bible into Greek which later became canonical and other Greek writings which did not become canonical. The original translation is called 'Old Greek' (OG) to distinguish it from later recensions. It is also important to make a distinction between the three pre-Hexaplaric revisions by Aquila, Symmachus and Theodotion, and post-Hexaplaric ones, the most important by Lucian (d. 312 CE). There are many witnesses to the LXX dating from the second century BCE to late Middle Ages. A few papyrus fragments have been discovered, but most extant materials are Greek uncials dating from the fourth to tenth century CE.[3]

---

[1] E. Tov, 'Three Dimensions of LXX Words', 529, 541.
[2] T. Muraoka, 'Towards a Septuagint Lexicon', 259.
[3] Cf. S. Jellicoe, *The Septuagint and Modern Study*, 74–5; Tov, *Textual Criticism*, 134–5.

The LXX was extremely important to the Jewish community
in the dispersion as they became less and less well acquainted with
Hebrew. It was also Holy Scripture for the first Christians. Their
frequent use of the LXX and disagreements about interpretation
caused Jews to distance themselves from it. These disputes partly
concerned discrepancies such as the rendering of עלמה in Isaiah
7:14 by παρθενος. Christians maintained that this was a Jewish
rendering, whereas Jews rejected it as inaccurate according to the
Hebrew. Christians also added to the text: in Psalm 95:10 the
phrase ὁ κυριος ἐβασιλευσεν was supplemented by ἀπο ξυλου
'from the wood'. As the Pre-Masoretic text became fixed during the
first century CE and a prominent school of rabbinic interpretation
laid emphasis on every letter of the sacred text, the LXX lost its
authority in Judaism and a Greek version which more accurately
reflected the Hebrew was required.

In approximately 125 CE Aquila translated every detail of his text
as precisely as possible into Greek: the first verse of the Bible in the
LXX read ἐν ἀρχη ἐποιησεν ὁ θεος τον οὐρανον και την γῆν. Aquila
seems to have aimed at providing a rendering of all Hebrew derivatives which was accurate even in regard to etymology: he translated
ראשית as a derivative of ראש by κεφαλαιον, a derivative of κεφαλη,
meaning 'main point, sum' rather than 'beginning', and even the
accusative marker את was translated separately by συν 'with'.[4]
Aquila was by far the most literal of the translators. Symmachus was
on the one hand very precise, but on the other hand, he translated the
sense rather than rendering Hebrew word for word. The third
pre-Hexaplaric version is known as *kaige*-Theodotion. Barthélemy
named an anonymous revision of the LXX καιγε because one of its
distinctive features is that גם 'also' is usually translated with καιγε 'at
least', apparently following the rabbinic hermeneutical rule that each
gam in the Bible refers not only to the word(s) occurring after it but
also to one additional word.[5] In antiquity this anonymous revision
was ascribed to Theodotion.

In 230–45 CE Origen organized a comprehensive edition of the
Bible in six columns (hence 'Hexapla'). This contained the Hebrew
text, a Greek transliteration, the work of Aquila and Symmachus,
Origen's annotated version of the LXX with symbols to indicate
whether material had been added (÷) or deleted (*) to bring it closer
to the Hebrew, and Theodotion's revision. The second column of

---

[4] Cf. A. Rahlfs, 'History of the Septuagint Text', lix.
[5] Tov, *Textual Criticism*, 145.

Origen's Hexapla provides the major source for transliteration of Hebrew. It is generally agreed it represents the actual reading of the Hebrew text less than two centuries after the destruction of the second temple. The importance of the Hexapla for this study is the witness it provides to the Greek texts.

The corpus of the LXX furnishes a whole field of study and scholars such as Jellicoe have insisted that it be studied as literature in its own right without reference to the Hebrew texts.[6] As Aejmelaeus has helpfully pointed out, 'textual criticism of the Septuagint, study of the Septuagintal translation technique, and use of the Septuagint for the purposes of OT textual criticism are three mutually dependent fields of study, each of which moves around the original Septuagint, the translation techniques, and the *Vorlage* – three more or less hypothetical entities – and benefits from advances made in the two other fields'.[7] This insight is vital to any exploration of how the LXX may assist in the investigation of meaning in the Hebrew Bible.

The LXX is considered to be the most important, even indispensable, witness to a Hebrew text many centuries earlier than the MT. It reveals, for instance, that *kethib-qere* variants were already evident.[8] It also reflects a greater variety of important variants than all the other traditions put together.[9] Hence when problems are encountered in Hebrew texts scholars have sought to compare the MT to the Hebrew text underlying the LXX. Indeed some would go so far as to say that the Greek and Hebrew texts provide two different and even equal witnesses to an earlier or original Hebrew text. The Greek texts may indeed be older than the Hebrew ones, but that does not automatically signify that they are more accurate or faithful to an earlier source. There is furthermore a multiplicity of Greek texts which may or may not derive from a single original text.

2.2 *Translation techniques*

The versions provide indirect witness to Hebrew texts: when scholars declare the LXX 'read' a particular Hebrew word, they mean that

---

[6] Jellicoe, *Septuagint*, 352; cf. I.L. Seeligmann, 'Problems and Perspectives in Modern Septuagint Research', 170.

[7] A. Aejmelaeus, 'What Can We Know about the Hebrew *Vorlage* of the Septuagint?', 60.

[8] Gordis, *Biblical Text in the Making*, xvii.

[9] Tov, *Textual Criticism*, 142.

the Greek text, if back-translated into Hebrew, would produce that word in the *Vorlage*. Although there are many thousands of differences between the MT and the versions, according to Tov, only a fraction of them was created by divergence between the MT and the *Vorlage*.[10] Most differences are not due to a different Hebrew text but to the translator and the process of transmission.

There is no guarantee that modern scholars can reliably reconstruct the Hebrew *Vorlage* of the Greek text because there are many possible relations between what the translators wrote in Greek (TEXT2) and the Hebrew text in front of them (TEXT1). The translator may have misread the Hebrew: the MT of Jeremiah 23:9 contains the word שִׁכּוֹר 'drunk', whereas Greek has συντετριμμένος 'broken', having read the Hebrew as שָׁבוּר.[11] The translator may have mistranslated the Hebrew. In the case of a difficult word or unknown phrase he may have guessed, or resorted to transliteration, used a more general word or attempted a paraphrase, or assimilated his text to another passage.[12] The translator may have sincerely translated the text in a way which according to modern scholars is 'wrong' thus giving the impression that they were reading a different Hebrew text. The translator may have made deliberate exegetical decisions on how the target text should be worded. Further divergences between the MT and the *Vorlage* may be due to errors made in the textual transmission of the translation.[13] These factors demonstrate the vital importance of knowing all the intricacies of the translator's exegesis and translation technique.

When the Greek translator employed very literal translation techniques, like mechanical word-for-word replacement, then the two texts approach 1:1 mapping and it is more likely that scholars can uncover, not the underlying written Hebrew text (TEXT1) but rather *the Hebrew that the translator had in mind*. There is no way of knowing if that was identical with the Hebrew *Vorlage*, although in practice scholars work as if it was. Reconstruction of the *Vorlage* can be determined more accurately the more consistently the translator used fixed translation equivalents for individual words and grammatical categories. If a certain element is freely rendered,

---

[10] Tov, *Textual Criticism*, 123.
[11] E. Tov, *The Text-Critical Use of the Septuagint in Biblical Research*, 82–3.
[12] E. Tov, 'Did the Septuagint Translators Always Understand Their Hebrew Text?', 55–6.
[13] Cf. Section 2.4 for examples.

however, it is much more difficult, if not impossible, to reconstruct the Hebrew source.[14] Despite these difficulties, discoveries of biblical texts at Qumran have supported some reconstructions of the LXX source by providing identical readings to those proposed by scholars through back-translation.[15]

Different parts of the LXX demonstrate the use of different translation techniques; therefore scholars need to be familiar with the whole section or book of the LXX on which they are working. Whether or not the translators themselves followed any clear or definite policy on how to render texts is debatable, they certainly worked without modern linguistic schooling and dictionaries, although there is evidence that the Pentateuch was used as a model for later translations.[16] Scholars should beware of judging ancient translations against modern standards; hence the urgent need for detailed commentaries on the nature of the translation activity resulting in each section of the LXX.

Linguists note that the meaning of a word is highly determined by its linguistic context. The question arises whether the same applies to the LXX, for it is not simply a literary creation encoded in one language; it is rather a recoding of an important religious Hebrew text. Some parts of the LXX employ a particular Greek word automatically for a particular Hebrew word and follow Aquila in attempting to model Hebrew morphology in Greek. The resultant translation is therefore not natural Greek; rather it is Hebrew text rendered directly into Greek symbols. This question is tied to both the translator's ability and the translator's intention. Was the translator working to produce a Greek text for those who could already read Hebrew? If so, the result might be expected to mirror the Hebrew text. However, if the translator was working towards producing a Greek text for those who had no knowledge of Hebrew, then easy comprehension of content would be expected to take priority over the form of the target text. In Brock's terms in the former case the translator would be *interpres* and in the latter *expositor*. The *interpres* is essentially oriented towards the source text, working on small units of translation (word or even morpheme), simply passing on any difficulties in the original, even if the translation makes nonsense. The *expositor* is oriented towards the reader, working on larger units of translation (phrase,

---

[14] Tov, *Textual Criticism*, 129.
[15] Tov, *Textual Criticism*, 117.
[16] S. Olofsson, *The LXX Version*, 26.

sentence or even paragraph), seeking to resolve any difficulties in the original, content to change grammatical categories and provide dynamic renderings.[17] The critical factor in the case of the LXX appears to be the high regard in which the very lettering of Hebrew text was held. The priority of translators such as Aquila was to mirror the form of the Hebrew text as closely as possible almost with disregard to meaning, although they must have had a basic understanding of the syntactic and semantic structure of the Hebrew text in order to make any attempt at translation.

Modern biblical translation aims to read well in the target language: it is 'free', dynamic, giving a sense of the passage as a whole, and making extensive use of paraphrase. It is extremely unlikely to employ direct 1:1 word-substitutions. By today's standards all of the Greek versions are literal translations but as Barr points out there are degrees of literalism. He suggests six distinguishable modes of difference between a more literal and a less literal rendering of a Hebrew text:

1.   *The division into elements or segments, and the sequence in which these elements are represented*: Hebrew temporal expressions have בְּ + infin. + noun or suffix. Less literal approaches turn the entire phrase into a typical Greek temporal expression: 2 Samuel 8:3 MT בְּלֶכְתּוֹ is rendered LXX πορευομενον αὐτοῦ. A more literal approach preserves in Greek a word for 'in' and an infinitive: thus Leviticus 22:16 MT בְּאָכְלָם אֶת־קָדְשֵׁיהֶם becomes LXX ἐν τῷ ἐσθιειν αὐτουσ τα ἁγια αὐτῶν.Aquila's literalism resorting to segmentation below word level can ruin the meaning of the Greek text: ἐκτισεν ὁ θεος συν τον οὐρανον και συν την γῆν. Such literal translation of important theological phrases can have very serious effects on the religious tradition.[18]

2.   *The quantitative addition or subtraction of elements* from the original means a loss of literality. This tendency is more marked in the Targums.

3.   *Consistency or non-consistency in the rendering*: the use of the same word in TEXT2 every time a particular word appears in TEXT1 is usually considered to be a mark of literalism. But such consistency in the use of vocabulary equivalences is not

---

[17]   S.P. Brock, 'To Revise or Not to Revise', 312.
[18]   J. Barr, 'The Typology of Literalism in Ancient Biblical Translations', 294–303.

in itself a guarantee of literalism. Sometimes a high degree of consistency is due to the fact that a particular word in the target language is the natural one to use and can be used repeatedly without strain: for example διαθήκη for ברית. Even literal translators yielded where words were polysemic, and some strange renderings may be understood as homonym mistakes.[19]

4. *The accuracy and level of semantic information*: a word's semantic range is dependent on its own language, therefore word **a** in language **A** will not have the same semantic range as word **b** in language **B**. Barr notes that παρθενος (used to translate עַלְמָה in Is. 7:14) had the general meaning 'young woman' but also carried a more specific sense 'virgin' (which עַלְמָה did not). Christians claimed this text spoke of a virgin birth. In cases of metaphor and idiom a literal translation preserves the metaphor, whilst a free translation renders the significance of the metaphor but in doing so destroys the metaphor itself. It restricts the reader's interpretation.[20]

5. *Coded 'etymological' indication of formal/semantic relationships obtaining in the vocabulary of the original language*: in Judges 5:3 (B text) ἐγω εἰμι ἀσομαι 'I will sing', εἰμι is purely a code marker signalling that Hebrew used the pronoun אנכי rather than אני. The 'etymological' style of translation classified together a group of Hebrew words having some common formal element and assigned to them all the semantic value of one dominant member – like Aquila's use of κεφαλαιον for בראשית.[21]

6. *Level of text and level of analysis*: sometimes translators analysed the source text lexically, deriving from it elements which were taken literally, and then combined in an entirely free syntactic arrangement as in LXX Proverbs.[22]

Adair questions the objectivity of Barr's criteria. He notes that qualities of translation such as accuracy and meaning are not easily quantifiable.[23] The formal factors of language are always more accessible to analysis than semantic aspects. Language meaning is a

---

[19] Barr, 'Typology of Literalism', 305–14.

[20] Barr, 'Typology of Literalism', 314–18.

[21] Barr, 'Typology of Literalism', 318–22.

[22] Barr, 'Typology of Literalism', 322–3.

[23] J. Adair, '"Literal" and "Free" Translations', 186.

function of language use and is tied to mental representations which cannot easily be formally quantified as evidenced by attempts at representing natural language by formal logic. Linguists inevitably rely to a certain extent on intuition, as no author or translator is completely consistent in the way that a computer might be.

Tov provides a similar set of criteria for the analysis of literal renderings:

1. *Internal Consistency*: the rendering of all occurrences of a Hebrew word, element, root or construction as far as possible by the same Greek equivalent. This tendency towards 'stereo-typing' was the rule rather than the exception and produced 'Hebraisms', that is, Greek words, phrases or constructions which transfer characteristic Hebrew elements into Greek regardless of Greek idiom even to the extent of always translating Hebrew words from one root with Greek words from one root, for example טוב = ἀγαθο-, צדק = δικαιο-.

2. *The representation of the constituents of Hebrew words by individual Greek equivalents*: literal translators segmented Hebrew words into semantic elements, which were then represented by their individual Greek equivalents, e.g. rendering the preposition ב by ἐν and מכתם = תם מך (Aq. τοῦ ταπεινοφρονος και ἁπλοῦ, Ps. 16:1).[24]

3. *Word order*: some translators adhered as much as possible to the word order of the Hebrew text; others followed the rules of Greek.

4. *Quantitative representation*: literal translators did their utmost to represent each individual element in the Hebrew text by one equivalent element in the translation. Others felt free to add clarifying elements or to omit other elements.

5. *Linguistic adequacy of lexical choices*: Tov notes that this is subjective and therefore cannot be used profitably in analysis of translation units.[25] Yet this is critical when referring to the versions in philological treatments.

These various criteria can be collapsed into four basic categories: consistency of renderings, level of segmentation, relative order of elements, and semantic adequacy of interpretation. Based on

---

[24] J. Barr, 'Vocalization and the Analysis of Hebrew among the Ancient Translators', 7.

[25] Tov, *Septuagint*, 24.

knowledge of linguistic behaviour typical of literal translators, Tov and Wright used computers to analyse five specific criteria for assessing literalness:

1. rendering of Hebrew preposition בְּ by ἐν;
2. rendering of conjunction כִּי by ὅτι or διοτι;
3. rendering of Hebrew third per. sing. masc. suffix by αὐτος and ἑαυτος;
4. frequency of prepositions added in the LXX in accordance with rules of Greek or translation habits;
5. frequency of Greek post-position particles δε, οὖν, μεν and τε in relation to και.[26]

They note that in some books such as the Minor Prophets, translators had relatively fixed ways of translating certain Hebrew words or phrases and other words or phrases were translated with greater flexibility depending on context.[27] Thus context does play a part in the wording of the LXX. Even extremely literal translators such as Aquila were not completely consistent: אֵת is not in every instance rendered by συν.

Adair suggests a more descriptive terminology in order to produce a full quantitative description of the translation technique of a given version. Data from four categories of consistency (lexical and grammatical), segmentation, word order, and quantitative analysis are first collected from the text. He examines only the category of consistency in detail, looking at five major subcategories of Lexical Consistency, Consistency in the Use of Word Classes, Grammatical Consistency in Rendering Verbs, Grammatical Consistency in Rendering Nouns and Adjectives, and Grammatical Consistency in Rendering Pronouns. First, the number of distinct Hebrew words occurring in the passage are counted. Greek words are counted per Hebrew word. Then the total number of Hebrew words that appear more than once is counted. Finally, the deviation factor from absolute consistency is calculated. This produces a number which can be compared to that for other passages. To know that a certain translation uses 1.51 words per Hebrew word or that 85.9 per cent of the time a Hebrew word is rendered by the primary word gives some idea of a translator's consistency. But it does

---

[26] E. Tov and B.G. Wright, 'Computer-Assisted Study of the Criteria for Assessing the Literalness of Translation Units in the LXX', 158.

[27] Tov and Wright, 'Criteria for Assessing Literalness', 183.

not help scholars to know whether on this particular occasion in this specific context the translator has read a certain Hebrew word.

The above criteria are based on formal equivalents. Several other factors need to be taken into account when looking at lexical consistency: the semantic range of the Hebrew word and its place in the appropriate semantic field; the comparable lexical and grammatical resources available in the target language; the demands of the target language with respect to form and content; and the translator's knowledge of Hebrew. Olofsson suggests a definition of consistency from the viewpoint of the target language: a Hebrew word which is always rendered by an equivalent in Greek which is never employed for any other Hebrew word could be called 'strictly consistent' or 'doubly consistent', in contrast to 'consistent': for example עשר is always rendered πλουτος, yet πλουτος renders nine Hebrew words: חיל, המון, הון, גדולה, אוצר, שפצ and רכלה, עשר, כבור.[28]

It is vital that the scholar gains a reasonable understanding of the translation techniques employed in the Greek text used to assist in comprehension of a Hebrew text. Statistical studies of literalness such as those by Tov and Wright can be helpful but they are not the same as gaining a 'feel' for the stylistic, lexical, exegetical and theological characteristics of the LXX translator. The next section provides an overview of the LXX of Judges which produces most of the examples of deviation from the MT.

2.3 *Greek texts of the book of Judges*

The Greek versions of Judges clearly demonstrate that the LXX is not a single entity. When claiming that the LXX provides a different reading of the Hebrew text, scholars need to clarify to which uncial or miniscule of the LXX they are referring, bearing in mind the known history and characteristics of that particular source. One question to be asked is whether the Hexapla has influenced the translation. The same factors apply in the clarification of the LXX text as they do in the clarification of the MT. An eclectic text of the LXX with a detailed critical apparatus is therefore needed.

The Greek texts of Judges as a rule keep close to the underlying Hebrew. The main problem is the existence of the two texts Codex Alexandrinus (A) and Codex Vaticanus (B). Paul de Lagarde contended that the A and B texts represent different translations and

---

[28] Olofsson, *LXX Version*, 18.

therefore they were printed on the same page with A above B, each with critical apparatus, in the edition of Rahlfs.[29] It is now generally agreed that the differences between the texts are due to extensive and repeated revision of the original translation. A is considered to be the superior text with B having been greatly influenced by systematic correction for closer conformity with the Hebrew. Tov and Wright classify Judges A as 'relatively literal'; they do not comment on B.[30] Barthélemy has demonstrated that it contains features of the *kaige* recension, but Lindars argues that B cannot be regarded as a consistent example of the *kaige* text of Judges, for some of its variations from A must be regarded as resulting from stylistic improvement.[31] But even A is not free from Hexaplaric influence. Lindars has asserted that for recovery of the original LXX recourse must be made to certain miniscules which are comparatively free from Hexaplaric influence. He had in mind here the cursives *glnw* of group AII,[32] particularly when supported by Old Latin. He warned that reliance on the great uncials A and B is liable to lead to false conclusions and so he emphasized the urgent need for an eclectic text of the Greek Judges.[33]

Once some understanding of the translation technique of a particular text has been gained (despite the statistical studies reviewed above, in practice this usually happens through intuition), then the scholar can begin to consider when it is appropriate to reconstruct the Hebrew *Vorlage*. The first step in the process is to attempt to establish a relationship between all the words in the MT and the LXX, thus revealing which elements do not appear to reflect the MT. At this point Tov introduces the notion of *deviation* which is 'any detail in the translation that differs from a literal rendering of the parent text'.[34] Any translation involves a certain amount of interpretation on the part of the translator, whether it is purely at the level of recognizing the forms and meanings of the Hebrew text, or at the subsequent stage of choice of content, reference, style or

---

[29] Cf. Jellicoe, *Septuagint*, 280.

[30] Tov and Wright, 'Criteria for Assessing Literalness', 37.

[31] B. Lindars, 'Some Septuagint Readings in Judges', 1.

[32] The groups of texts are: B plus the cursives *efjqsz* (B); A and the cursives *abcx* (AI); the 9 cursives *dglnoptvw* (AII); the uncials MN and the cursives *yb*$_2$ (AIII) according to A.V. Billen, 'The Hexaplaric Element in the LXX Version of Judges'.

[33] B. Lindars, *Judges 1–5*, ix.

[34] Tov, *Septuagint*, 39.

theological exegesis.[35] The scholar needs to be able to identify the
source or type of divergence from the MT and only when all other
possible factors have been dismissed should it be assumed that
the LXX is based on a different Hebrew text. The final step in the
process is the weighing of the different Hebrew readings to determine whether the reconstructed LXX *Vorlage* or the MT is the
superior text.

2.4 Some sources of deviation from the MT

The process of exegesis may result in the addition of elements
to improve readability and clarify the meaning of the Hebrew:
in Judges 4:8, where Barak refuses to go without Deborah, both
A and B add the explanation ὅτι οὐκ οἶδα την ἡμεραν ἐν ᾗ
εὐοδοι κυριος τον ἀγγελον μετ’ ἐμοῦ. ‘For I do not know the day
on which the LORD prospers his angel with me’. Then, in verse 9
A adds προς αὐτον Δεββωρα which does not appear in the Hebrew
but does improve the style and both Greek versions add the phrase
πλην γίνωσκε ὅτι where there is no verb in Hebrew. In verse
21 A reads και αὐτος ἀπεσκαρισεν ἀνα μεσον τῶν γονατων
αὐτες και ἐξεψυξεν και ἀπεθανεν, adding the further details
‘and he jerked between her knees and lost consciousness and
died’, whereas B reads και αὐτος ἐξεστως ἐσκοτωθη ‘and he
collapsed dead’, more or less following the very concise style of
the Hebrew.[36]

Similarly, items may be omitted or condensed if they are considered to be superfluous or if the Hebrew text was misread. At the
beginning of Judges 4 A omits mention of Ehud, who is unexpected
as Shamgar was the last Judge mentioned. In the Song of Deborah
(Jdgs. 5) the situation is rather more complicated. The translators
obviously struggled with verse 10:

MT: רֹכְבֵי אֲתֹנוֹת צְחֹרוֹת יֹשְׁבֵי עַל־מִדִּין וְהֹלְכֵי עַל־דֶּרֶךְ שִׂיחוּ
you who ride on tawny asses, sitting on saddle-cloths, and you who
pass along the way, give praise

A: ἐπιβεβηκοτες ἐπι ὑποζυγιων, καθημενοι ἐπι λαμπηνων
you who ride on asses, who sit in covered waggons

---

[35] Cf. Barr, ‘Typology of Literalism’, 16–17; Tov, *Septuagint*, 45–6.
[36] Cf. Soggin, *Judges*, 67.

B: ἐπιβεβηκοτες ἐπι ὀνου θηλειας μεσημβριας, καθημενοι ἐπι κριτηριου και πορευομενοι ἐπι ὀδους συνεδεωϖ ἐφ' ὀδῷ,

you who ride on female asses at noon, who sit in judgement, and who go the way of the council go along the way

A omits both צחרות and והלכי על־דרך, the latter phrase most probably due to its similarity to the preceding verse. The loss of צחרות 'tawny' is more difficult to explain. It is fairly obvious that the translators did not know this word, B has μεσημβρίας 'at noon' possibly due to misreading Hebrew as צהרים and the Hexapla has λαμτούσων which Lindars believes represents צחחות 'gleaming'. מדין also caused difficulties: A's λαμπηνων 'covered wagons' mis-reads an Aramaic plural of מד 'measure', 'long robes' or possibly 'rich carpets'. B's κριτηριου implies Hebrew read as מָדוֹן meaning 'strife', often in a judicial sense. The great men who ride on tawny she-asses are likely to be those who sit at the court of justice too. Hence, the Targum reading: 'those who ride asses go through every district of Israel, and after giving judgement go on their ways to tell of God's deeds'.[37]

LXX translators tended to avoid using anthropomorphic expressions of God. The phrase בְּעֵינֵי יהוה occurs fifteen times in the MT of Judges. But ἐν ὀφθαλμοις is not used before the divine name. In Judges 4:1 בְּעֵינֵי יהוה is rendered ἐναντι κυριου 'against the LORD' in A and ἐνωπιον κυριου 'before the LORD' in B.[38] Further examples include the use of δοξα 'glory' for תמנה the 'form' of God in Numbers 12:8 and Gideon being visited by ὁ αγγελος κυριου 'the angel of the LORD' in Judges 6:14, 16 instead of by 'the LORD' (MT יהוה). Yet, the translator of Judges 13:22 did not attempt to modify Manoah's exclamation after seeing the angel, 'We shall surely die for we have seen God', מוֹת נָמוּת כִּי אֱלֹהִים רָאִינוּ, rendering it θανατω ἀποθανούμεθα, ὁτι θεὸν ἑωράκαμεν (εἰδομεν B), although in the rest of this passage the visitor is referred to as ἀγγελος κυριου 'the angel of the LORD'.[39] When seeking to illuminate the meaning of the Hebrew text through reference to the versions, scholars should be mindful of theologically motivated exegesis such as the avoidance of anthropomorphisms.

---

[37] Cf. B. Lindars, 'Some Septuagint Readings in Judges', 5–9.

[38] Cf. Lindars, *Judges*, 118.

[39] Cf. A. Hanson, 'The Treatment in the LXX of the Theme of Seeing God', 557–68.

When encountering difficulties some translators merely transliterated Hebrew. In Judges 5:7 A transliterates פְרָזוֹן as φραζων in
ἐξέλιπεν φραζων ἐν τῷ Ισραήλ for חָדְלוּ פְרָזוֹן בְּיִשְׂרָאֵל.
Unknown words were transliterated in exact Hebrew form
including prefixes and suffixes: in Judges 5:22 A reads αμαδαρωθ
δυνατων αὐτοῦ for Hebrew מִדַּהֲרוֹת דַּהֲרוֹת אַבִּירָיו.[40] In Judges 4:6
A has Κεδες whereas B has Καδης. The different place names
could be due either to differences in transliteration of קֶדֶשׁ, or to
the existence of more than one location with very similar names.[41]

Translators may have been unable to identify the referent of a
noun. In Judges 4:11, A takes חֶבֶר to refer to a group of Kenites,
whilst B takes it to be a proper name and transliterates it. Commentators have speculated as to the identity of the article in verse 18
with which Jael covered or hid Sisera – suggestions range from a
rug with a generous pile (but surely he would have been hot after
his frantic flight on foot) to a fly-net (but that would hardly
have hidden him). The problem is the *hapax legomenon* בַּשְּׂמִיכָה. A
indicates that Jael hid Sisera with 'a curtain' (possibly of goat hair)
by employing the unusual technical term δερρει which refers to
the skin hung at the entrance to the tent.[42] B is more vague in its
rendition: και περιεβαλεν αὐτον ἐπιβαιῳ, 'she covered him with
a covering'.

עַד־אֵלוֹן בְּצַעֲנַּים caused further problems for translators in verse
11. The *qere* took בְּ as a preposition and adopted spelling from
Joshua 19:33 מֵאֵלוֹן בְּצַעֲנַנִּים, possibly connecting this form with
צָעַן, meaning 'to wander, travel', thus providing Soggin's 'oak of
the caravanners'.[43] The LXX appears to interpret בְּצַעֲנַּים as deriving
from בָּצַע meaning 'to cut off' giving ἀναπαυομενων in A, or 'to
plunder' for πλεονεκτουντων in B.[44] Some commentators prefer
to transliterate the Hebrew retaining the place name 'Oak of
Zaananim' which contrasts with Deborah's Palm mentioned in
verse 5. This is one example of a text which translators of versions
found just as difficult as today's scholars.

As mentioned above, verse 21 caused difficulties:

[40] E. Tov, 'Septuagint Translators Always Understand Their Hebrew
Text?', 55–6.
[41] Cf. Lindars, *Judges*, 185.
[42] Soggin, *Judges*, 67.
[43] Soggin, *Judges*, 66.
[44] Cf. Lindars, *Judges*, 192.

A: Ιαηλ ... και εἰσῆλθεν προς αὐτον ἡσυχῇ και ἐνεκρουσεν τον πασσαλον ἐν τῇ γναθῳ αὐτον και διηλασεν ἐν τῇ γῃ

B: Ιαηλ ... και εἰσῆλθεν προς αὐτον ἐν κρυφῇ και ἐπηξεν τον πασσαλον ἐν τῷ κροταφῳ αὐτου και διεξῆλθεν ἐν τῇ γῃ

The verb בָּלָט means 'secretly', but here implies 'silently'; hence ἡσυχῇ 'quietly' in A becoming ἐν κρυφῇ 'in secret' in B. Both verbs ἐνεκρουσεν and ἐπηξεν describe the action of pitching a tent. The precise referent of Hebrew בְּרַקָּתוֹ is obscure, although it appears to indicate a visible part of the head (cf. Song. 4:3; 6:7) and somewhere vulnerable. A interprets it as 'jaw' γναθος, and B as 'temples' κροτφος, as in verse 22. The meaning of the verb in וַתִּצְנַח בָּאָרֶץ was unknown to the translators. צנח only occurs elsewhere in Judges 1:14 and Joshua 15:18. Here it obviously refers to the tent peg. A assumes Jael is the subject of the action, whilst B takes the peg to be the subject; and its correction excellently expresses the meaning of the Hebrew 'it went right through into the earth'.[45]

Matters of style include explicit use of the definite article after prepositions, which is evident in B, choice of word order (B tending to follow Hebrew more closely), and the use of different prepositions. Most of these result in minor deviations from the sense of the MT, and hence for this study it does not matter whether they are due to the translator or to a different *Vorlage*.[46] The disparities between the LXX and MT of Judges 4 are minor and do not significantly alter the sense of the chapter, whereas the greater differences with respect to the poem in Judges 5 reveal the difficulties the translators had in understanding that text. Slight variations in wording, explicit use of the definite article and even the addition of explanatory words and clauses do not change the meaning of the original text. They serve rather to clarify the message for contemporary readers and in some instances to mirror more closely the precise form of the Hebrew text.

As well as these exegetical issues, scholars need to consider scribal developments in the LXX, haplography or dittography and parablepsis, along with the confusion of graphically similar letters and wrong word division.[47] Some apparent additions in the Greek versions may reveal an accidental omission from the Hebrew

---

[45] Lindars, *Judges*, 201–2.
[46] Cf. Aejmelaeus, 'Hebrew *Vorlage*', 68.
[47] Cf. Tov, *Septuagint*, 50–1.

text. In the well-known example from Judges 16:13–14 Samson's instruction to Delilah to weave his hair into the loom merges into the account of her doing so. This is a case of parablepsis: the scribe has slipped from מַסֶּכֶת 'web' in the instructions to the same word in the narrative on the next line.[48] It is only when all of these possible factors have been eliminated that scholars should attempt retroversion of an element of the LXX text into Hebrew.

2.5 Reconstruction of the Vorlage

Tov makes a distinction between 'content' elements, which can be retroverted with reasonable certainty on the basis of knowledge of the translator's vocabulary, and 'grammatical' elements such as prepositions, conjunctions and particles, for which there is insufficient data for identification.[49] Knowledge of the translator's vocabulary in practice means reference to a concordance such as Hatch-Redpath, which merely records extant formal equivalents without commenting on any semantic correlation between them.[50] Scholars must consider the way in which the translator handles the whole context, and retroversion should aim to follow the grammar and lexical understanding of the translator rather than the modern scholar's understanding of Hebrew philology. The retroversion is based not only on the meaning of the Greek but also on the graphic form of the Hebrew text, thus taking into account the orthography of the time and allowing for typical textual errors.

Any retroversion is inevitably derived with reference to the MT (it is based on vocabulary equivalences between the MT and LXX) and is in effect grafted back into the MT. Tov asserts that correct retroversions should be probable from a textual point of view and plausible from the perspective of grammar, vocabulary and style of the Hebrew Bible, and in particular of the book in which the reading is found. Some retroversions may also be supported by identical readings elsewhere.[51]

It should be remembered that any retroversion is not claimed to be exactly equivalent to the Hebrew *Vorlage* of the version: there is

---

[48] Cf. B. Lindars, 'A Commentary on the Greek Judges?', 174–5.

[49] Tov, *Septuagint*, 59, but see bibliography at 69–70; cf. J.R. Adair, 'A Methodology for Using the Versions in the Textual Criticism of the Old Testament', 116–17.

[50] Cf. Tov, *Septuagint*, 90–1.

[51] Tov, *Septuagint*, 59–60.

no way of knowing whether it existed in the mind of the translator or in a Hebrew text or at all. Therefore, no retroversions are beyond doubt, but some are more reliable than others. Those supported by scribal errors in Hebrew and by Hebraisms in the LXX which are not supported by any corresponding element in the MT are considered to be more reliable, whereas retroversion of any element in a non-literal translation is doubtful, as are the attempted retroversions of additions and omissions of personal names, harmonizations and *hapax legomena*.

2.6 Evaluation of retroverted variants

In principle the evaluation of Hebrew and retroverted variants is identical, as long as the retroversion is reliable.[52] The LXX provides the greatest number of significant variants to the biblical text and many have been incorporated into the *BHS*. This factor must be borne in mind when seeking to gain meaning from the biblical text because the compilers of the *BHS* have already made decisions about the meaning of the Hebrew text. All evaluations of variant readings are by nature subjective and therefore open to debate. The decision to use the *BHS* as the source text for the study of meaning in CH does not preclude criticism of its evaluation and inclusion of retroverted variants.

Tov insists that common sense should be the main guide for locating the most contextually appropriate reading.[53] Various abstract rules are nevertheless recommended, a distinction usually being made between internal and external criteria. Internal criteria concern the intrinsic value of the reading itself whilst external criteria relate to the document in which the reading is found. It is often stated that all things being equal the MT reading should be preferred.[54] As Tov has pointed out, in practice the MT readings are usually preferable, but this statistical information should not be used to influence decisions in individual cases.[55] Another external criterion is the breadth of witness to a particular variant, but several versions can be interdependent, so the relationships

---

[52] Tov, *Septuagint*, 213–14.
[53] Tov, *Septuagint*, 219; cf. M.L. Margolis, 'Complete Induction for the Identification of the Vocabulary in the Greek Versions of the Old Testament with Its Semitic Equivalents'.
[54] R.W. Klein, *Textual Criticism of the Old Testament*, 74.
[55] Tov, *Septuagint*, 223.

between the various versions must be taken into account when evaluating variants. As Barr notes, even where one version has not been influenced by another, both may have been influenced by the same tradition of interpretation.[56] It is a dictum therefore that variants should be weighed not counted. Older witnesses are often preferred to more recent ones, but again there is no guarantee that an older witness is less corrupt than a more recent one.

Internal criteria include the rule *lectio difficilior probabilior* – the more difficult reading is to be preferred. The more difficult reading must also fit the context and make better sense than its rivals. In the well-known example from Genesis 2:2, which states when God finished the work of creation, the MT has the more difficult reading השביעי 'on the seventh day' and the LXX, Peshitta and Samaritan Pentateuch witness to הששי 'on the sixth day'. In this case it is suspected that the variant was introduced to protect the Sabbath. The relative difficulty of readings is a subjective decision made by scholars today whose working definition of 'difficult' may be quite different from that of the LXX translators and who of course are not always in agreement. *Lectio difficilior probabilior* fails to take into account the existence of simple scribal errors.[57]

A second internal criterion is *lectio brevior potior* – the shorter reading is to be preferred. As Klein explains, 'Unless there is clear evidence for homoeoteleuton or some other form of haplography, a shorter text is probably better.'[58] Translators expanded the text by making explicit the subject and object of sentences; they added other words to clarify difficult sentences; and when faced with different readings in manuscripts they tended to include both (conflation) to ensure preservation of the original. This rule presumes that ancient scribes were more likely to add details than to omit anything, but it too fails to allow for accidental scribal omissions as in Judges 16.

2.7 *The LXX and meaning in Hebrew*

The LXX can provide useful information about the meaning of BH words, particularly with respect to flora and fauna and technical

---

[56] Barr, *Comparative Philology*, 259.
[57] Cf. B. Albrektson, 'Difficilior Lectio Probabilior', 5–18.
[58] Klein, *Textual Criticism*, 75.

terms for which modern scholars have no other information.[59] But before adopting a new meaning for a known Hebrew word, the possibility of a different *Vorlage*, the effects of textual transmission and all the intricacies of the relevant translator's techniques should be taken into consideration. This process includes a comprehensive analysis of both the translator's basic linguistic competence and potential deliberate exegesis. As noted in the introduction to this chapter, scholars are reading TEXT2 to uncover TEXT1, which may or may not be identical to the MT. The meaning gained from such study is inevitably a result of the philological process, a reflection of how modern scholars believe the LXX translators read their Hebrew text. Meanwhile there is much more work to be done on the language of the LXX and the methods used by translators of each section. Scholars referring to LXX texts when encountering difficulties with words in the MT must remain aware of the wider context of both the MT item and the formal LXX equivalent each within their own language and literature, for to take such pairs out of context deprives them of their significance.

3. Targums

3.1 *The data*

'Targum' means explanation, commentary or translation, later referring specifically to translation into Aramaic. On the basis of Nehemiah 8:8 it has been suggested targumic tradition started with Ezra. The custom of interpreting the synagogue reading of the Hebrew Bible with a Targum after each verse of the Torah, or every three verses of the prophets, in the presence of the congregation, so as to permit a translator to repeat it in Aramaic, is attested in the Mishnah.[60] Every effort was made to avoid confusing the Targum with written scripture. Scripture had absolute authority; the Targum was only an aid to understanding. It had a double purpose: to explain the Bible reading in language understandable to most people, and to some extent to apply the text to the contemporary situation. The targumists were therefore acting as *expositor* rather than *interpres*.

---

[59] Cf. T. Muraoka, 'The Semantics of the LXX and Its Role in Clarifying Ancient Hebrew Semantics'.

[60] B. Grossfeld, 'Ancient Versions: Aramaic', 841.

Jewish Targums had a special place in Judaism and medieval commentators often quoted from them – their texts were printed alongside the Hebrew in the rabbinic Bible. Written Targums were made of almost all biblical books. Both free and literal Targums were made and it is generally assumed that the freer translations were earlier. All Targums, however, retain a prominent interpretative element often resorting to paraphrase and are therefore not comparable to the LXX as versions of the Hebrew Bible.

The best known Targum, Onkelos, was composed in Palestine in the second century CE. It was revised in Babylonia during the third century and became the official Aramaic version of the Pentateuch. Targum Onkelos is a literal translation, closely following the grammatical structure of Hebrew, but in poetry it resorts to paraphrase and adds many exegetical elements. Figurative language is also explained rather than translated literally. The Targum avoids anthropomorphisms, tends towards idealization of the patriarchs and replaces some archaic names with more modern forms.[61] When its *Vorlage* can be recognized beneath layers of exegesis, Onkelos almost invariably reflects the MT.

Fragments of a Palestinian Targum were discovered in the Cairo Geniza. Other unofficial Targums to the Pentateuch are Targum Pseudo-Jonathan and the Fragmentary Targum. While differing among themselves, such texts as Neofiti, the Fragmentary Targum, and sections of Pseudo-Jonathan have basically the same paraphrase, which seems to argue for the existence of a common tradition which was not fixed verbally.[62] While numerous Targums have been found at Qumran, most are fragmentary; but the Hebrew text reflected in them is very close to that of the base MT.[63]

Targum Jonathan, the official Targum to the prophets, was written in Palestine and revised in Babylonia during the early centuries of the Common Era. It is generally more paraphrastic than Onkelos and integrates elements from it in quotations and parallel passages: Judges 5:8 = Deuteronomy 32:17 and Judges 5:26 brings to mind Targum Onkelos of Deuteronomy 22:5.[64] The usual rules of targumic interpretation are followed with avoidance of anthropomorphisms and geographical locations sometimes given their

---

[61] B.J. Roberts, *The Old Testament Text and Versions*, 204.
[62] M. McNamara, 'Targums', 860.
[63] Tov, *Textual Criticism*, 149.
[64] Grossfeld, 'Aramaic', 847.

contemporary name.[65] Jonathan often modernizes biblical customs to fit in with its own time: judges are called 'leaders' and in Judges 4:5 Deborah resides in a city because that is where the courts were. Sometimes the Targum translates the *qere* rather than the *kethib* and where the MT is unclear the Targum provides an interpretation. Poetic passages such as Judges 5 are drastically paraphrased and the influence of religious or dogmatic ideas of the author's time is more noticeable than in Onkelos.[66] The targumist turned The Song of Deborah into an illustration of Israel's relationship with God: whenever Israel rejects the law, its enemies triumph; whenever it returns to the law, it triumphs over its enemies.[67]

Although there are Targums to the Hagiographa, there is no evidence of an officially recognized one. The books which do exist originate from a later period and were written at different times by various authors, yet they do contain some much older material. In translation technique they vary from strict adherence to the text to amplified Midrash.

3.2 Translation techniques

Alexander distinguishes two basic types of Targum: A and B. Type A consists of a base translation plus detachable glosses. The expansions are unevenly distributed with some sections of the text being rendered more or less literally, whilst others are expanded many times over in order to supply the sort of circumstantial detail which an audience would demand from the retelling of a biblical story.[68] Type B is similarly paraphrastic and all elements of the original are represented, but unlike type A a base translation cannot be recovered from this type because the original is dissolved in the paraphrase.[69]

As paraphrases, aimed at the understanding of Jewish worshippers, Targums are of more value as examples of Jewish homiletical procedures and trends than as precise instruments of textual transmission. In theology the contribution of Targums is of special

---

[65] P.S. Alexander, 'Jewish Aramaic Translations of Hebrew Scriptures', 226–7; D.J. Harrington and A.J. Saldarini, *Targum Jonathan of the Former Prophets*, 5–6.

[66] Roberts, *Text and Versions*, 208.

[67] Harrington and Saldarini, *Targum Jonathan*, 11; cf. Harrington, 'The Prophecy of Deborah'.

[68] Alexander, 'Jewish Aramaic Translations', 229–34.

[69] Alexander, 'Jewish Aramaic Translations', 234–7.

importance as most are consistent in the way theological motives are presupposed. There is a universal tendency to avoid all reference to the divine name and anthropomorphisms are usually paraphrased, thus God is מימרא דיהוה 'the Word of Jahweh'. In the Jerusalem Targum to the Pentateuch, Genesis 1:26 records that man was created not in the image of God but of the angels.[70] There are even cases where the Targum presents a direct contradiction of the Hebrew text, usually where the Hebrew implicitly or explicitly violates theological, ethical or aesthetic values. In Genesis 4:14 where Cain complains that God is driving him from the land and 'I will be hidden from your presence', Targum Onkelos reads, 'it is impossible for me (man) to hide from before you (O LORD)' and Targum Jonathan ben Uziel 'is it possible for me to be hidden from before you?'[71]

Unless evidence from Targums is used solely to confirm readings from other versions, divergences from the MT must be taken to reflect Targumic tendencies and do not, as a rule, indicate textual corruption in the Hebrew. A Targum does not generally offer adequate independent proof of a variant text or reading which can be taken back beyond the consonantal text adopted by the Masoretes, although Levine argues that there are some cases where the Targum retains the correct reading, as in Exodus 30:35 and Deuteronomy 22:5.[72]

3.3 Targums and meaning in Hebrew

When consulting Targums to throw light on the meaning of a Hebrew text, there are several important factors to be considered. Targums are translations; therefore, as with the LXX, any attempt to uncover the Hebrew *Vorlage* needs to be made with caution: scholars are trying to discover the meaning of TEXT1 through the form of TEXT2. Hebrew and Aramaic furthermore are closely related languages sharing many lexical items and grammatical structures. This can lead to confusion as the same root may have different forms in each language and the same form will not necessarily have the same meaning in Hebrew and Aramaic. The semantic range of a word will be dependent upon the other words available in its own

---

[70] Roberts, *Text and Versions*, 199; cf. M.L. Klein, 'The Translation of Anthropomorphisms and Anthropopaphisms in the Targumim', *VTS 32*.
[71] M.L. Klein, 'Converse Translation'.
[72] E. Levine, *The Aramaic Version of the Bible*, 31–2.

language. When encountering an ambiguous Hebrew word, the Targumist may have deliberately rendered that word by an Aramaic cognate, thus retaining the ambiguity.

Many Targums are fragmentary and moreover they contain very free translations, or rather interpretations, of the Hebrew text. One of the first tasks of the scholar therefore is to identify whether a particular Targum is of type A or B. Can the underlying Hebrew text be distinguished from the exegetical material? In type A Targums it is possible to determine which Aramaic words correspond to the Hebrew text and the exegetical material should give added indication of how the targumists interpreted that Hebrew text for their day. It must be remembered that Targums were created to be used alongside the Hebrew text rather than to be translations to replace it; therefore they reveal what the targumists saw as the significance of the Hebrew passage (like homiletics). The Targums provide valuable insight into the interpretation of biblical verses widely accepted in contemporary Judaism. They are most useful for reconstructing BH texts when they agree with other versions.

4. Peshitta

4.1 The Data

The Peshitta is the standard version of the Hebrew Bible in Syriac, an Aramaic dialect. 'Peshitta' means 'the simple translation', possibly to distinguish it from the Syro-Hexapla translation of the Greek Hexapla into Syriac. There are only two manuscripts from the fifth century, one containing Genesis and Exodus; the other, parts of Isaiah and Ezekiel. There are also a few manuscripts from the sixth to ninth century for all parts of the Old Testament.[73] The Hebrew text reflected in the Peshitta is very close to the MT which suggests that the Peshitta originated after the MT had already been established, that is mid-first century CE.

There are nevertheless a number of places where the Peshitta together with the LXX, Targums, or both, may reflect a different Hebrew *Vorlage*. On the whole translators of the Peshitta produced a reasonably literal rendition of the Hebrew whilst varying their version according to the demands of Syriac idiom. Their stylistic

---

[73] P.B. Dirksen, 'The Old Testament Peshitta', 257.

modifications include pluses, minuses, variation in word order, avoidance of the construct state, modifications in tense, number, suffixes, and avoidance of rhetorical questions.[74] Differences from the Hebrew may also be due to exegetical, theological modifications, and the influence of Jewish exegetical traditions. The LXX appears to have influenced some of the Peshitta.[75]

4.2 Translation techniques

Variations in wording, style and text point to a long period of development for the Peshitta. Certain books render the Hebrew quite literally (Judges, Song of Songs, Ecclesiastes); some even slavishly (Job); others show more freedom (Psalms, Isaiah and the Twelve Prophets); some display a surprising paraphrastic freedom (Ruth); others reflect Targums (Pentateuch, Ezekiel, Proverbs), and some appear to be Midrashic (Chronicles).[76] Thus translation technique and external influence must be studied for each book or group of books separately.

Scholars disagree as to whether the Peshitta was produced by a Jewish or Christian community. There is undoubtedly a distinctive substratum of Jewish exegesis, especially in the Pentateuch. Another common argument for Jewish origin of the Peshitta is the existence of many verbal parallels with Targums, but the hypothesis of a targumic origin lacks convincing evidence. As Weitzman has pointed out, some scholars seem to forget how much similarity is inevitable between translations of the same text into dialects of the same language, even when those translations are made independently.[77] The Peshitta has only been preserved by the Church, yet the number of places which might indicate Christian authorship is actually quite small. The best known example is the translation of הָעַלְמָה 'young woman' in Isaiah 7:14 as *b*^e*tulta* 'virgin' instead of *^{ce}laym*^e*ta*, as elsewhere. But this accords with παρθενος in the LXX and Peshitta translators seem to have often consulted the Greek of the LXX. Dirksen is forced to conclude, 'No decisive arguments for either Christian or Jewish authorship have been advanced.'[78]

---

[74] Dirksen, 'Peshitta', 259.
[75] Dirksen, 'Peshitta', 259.
[76] A. Vööbus, 'Syriac Versions', 849.
[77] M. Weitzman, 'From Judaism to Christianity: The Syriac Version of the Hebrew Bible', 148.
[78] Dirksen, 'Peshitta', 295.

Much of the Peshitta appears to have been corrected in line with the LXX, especially Isaiah and the Psalms. It incorporates some passages found in the LXX but not the MT. This is particularly evident in Proverbs, which may have been based on the LXX.[79] The Isaiah scroll from Qumran also reveals close affinities with the Peshitta.[80] Tov nevertheless concludes that the Hebrew source of the Peshitta is close to the MT, containing fewer variants than the LXX, but more than the Targums and the Vulgate.[81] Probably the greatest deviations from the MT occur in Chronicles which has several substantial additions. Weitzman suggests that these may be due to the translators working from a severely damaged Hebrew text.[82]

4.3 The Peshitta and meaning in Hebrew

Once again, when looking to the Peshitta for assistance in investigating the meaning of a Hebrew text, matters of translation technique and external influence are fundamental. These must be studied for each book or groups of books separately. If the Peshitta is dependent on the LXX, then it cannot be legitimate to count these versions as two equal witnesses for a particular reading. The relationship between the different versions of the text under investigation needs to be clarified before such decisions can be made. The cautions sounded above with respect to both the LXX and Targums are also to be heeded with reference to the Peshitta.

5. Latin Translations

5.1 Old Latin

The first translation of the Hebrew Bible into Latin was undertaken in about 150 CE. Old Latin (OL) translations were based mainly, if not exclusively, on the LXX. They therefore witness to an earlier form of the LXX than extant manuscripts.[83] Translators believed they were handling the very word of God, every word counted and even the order of words was important; therefore they sought

---

[79] Tov, *Textual Criticism*, 152.
[80] Vööbus, 'Syriac Versions', 849.
[81] Tov, *Textual Criticism*, 152.
[82] Weitzman, 'Syriac Version', 151–8.
[83] B. Kedar, 'The Latin Translations', 302.

to produce a word-for-word translation. Kedar notes that the scrupulous adherence of OL to the Greek text is most conspicuous, particularly when Latin faithfully follows Greek blunders.[84] The LXX itself closely follows the original and so OL is littered with Hebraisms and un-Latin word order.

5.2 The Vulgate

Jerome is famous for the translation of the Hebrew Bible which produced the authoritative Latin Vulgate in 390–405 CE. The Vulgate was prepared in harmony with 'Hebrew Truth' rather than merely following the LXX. Jerome enlisted the help of Jewish teachers (most probably communicating with them in Greek) and his translation closely followed its Hebrew source. Barr concludes that the reading tradition Jerome received from his Jewish teachers differs little from the later MT.[85] Jerome also used earlier Latin translations like a modern scholar would make use of dictionaries and concordances.

   The resultant version varies greatly with respect to its translation technique: in places it is extremely literal; in others relatively paraphrastic. The Psalms and Prophets exhibit adherence to the linguistic structure of Hebrew, while Joshua, Judges, Ruth and Esther abound in free renderings. The former were the early products of Jerome's labour, while the latter comprise the concluding part.[86] As might be expected, many of Jerome's interpretations reflect the exegetical traditions of his day with some words translated according to rabbinic explanation. His translation and comment-aries generally agree with the semantic content of the MT against such versions as the LXX and Aquila.[87]

5.3 Latin versions and meaning in Hebrew

The extant OL texts bear witness to the LXX rather than to any Hebrew *Vorlage*. The Vulgate along with Jerome's linguistic obser-vations and commentaries provide a wealth of material witnessing to interpretation of the Hebrew Bible at the turn of the fourth century. As with other versions, the translation technique employed

---

[84] Kedar, 'Latin Translations', 306.
[85] J. Barr, 'St. Jerome and the Sounds of Hebrew'.
[86] Kedar, 'Latin Translations', 326.
[87] Grabbe, *Comparative Philology*, 190.

for a particular book provides an important guide to the feasibility of attempting retroversions.

6. The Versions and Meaning in Hebrew

This chapter has detailed several fundamental factors concerning the use of the versions in investigating meaning in BH. It must be remembered first that the versions are translations and secondly that they constitute but one piece of evidence among many. As with the application of comparative philology in the investigation of the meaning of a Hebrew word, the versions should be referred to only after all available Hebrew material has been exhausted.

It should be noted, however, that the versions may provide valuable information in the special case of a *hapax legomenon* where, although the word appears only once within the BH text, its meaning may have been well known beyond that corpus.

When referring to versions, the key to the whole operation is the translator, the reader of a Hebrew source (TEXT1) and author of a version (TEXT2). Knowledge of the translator's intention is vital to the process. Therefore the following questions should be posed: What was the prime objective? Who were the intended readers? Did the translator function as *interpres* or *expositor*? How literal is the result?

A further critical factor is the translator's linguistic competence in both source and target language: the Hebrew text may have been misread or misunderstood. Translation involves both a basic recognition of linguistic forms and their meaning in the source text, and an element of interpretation in the choice of wording in the target text. Each word carries its own connotations and can subtly alter the meaning of the resultant text. Furthermore, two distinct languages will not have identical linguistic resources: both items and their arrangements will differ.

Linguistic context places some restriction on suitable encoding and so does pragmatic context. The translator's cultural and theological perspectives inevitably influence the choice of expression: there may be deliberate exegesis – the addition of explanation, subtraction of sensitive material, updating of names and places, or the use of paraphrase to avoid inappropriate reference to the divine.

The possibility of the translator's dependence on another version also needs to be considered, with the reasons for such reliance, and discussion as to the identity of the source text in such instances.

There is furthermore no single target text; there is a multiplicity of witnesses to the versions, all of which have undergone a process of transmission, allowing for scribal error and emendation.

Modern scholars try to understand the MT (which may or may not be identical to TEXT1) through reference to TEXT2 which results from translation and transmission. There is no guarantee that back-translation can reverse the process and obtain the form and, more significantly, the meaning of the *Vorlage*. Versions rarely consist of strings of 1:1 word-substitutions; they are usually a mixture of literal and free renderings. It is vital that scholars familiarize themselves with the techniques employed by the translator of the particular section of the version on which they are working and acknowledge the potential gap between their reconstruction and the translator's Hebrew source.

The versions may reveal how the Hebrew Bible was understood by certain translators at particular stages in its history, and furthermore how they chose to transmit that sacred literature in their own language for their religious community.

Part Three

Modern Linguistic Methods

6

Lexical Semantics

1. Introduction

Lexical semantics arises out of structural linguistics and particularly the work of Ferdinand de Saussure. One difficulty with any description of this theory is the lack of agreement among linguists in terminology. This situation is further complicated by philosophers and cognitive scientists using very similar and sometimes overlapping terminology. Many biblical scholars turning to lexical semantics for assistance in Hebrew lexicography and exegesis have failed to clarify their terms; thus in biblical studies 'lexical fields', 'semantic fields' and 'associative fields' are used interchangeably. The first part of this chapter therefore concentrates on the description of theory and definition of terms. The second part looks at the practical difficulties encountered in any attempt to categorize language formally. The third section surveys semantic field studies of BH and the final section analyses the value of this theory in the investigation of meaning in CH.

1.1 The linguistic sign

Saussure defines the linguistic sign as the association of a form (signifier) with a meaning (signified). The linguistic sign is an abstract unit which is not to be confused with either the actual sequence of physical sounds or the referent. If 🍎 is the signified, then 'apple' is the signifier in English, and the sign is the relationship between the two. 'Apple' can only be a sign because of the concept it carries with it; 'paple' would not be a sign in English because it carries no meaning. Saussure insists that the sign does not unite word and object; it is not simply a name or label, but is a psychological entity uniting a signifier (sound-image) with a signified (concept) which can be observed as sounds and meanings.

The relationship between signifier and signified is completely arbitrary, there is no reason why a particular concept should be linked with one linguistic form rather than another: there is no reason why 🍎 should be linked with 'apple' rather than 'pear' or 'print'. Linguists cannot attempt to explain individual signs but must refer to the system within which they exist: the 9.15am train from Kings Cross to Cambridge is thought of as the same train each day even though it does not always comprise the same engine, carriages and crew. The 9.15am is not a substance but a form, defined by its relation to other trains in the timetable. Its identity is independent of its physical manifestations.[1]

1.2 *The lexicon as a network*

According to John Lyons, the central thesis of structuralism is 'that every language is a unique relational structure, or system, and that the units which we identify, or postulate as theoretical constructs, in analysing the sentence of a particular language (sounds, words, meanings, etc.) derive both their essence and their existence from their relationships with other units in the same language system'.[2] Thus in lexical semantics the lexicon is understood as a system or network of interrelated items. Each lexical item derives its linguistic validity from the place it occupies within that network of operational relations and it cannot be identified independently of those interrelations. The meaning of a lexical item is therefore dependent upon the lexicon within which it operates.

The language-specificity of the system becomes evident in the task of translation. This is not simply a matter of finding a lexeme with the same meaning in another language and then arranging words in the correct order. A translation equivalent ('gloss') is not a lexical meaning although it may *represent* the meaning of a word in a particular context. Lexemes are not likely to be semantically equivalent across languages because in any two languages the sets of meanings never completely correspond: French has *mouton*, whereas English has 'sheep' and 'mutton'. Further problems arise when two or more meanings are associated with homonymous lexemes in one language but not in another. When comparing

---

[1] Cf. F. de Saussure, *Course in General Linguistics*, xviii, 65–66.
[2] J. Lyons, *Semantics*, I:231–232.

Hebrew roots there appear to be numerous examples of homonymy (or homography), when comparing words there are far fewer.[3] In any language it is context which helps resolve ambiguity and assists in the identification of a suitable gloss.

One language may lexicalize a meaning while another does not: some languages of central Africa have no word for snow, thus requiring a phrase or sentence to convey the meaning of one word. The boundaries between meanings of what at first appear to be semantically equivalent words in different languages are very often incongruent – words only partially overlap between languages: the English word 'brown' has no single equivalent in French; the range of colours denoted by 'brown' would be described as *brun, marron* or even *jaune*. There are no genuine synonyms between languages (nor are there technically any complete synonyms within any one language).

The meaning of a word cannot be adequately explained by quoting a word from another language because meaning is internal to the lexicon to which the word belongs and each lexicon has its own semantic structure. Classical structural linguistics asserts that single lexical items across different languages cannot be legitimately compared; rather entire systems and the values of items within those systems must be compared. It also assumes that all terms in a system (all items in a lexicon) have equal status ('red' might be used more frequently than 'scarlet', but both words have equal value in the system) and all referents of a term have equal status (two items might be called 'red', but there is no place in the system for declaring that one is 'more red' or 'redder' than the other). The only legitimate object of study therefore is the language system and not individual terms.[4]

1.3 Relations within the lexicon

Saussure identified two key relations between words in the lexicon: syntagmatic and paradigmatic. The former describes the relationship between words which combine to form a linear linguistic sequence called a syntagm. English syntax requires the word order article + adjective + noun as in the noun phrase 'the green apple'. This relationship is syntagmatic. The same relationship is found in 'the young woman', 'a fine day', 'the green woman' and 'a

---

[3] Cf. J.H. Hospers, 'Polysemy', 114–115.
[4] J.R. Taylor, *Linguistic Categorization*, 7–8.

young day'. However, the choice of words in the last two phrases is unusual. They are syntactically well formed but semantically anomalous. The adjective 'green' and noun 'woman' do not often co-occur. The habitual co-occurrence of two or more words is called collocation: during the weather report 'fine weather', 'torrential rain' and 'light drizzle' might be expected, whereas 'torrential drizzle' is incongruous. Syntagmatic relations are to a large extent determined by syntax; it is paradigmatic relations which are related to information.

In 'the old man' and 'the young man' different adjectives are employed. The choice between adjectives to occupy this slot demonstrates the paradigmatic relationship. Lexemes which are related paradigmatically may be semantically unrelated like the adjectives 'old', 'fine' and 'green'; semantically incompatible as in 'Monday', 'Tuesday' and 'Friday'; antonymous: 'old' and 'young'; hyponymous as in 'cat' and 'animal'; or in a converse relationship: 'parent' and 'child'.[5] The selection of a particular lexeme is always made against the background of various possible alternatives, for example, between 'girl', 'lady' and 'woman'. This does not necessarily entail a different meaning descriptively, although it will involve at least a different social or expressive connotation, for the paradigmatic relationship is one of contrast.

Structuralism maintains that the meaning of a linguistic form is determined by its place in the language system. The world and how people interact with it, how they perceive and conceptualize it, are extra-linguistic factors which do not impinge on the language system itself. Of course, people use language to talk about, to interpret and to influence the world around them. It is therefore necessary to recognize the influence of factors such as sender, recipient, form of the message (poetry / narrative / official report, etc.), content, channel of communication (written or spoken) and overall setting or environment (*Sitz im Leben*) on the selection of a lexeme. In other words, context in its broadest possible sense influences the choice of wording, although it will not directly affect the language system.

1.4 *Categorization*

The strict form of structuralism insists that linguistic categories are discrete entities with well-defined boundaries. Thus the linguistic

---

[5] Cf. section 1.6.

category 'word' should be clearly differentiated from 'morpheme' and 'phrase'. Whereas in writing spaces separate words, in speech this is not the case, although pauses may be inserted between words. The definition of a word as 'the smallest unit of grammar that can stand alone as a complete utterance'[6] is useful but not perfect: according to this definition 'kick the bucket' comprises three words, yet it functions as one word. Linguists continue to debate satisfactory criteria for the definition of 'word'. Lexical semantics therefore uses the linguistic category Lexeme which is defined as 'the smallest contrastive unit in a semantic system'.[7] The lexeme WALK can occur in the various items (or words) 'walks', 'walked' and 'walking'; it contrasts in the semantic system with RUN, CRAWL, HOP. Lexemes often appear as the headword in dictionary entries; therefore Hebrew scholars are tempted to identify the Hebrew root with the lexeme. Brenner, in *Colour Terms in the Old Testament*, makes a useful distinction between 'lexemes' which are different patterns of the same root and 'words' which are inflectional forms derived from 'lexemes' and exhibiting some formal similarities with their base.[8]

Structuralism defines categories in terms of a conjunction of necessary and sufficient features. All features are considered to be binary, primitive, universal and abstract.[9] In lexical semantics the usual example given is 'bachelor' which can be reduced to the semantic features + Human, + Male, + Adult, – Married. 'Spinster' would differ only with respect to the feature – Male, whereas 'spouse' would necessitate + Human, + Adult and + Married. This example is relatively straightforward but it soon becomes apparent that the number of binary distinctive features needed to describe the lexicon of any natural language is potentially vast and liable to increase without limit. The identification of semantic features is not straightforward and the results are usually subject to the thinking of the scholar concerned. Studies by cognitive scientists during the last twenty years have further challenged the validity of such categorization.[10]

---

[6] D. Crystal, *The Cambridge Encyclopedia of Language*, 433.

[7] Crystal, *Encyclopedia*, 424.

[8] A. Brenner, *Colour Terms in the Old Testament*, 27.

[9] Cf. Taylor, *Categorization*, 21–2.

[10] Cf. section 1.6.

1.5 Semantic fields

The term 'semantic field' assumes that field theory is concerned with the analysis of sense. Following terminology employed by Lyons, the colour spectrum can be thought of as a conceptual area. This conceptual area becomes a conceptual field by virtue of its strict organization, or articulation, by a particular language system. The colour spectrum can be organized in various ways linguistically – the example of English 'brown' and French *brun, marron* and *jaun* has already been mentioned; Russian has no word for 'blue': *goluboy* 'light, pale blue' and *siniy* 'dark, bright blue' are different colours, not different shades of the same colour. Kinship relations is another conceptual area which is organized differently in individual language systems: English has no single words for expressing 'mother's brother', 'father's brother' ('uncle' is used for both), 'mother's sister' and 'father's sister' ('aunt' is used for both); many languages do.

The set of lexemes used by a language to describe the conceptual field comprises the lexical field. The sense of a lexeme is therefore a conceptual area within a conceptual field.[11] As Trier wrote, 'The value of a word is first known when we mark it off against the value of neighbouring and opposing words. Only as part of the whole does the word have sense; for only in the field is there meaning.'[12]

Coseriu described a semantic field as 'a primarily paradigmatic structure of the lexicon', but as mentioned in section 3 this does not entail semantic relationship between items. Fronzaroli defines 'semantic field' as 'a group of words that stand in paradigmatic opposition to one another and share at least one semantic component'.[13] Lyons, having already pointed out that a lexical field covers an area of meaning, asserts that 'A lexical field is a paradigmatically and syntagmatically structured subset of the vocabulary.'[14] The terms 'lexical field' and 'semantic field' appear to be interchangeable in the linguistic literature and are treated as such for the purposes of this study.

'Associative field' as used by Sawyer moves beyond the paradigmatic and syntagmatic relations of the lexicon: 'Theoretically a word's associative field includes, not only words of related meaning

---

[11] Lyons, *Semantics*, I:253–4.
[12] J. Trier, *Der Deutsche Wortschatz im Sinnbezirk des Verstandes*, 6.
[13] P. Fronzaroli, 'Componential Analysis', 79.
[14] Lyons, *Semantics*, I:268.

(synonyms, opposites, etc.), but also words which occur a number of times in the same context, words which rhyme with it, and even words which look like it or sound like it, in short, words which are associated with it in any way at all.'[15] The associative field of a word moves beyond the semantic field of structural linguistics into the realm of cognitive science because some of the associations will be formed across the boundaries of the linguistic system in the world of individual experience: whenever I read the Hebrew word יָרֵן, I instantly think 'garden', because the Hebrew word sounds vaguely similar to French 'jardin', which I learnt at school was equivalent to English 'garden'. An individual's associations between words will inevitably influence reading and writing both in their native language and in other languages. Modern scholars' intuitive reconstruction of the associative fields of Hebrew words may be very different from those of the producers of the Hebrew Bible.

The different definitions in lexical semantics have created some confusion in Hebrew studies. One example is the work of Chmiel who refers to the reduction of the 'five Hebrew semantic fields of *qûm, 'ûr, qîs, hayah* and *'amad* to the two Greek semantic fields of ἐγείρω and ἀνίστημι'.[16] It is perfectly legitimate to compare the semantic fields of two languages, but Chmiel appears to have looked at a semantic field of Hebrew and the translation of its lexical items into Greek, which is not the same thing. Furthermore, a word is not a semantic field; it may have a place in one or more semantic fields and its semantic range will depend on its relations with other items within each particular field. It is appropriate to talk about the associative field of a word, or the semantic field within which a word functions.

The most important idea to be retained from this discussion of definitions is that a semantic field (= lexical field) consists of a group of words which cover a conceptual field (therefore there is some semantic component common to these lexical items), and that their relations to one another can be described in terms of sense relations.

1.6 Sense relations

Relations of similarity include overlapping or partial synonymy where terms are similar enough to be mutually interchanged in some contexts ('ooze' and 'seep'; 'ooze' and 'trickle'). The

---

[15] J.F.A. Sawyer, 'Hebrew Words for the Resurrection of the Dead', 219.
[16] J. Chmiel, 'Semantics of the Resurrection', 62.

complete synonymy of two lexemes would entail interchangeability in all contexts, which is extremely rare. In contiguity or improper synonymy terms share some semantic features but can never be interchanged ('ooze' and 'pour'). Hyponymy is an inclusive relation between a more specific lexeme and its superordinate ('blood' and 'fluid'). The superordinate 'fluid' can take the place of its hyponym 'blood' in many sentences, whereas the hyponym 'blood' can only take the place of the superordinate when other types of fluid are not meant. Bilateral hyponymy would be synonymy: interchangeability in all contexts. Hyponymous relations can be transitive: 'bullock', 'cow', 'animal'.

The relation of antonymy is dependent on dichotomization, as in the binary opposition of 'dead' or 'alive'. The majority of sense relations, however, is concerned with grading rather than dichotomization. Grading involves an element of comparison. The sentence 'X is not cold' is not synonymous with 'X is hot', for X could be described as 'warm'. The lexemes 'hot' and 'cold' are contrary, along opposite poles of a spectrum, rather than contradictory. An example of the latter relation would be 'male' and 'female'. Grading may be semi-explicit, or marked, as in the case of comparative adjectives: 'smaller', 'smallest'. Their explicitness is usually indicated morphologically. Morphological variation can convey various sense relations: 'friendly', 'unfriendly', 'friendless'; 'possible', 'impossible'; 'lion', 'lioness'. The unmarked lexeme may be the generic form; it is usually less specific and more frequent. More common lexemes tend not to be related morphologically: 'hot', 'cold'; 'good', 'bad'. This serves to enhance semantic distinction.

Within sense relations there is often a positive–negative polarity. In the spectra 'good'–'bad', 'tall'–'short' the first lexeme is the positive pole and the second negative. This phenomenon is illustrated by 'How good is it?' or 'How tall is he?' – the expected forms of questions. To be asked 'How bad is it?' or 'How short is he?' usually indicates that context has already focused attention on that end of the spectrum. Similarly binomials tend to be irreversible: 'male and female', 'fish and chips' are expected, whereas 'female and male' or 'chips and fish' cause the hearer to double-take. The reversal of a standard binomial serves to emphasize a point or reveal a non-native speaker.

Oppositions between lexemes such as 'dead' and 'alive', which are considered dichotomous or non-gradeable, can also be explicitly graded to create alternative connotations. This is exemplified by the following fictional conversation between a nurse and the doctor after theatre:

Nurse: 'Is he dead?'
Doctor: 'Well, he certainly isn't alive!'
Nurse: 'But, will he survive?'
Doctor: 'I expect so.'

Comprehension will be dependent on knowledge of the context and non-native speakers may miss the significance of the interchange.

The two concepts of localism and motion provide contexts for directional opposition: 'up', 'down' and 'come', 'go'. Lexemes may also be ordered serially or cyclically: 'January', 'February', 'December'. They may be ranked: 'excellent', 'good', 'fair', 'bad', 'atrocious'. The same lexemes may appear in different ranks according to appropriate context: the above rank could refer to the weather but is unlikely to be used as an academic grading system. In the latter instance 'poor' could be included and 'atrocious' might be replaced by 'fail'.

It is believed that most of these types of sense relations occur in all languages although they may not all be expressed within the lexicon. Individual semantic fields furthermore can only be expected to contain a subset of relevant relations.

1.7 Componential analysis and semantic features

One way in which the lexemes within a semantic field may be differentiated is via componential analysis. This method consists of 'reducing a word's meaning to its ultimate contrastive elements'.[17] Lexical items are analysed into their distinctive features or 'semes'. Semes are defined as the minimal distinctive features of meaning operative within a single lexical field. They serve to structure the field in terms of various kinds of opposition. A typical example is:

	man	woman	boy	girl
human	+	+	+	+
adult	+	+	−	−
male	+	−	+	−

---

[17] G.N. Leech, *Semantics*, 91.

The categories 'human', 'adult' and 'male' in the left column are the distinctive features or components of meaning which have been abstracted from the lexical field. It is debatable whether such components are purely dependent upon the linguist's intuition or whether they represent some more objective criteria within the lexicon. The abstraction of distinctive features in componential analysis is comparable to the process of Internal Reconstruction in Comparative Philology. In both cases they can be useful procedures in linguistic analysis, but there is no way of knowing whether the abstracted elements exist(ed) in reality. As Lyons points out, 'it has yet to be demonstrated that sense-components of the kind that linguists have tended to invoke in their analysis of the meaning of lexemes play any part whatsoever in the production and interpretation of language-utterances'.[18] Different scholars may produce different results from the same data. There is also reason to question why 'male' rather than 'female' should be the standard label for the distinctive feature as this is not universal in language: 'cow' is the superordinate from which 'bull' is differentiated. Some features prove to be language bound and are therefore neither primitive nor universal.

Componential analysis fails to encapsulate the complexity of relations even within the small example field of vocabulary, because 'man' and 'boy' are sharply opposed to one another in a way that 'woman' and 'girl' are not. It could be argued that this is a feature of language use or connotation rather than of the system. Yet the lexical fields which have been subjected to componential analysis tend to be referential, for example, human relations, colours, body parts, and furniture. Components are therefore related to world experience rather than restricted to sense relations between words. It is questionable whether 'with a back' and 'for one person' are components of the meaning of the word 'chair' or relate to people's experience of calling the object they have learned to sit on a chair. Such discussion crosses into the field of cognitive science, language acquisition and the mental lexicon. Componential analysis is more obviously applicable to some parts of the lexicon than others. In practice it appears to apply only to referential meaning where 'meaning consists of that particular structured bundle of cognitive features, associated with the lexical unit, which make possible the designation of all the denotata by the lexical unit in question'.[19]

---

[18] Lyons, *Semantics*, I:333.
[19] E.A. Nida, *Componential Analysis of Meaning*, 26.

1.8 Lexical gaps

As Ullmann notes, 'the neatness with which words delimit each other and build up a kind of mosaic, without any gaps or overlaps has been greatly exaggerated'.[20] Nevertheless attempts have been made to describe the lexical fields of complete languages, so far without success. Individual lexical fields are not necessarily complete in themselves. There may not be individual lexemes for some parts of a semantic field: in everyday English there is a lexeme for the body of a dead person, 'corpse', and for the body of a dead animal, 'carcass', but not for the body of a dead plant. This could be culturally conditioned: there are extensive funeral and burial rites in British culture; there is a whole industry of abattoirs and butchers; there is no equivalent for dead plants. This illustrates the fact that lexemes do not usually exist when they are not needed.

1.9 Summary

Lexical semantics views the lexicon of a language as a network of interrelated elements. These elements relate to one another syntagmatically and paradigmatically. The lexicon is subdivided into lexical fields which categorize conceptual fields. Individual lexemes relate to each other in a variety of sense relations and those belonging to the same semantic field may be differentiated through componential analysis.

2. Language and Life

A further distinction made by Saussure was between the language system *la langue* and language behaviour, that is, evidence of the system in use, *la parole*.[21] The primary task of linguists was to study *la langue*. But, as has been demonstrated above, language cannot be studied apart from its environment. In practice *la langue* is abstracted from observation of *la parole*. The lexicon of CH is abstracted from available data.

As Ullmann points out, the meaning of a word can be ascertained only by studying its use.[22] Some words do have meaning apart from

---

[20] S. Ullmann, *Semantics*, 249.
[21] Saussure, *General Linguistics*, xvii.
[22] Ullmann, *Semantics*, 67.

their place in the system. At least certain items in the vocabularies of all languages can be put into correspondence with 'features' of the physical world, extra-linguistic objects or entities: the words 'chair', 'sofa' and 'stool' refer to, or denote, particular pieces of furniture. Any dictionary definition of the word 'chair' incorporates a description of the object to which it typically refers. This notion of reference furthermore cannot be limited to physical entities: the words 'law' and 'sin' refer to particular concepts. As Silva observes, 'Once we admit the existence of denotation we have to face the fact that many words do have their own value; even words depending mostly on their relationship with other words can occasionally *mean* something by themselves.'[23]

While proper names and a few other lexical items can be understood fully by invoking the notion of reference, most vocabulary cannot be treated in such a way. The vast majority of words have at least some significant relational value and this relational value influences denotation. The choice of a word employed on a particular occasion will depend on the alternative words available. This is not so obvious when referring to a typical armchair, but it becomes more so when referring to an untypical item of furniture.

Linguistic categories are vague, they have fuzzy boundaries, and the choice of a word in a particular context is dependent on extra-linguistic factors such as the form and function of the object being referred to. Traditional feature representation does not provide for the interdependence of such conditions. It is nevertheless useful to conceive of the meaning of a word as the set of conditions which must be fulfilled if that word is to be employed. But the meaning of all words are to a lesser or greater degree vague, such that, the boundary of the application of a term is never a point but a region where the term gradually moves from being applicable to non-applicable. The problem of vagueness is seen most clearly when there are a large number of objects which differ by only small degrees from each other. A typical example is the colour spectrum: two speakers of English may not agree on whether a particular shade should be labelled 'green' or 'blue'. Yet they will usually agree on the focal or central point of reference for a lexical item: they immediately recognize and agree on obvious instances of 'blue' and 'green'. There is a difference in character between the central or focal denotation of a lexical item and its total denotation. Two languages may differ with respect to the position of the boundaries

---

in the denotational continuum but agree with respect to the focal or central point in the denotation of roughly equivalent words.

Some linguists have posited a centre to the denotational range of a word, others have suggested a centre to the semantic range of a word. Ullmann affirms, 'There is usually in each word a hard core of meaning which is relatively stable and can only be modified by the context within certain limits.'[24] The central or core meaning of a term can be distinguished as the least marked, the sense which is least conditioned by context, this is the 'lexical meaning'. Louw insists that a distinction be made between lexical meaning and contextual meaning: 'That is, between what a word in itself, on its own, contributes to the understanding of an utterance (lexical meaning) and what features of meaning, derived from the context, enable one to define the event more precisely by adding particular contextual features.'[25] According to Cotterell and Turner, 'The lexical meaning is the range of senses of a word that may be counted on as being established in the public domain.'[26] They readily admit that to distinguish lexical meaning from contextual meaning is not always easy. The attempt to do so can lead to 'Illegitimate Totality Transfer'. The lexical meaning should be thought of as the minimum meaning that a word brings to a sentence or utterance. Cotterell and Turner define the sense of a word as a discrete bundle of meaning, the content of which may be clarified using two approaches:

1. Compare and contrast the word under investigation with others with related senses, ideally this means plotting the semantic fields to which the word belongs.
2. Attempt to stipulate those features which are essential to the sense, and which components would be regarded as belonging to a typical member of the class of thing denoted.[27]

The first approach is within the remit of structural linguistics: investigating the lexicon as a system of interrelated items, whilst the second considers reference or denotation, the relationships between words and the extra-linguistic world. Both are necessary to a comprehensive understanding of meaning.

---

[24] Ullmann, *Semantics*, 49.
[25] J.P. Louw, 'How Do Words Mean?', 137.
[26] P. Cotterell and M. Turner, *Linguistics and Biblical Interpretation*, 140.
[27] Cotterell and Turner, *Linguistics*, 180.

3. A Survey of Some Semantic Field Studies

In 'The Image of God in the Book of Genesis: A Study of Terminology', Barr notes that much traditional exegesis has sought a
referential meaning for the phrase 'image of God'.[28] He is more
interested in why P employed the words צֶלֶם and דְּמוּת rather than
the available alternatives. Barr insists 'it is the choice, rather than
the word itself, which signifies'.[29] He chose a group of eight words
within which to place צֶלֶם. He readily acknowledges that there is
no objective criterion to guide this choice. He works from his intuitive knowledge of Hebrew; he knows that צֶלֶם can be used to refer
to a physical representation like the statue of a deity; therefore he
includes three other words for such representations: מַסֵּכָה, פֶּסֶל and
סֶמֶל. דְּמוּת is added because of its place in Genesis and therefore so is
מַרְאֶה which occurs with דְּמוּת in Ezekiel. תְּמוּנָה is included because
of its associations both with פֶּסֶל and in passages concerned with
seeing God. Finally he adds תַּבְנִית because of its use in a parallel
construction with בְּ concerning the building of the tabernacle, in
Exodus 25:40.

Barr has reconstructed a group of words which in his mind are
related in meaning, or rather could be used to refer to the same
referent. They may or may not have been in the mind of P, a hypothetical author constructed from the text.

Barr then suggests why some of these words were unsuitable for
use by P in the current context. Some of the nouns are transparent;
they carry associations from the verbs to which they are related; thus
מַרְאֶה clearly suggested that God might be seen, while תַּבְנִית suggested
the human activity of building. Others carry inappropriate connotations: both פֶּסֶל and מַסֵּכָה were used for objects which were evil and
explicitly forbidden by law. סֶמֶל is also invariably negative. תְּמוּנָה
did occur in favourable contexts, but also in highly unfavourable
contexts; it was furthermore connected with the idea of seeing.
(Barr was aware of all these factors when he suggested the potential
alternatives.) צֶלֶם on the other hand seems to have been somewhat
ambivalent. It was used as the name of a physical imitation of something, but this was not necessarily negative, idolatrous or evil. צֶלֶם
could therefore be adopted as a positive theological term relatively
free from a negative heritage. It was, however, rather ambiguous.
Barr suggests therefore that דְּמוּת was added to צֶלֶם in Genesis 1:26

---

[28] J. Barr, 'The Image of God in the Book of Genesis', 12.
[29] Barr, 'Image', 15.

'in order to define and limit its meaning, by indicating that the sense intended for צֶלֶם must lie within that part of its range which overlaps with the range of דְּמוּת'.[30]

Whereas Barr relies on his intuitive understanding of the meanings of various nouns and their connotations,[31] Sawyer looks at the syntactic structure within which the term appears. In 'The Meaning of בְּצֶלֶם אֱלֹהִים in Genesis 1–11', Sawyer takes the final form of the text to be his context.[32] He notes twelve prepositional terms in Genesis 1–11 which express a relationship of similarity between two entities, six with the prepositional prefix כְּ and six with the prepositional prefix בְּ, and suggests that these present a lexical group within which a contrastive study of the meaning of related terms may help to define more precisely the term בְּצֶלֶם אֱלֹהִים.[33] He also looks at the verbs used in each context. This detailed study demonstrates the value of investigating paradigmatic relationships in order to clarify the semantic significance of a particular term.

A more extensive survey by Sawyer is his study of הוֹשִׁיעַ and related terms. He begins by restricting his study to passages where God is addressed. Sawyer insists that 'An adequate definition of context must precede every semantic statement.'[34] This begins with a precise definition of the corpus; then the historical context; the situational context is carefully defined and finally distinctions are drawn in terms of style or literary form. 'A register is the variety of language proper to a particular situation.'[35] The object of this study, the language variety adopted by people addressing their God, can be readily identified because it is marked by an introductory formula 'he said to the LORD', or by the occurrence of one of the names of God in the vocative 'my God', 'O LORD', or both.[36] The precise specification of context is a vital preliminary to any semantic study.

Sawyer pays particular attention to the paradigmatic relations obtaining between words. His method was first to assemble all utterances in the register; many of them were then grouped

---

[30] Barr, 'Image', 24.
[31] Cf. J. Barr, *Biblical Words for Time*.
[32] J.F.A. Sawyer, 'The Meaning of בְּצֶלֶם אֱלֹהִים in Genesis I–XI', 420.
[33] Sawyer, 'בְּצֶלֶם אֱלֹהִים', 421.
[34] Sawyer, *Semantics*, 112.
[35] Sawyer, *Semantics*, 17.
[36] Sawyer, *Semantics*, 18.

according to introductory formula. Nine styles were distinguished. In the *hitpallel*-style, associated with cultic locations or activities, the speakers were normally the leaders of Israel, and הושיע and הִצִּיל occurred frequently. The *ša'al* (*daras*)-style appeared between the death of Joshua and the time of Elisha. It was short, interrogative, and the name of God was never mentioned. Instances of the *qara'*-style were all short, most beginning with the vocative. The *ša'aq*-style similarly consisted of short utterances but without any specific association with the cult. The four occurrences of the *nadar*-style were in pre-monarchical contexts. All of these were short, consisting of protasis introduced by אָם. The *šir*-style included the phrase 'on that day' in three of its four occurrences. All were of considerable length, the vocative was frequently present, as were הושיע and הִצִּיל. Both occurrences of the *berek*-style stood at end of a book at the end of long life. In the *'ana*-style both utterances occurred among legal formulations in Deuteronomy. And finally, the *miktab*-style found in Isaiah 38:9–20 was very similar to the *hitpallel*. The *ša'al, nadar, berek* and *miktab* styles were set aside because none of the terms to be discussed occurred in them. The rest were almost invariably distinguished from the style of language immediately preceding and following the utterance addressed to God.

Within the large associative field of הושיע, Sawyer isolated a core lexical group of eight items: הושיע, הִצִּיל, עָזַר, חִלֵּץ, מִלַּט, פִּלֵּט, פָּצָה, פָּרַק with their nominalizations. He appears to rely on intuition to guide him in this choice. One criticism is that he did not treat verbs separately from their nominalizations. This suggests that he did not consider them to be separate lexemes but rather alternative forms of the same lexeme.

Sawyer observes that הושיע is approximately five times more frequent in language expressed to God than either הִצִּיל or עָזַר. Concerning the element of separation, הִצִּיל is almost always used with the preposition מִן, whereas הושיע occurs with it only four times and עָזַר only once. הושיע is properly used only of God's activity and this verb occurs 50 per cent of the time as one of four nominalizations. Such observations of the relative frequency of related terms in particular constructions are valuable indications of the differences between them.

Wernberg-Moller questions Sawyer's selection of terms and omission of antonyms: 'Sawyer concentrates on the synonyms or near-synonyms of הושיע (הִצִּיל, עזר, פלט, מלט, חלץ, פצה, פרן) and presents, not a study of the הושיע field, but rather an analysis of the contexts of הושיע and similar words.'[37] The relations of synonymy and antonymy, while essential to the semantic field, are not necessarily characteristic of the associative field. According to Saussure, associative relations are those formed outside discourse, they are not supported by linearity: 'Their seat is in the brain; they are the inner storehouse that makes up the language of each speaker.'[38] The associative field is not necessarily encoded in linguistic form; it is a product of the individual's mind.

Sawyer distinguished between the eight core words on the basis of frequency, nominalization, transitivity, element of separation and religious context – significant structural features. He concludes that the element of separation appears to be context bound and varies in degree between members of the lexical group. His conclusions are largely formalistic and compare the linguistic context of terms, but tell relatively little about the comparative semantic content of each term. His study is nevertheless a valuable one as it demonstrates methods for the comparison of terms. The precise definition of context and the calculation of the comparative frequency of individual terms in particular contexts are important parts of any investigation of a semantic field.

More recent is the ambitious work on the lexical field of 'separation' by Angelo Vivian. He distinguishes four stages of the Hebrew language: Pre-exilic Biblical, Post-exilic Biblical, Qumranic, Mishnaic. He further classifies Pre-exilic Hebrew as consisting of four distinct forms: narrative, poetic, dialectal-poetic (Amos) and legal-ritual. Vivian provides distributional tables on verb morphology and brief syntactical notes on the passages where each verb occurs. The author limits his study to twelve verbs and applies componential analysis to them. The following chart summarizes a small part of his results for pre-exilic biblical legal-ritual:

	1	2	3	4	5
בדל	+	+	+	–	–
חרם	+	+	–	+	–
קדש	+	+	–	+	+

---

[37] P. Wernberg-Moller, 'Review of J.F.A. Sawyer's *Semantics in Biblical Research*', 216.

[38] Saussure, *General Linguistics*, 123.

1 indicates the semantic component of 'separation' itself, 2 that the verb may be used without reference to a spatial dimension, 3 indicates use with a spatial dimension, 4 a sacral component, and 5 that it is used absolutely.[39]

Vivian does not explain how he selected the verbs or antonyms. The results are interesting but the author does not demonstrate how he determined which semantic components are shared by particular verbs. To a certain extent all linguists rely on their own intuition, a fact which needs to be openly acknowledged, and furthermore analysed, in order to determine where such intuition derives from, and to facilitate comparison between the intuition of different scholars, because what is obvious to one linguist may not be to another. It seems excessive that eighteen semes are needed to distinguish eleven lexemes. There also seems to be some confusion between the lexical and contextual meanings of terms: Vivian uses the feature 'with/without instrument'. There is no doubt that in 1 Kings 3:25–26 the verb גזר is used in a context where an instrument (a sword) is in view. But Silva questions whether that feature derives from the contribution of the verb to the context, or the contribution of the context as a whole.[40]

Zatelli studied the field of purity adjectives in BH, beginning with an analysis of the distribution of terms in ancient Hebrew narrative, legal material, poetry, and the book of Amos, later narrative, poetry, and the book of Job. She adopted the notion of 'dimension' to analyse the field. The basic dimensions were /natural/, /ethical-religious/ and /material-religious/. Within these dimensions the fundamental distinction is /pure/:/non-pure/.[41] Zatelli underlines caution in the designation of classes because of the restricted nature of biblical material and the lack of external verification.[42]

In both her studies of colour terms and humour Brenner adopts Ullmann's definition of a semantic field as, 'a closely knit and articulated lexical sphere where the significance of each unit is determined by its neighbours, with their semantic areas

---

[39] A. Vivian, *I campi lessicali della "separazione" nell' ebraico biblico, di Qumran e della Mishna*, 180.

[40] M. Silva, 'Review A. Vivian's, *I campi lessicali della "separazione" nell' ebraico biblico, di Qumran e della Mishna*', 395.

[41] I. Zatelli, *Il campo lessicale degli aggettivi di purità in ebraico biblico*, 71.

[42] Zatelli, *Purità*, 31.

reciprocally limiting one another and dividing up and covering the whole sphere between them'.[43] She also echoes discoveries of cognitive scientists in viewing the semantic field as a hierarchy whose structuring is predetermined by certain criteria. A term is considered to be primary when it is monolexemic, its signification is not included in any other term, its application is wide, it is psychologically salient and easily identified, it is not a transparent loanword from another language or another linguistic sphere, and it is morphologically of a simple construction.[44] A secondary term is defined as either monolexemic but with limited signification and/or restricted specification, or morphologically derived from another term which has already been classified as primary. The signification of the secondary term is included in that of a primary term and the distributional potential of a secondary term is more restricted than that of a primary one. Tertiary terms are relatively rare, compounds are tertiary and the signification of the tertiary term is limited and its application restricted.[45] Indirect terms are lexemes or syntagms which may be associated with higher levels of the field through etymological, phonetic or semantic links. These can be thought of as part of the wider associative field. This important distinction between primary, secondary and tertiary terms should be borne in mind in every semantic field study.

Brenner is not interested in semantic differences between primary terms, but she does suggest some useful criteria for considering the relative position of a given term (root) within its field: the occurrence of single or recurrent parallels, the existence of stable verb phrases, and other recurrent syntagms.[46] Once again the author does not explain the process by which she came to the categorization of terms, although she does refer to *BDB* and Jastrow, which suggests that she may have been working from the English semantic field. In the article about humour, Brenner comments that 'the inevitable conclusion is that the field of humour, laughter and the comic in Biblical Hebrew is sadly depleted and lopsided'.[47] This could be due to the restricted corpus or to a different

---

[43] S. Ullmann, *Principles of Semantics*, 157.

[44] A. Brenner, 'On the Semantic Field of Humour, Laughter and the Comic in the Old Testament', 45.

[45] Brenner, *Colour Terms*, 42–4.

[46] Brenner, 'Humour, Laughter and Comic', 48.

[47] Brenner, 'Humour, Laughter and Comic', 57.

concept of humour from that expressed in English. Humour is not universal; jokes are often the most difficult aspect of a foreign language to understand.

Donald, in his study of the semantic field of rich and poor in the wisdom literature, attempts to 'derive meaning from an examination of the system of opposition and balance found in the texts'.[48] The study is restricted to the biblical books of the Psalms, Ecclesiastes, Job and Proverbs. The field includes general adjectives for rich and poor and general substantives for riches, poverty and destitution. He notes that there are four common adjectives for poor: אֶבְיוֹן, עָנִי, דַּל and רָשׁ but only one for rich: עָשִׁיר, and that the situation is reversed in the case of substantives. He does not explain how he selected these terms. He notes that a comparison of the fields in Hebrew and Accadian reveals a general agreement in the number of terms used and the internal structure of the fields. He also points out that common terms show no etymological correspondence between the two languages, which accords with Brenner's classification of primary terms. Donald provides tables demonstrating the occurrence of parallelism between the different words in each of the biblical books and a table of the distribution of terms. He has not, however, derived a semantic analysis from his study.

In a study of the semantic field of folly in the same four books, Donald again uses parallelism to establish the relationships between words. In this article he attempts to present in a diagram the relative position of different terms as they appear in each book along the axis of 'mental and moral inculpability'–'mental and moral culpability'. He also indicates opposite and related terms.[49] The diagram is a useful visual aid.

Fox in 'Words for Wisdom' acknowledges that boundaries between words are vague and the goal is to discover why a certain word was chosen for a specific context, but he writes, 'it is dogmatic to think that only one word in the semantic field could have served'.[50] He knows that each word has its own particular slant or focus but that such detail is often only recovered with the help of living informants. Any semantic study of ancient texts therefore must be partial and uncertain.

---

[48] T. Donald, 'The Semantic Field of Rich and Poor in the Wisdom Literature of Hebrew and Akkadian', 28.

[49] T. Donald, 'The Semantic Field of "Folly" in Proverbs, Job, Psalms, and Ecclesiastes', 292.

[50] M.V. Fox, 'Words for Wisdom', 149.

Fox views a word as 'offering a single, flexible "packet" of meaning (= lexical meaning) that assumes different shapes ("senses") under pressure of context (= contextual meanings or applications)'.[51] He claims to study the lexical (as opposed to contextual) meaning of eight words in the semantic field of wisdom and knowledge. He begins by determining how בִּינָה and תְּבוּנָה differ from each other and notices that there are some significant differences in syntactic usages: one is said to do things 'in' or 'by' תְּבוּנָה, but not 'in' or 'by' בִּינָה. בִּינָה is not a *means* of activity. People are said to 'know בִּינָה' but not 'know תְּבוּנָה'.[52] The terms also differ with respect to their collocations. תְּבוּנָה always refers to practical astuteness or common sense, whereas בִּינָה is the faculty of intellectual discernment or interpretation, which can produce בִּינָה. Fox then looks at the relationships with other words in the semantic field of wisdom: תְּבוּנָה is the hyponym of חָכְמָה. בִּינָה is in most regards encompassed by חָכְמָה, but it can refer to mental activity in a way that חָכְמָה would not. This detailed study of syntagmatic, paradigmatic and collocational relations produces a nuanced commentary on the different items in the semantic field of wisdom. It is exemplary.

Botha took eight words for Torah in Psalm 119 as an example of a lexical field. These words (דבר, מצות, חקים, פקדים, עדוה, תורה, משפטים and אמרה) are used in an intentional lexical relationship as can be deduced from their equal frequency and fairly regular repetition.[53] Botha notes that any results from a study on such a closed corpus are relevant only to this context. His procedure is 'to compile semantic categories from the associative fields of the Torah terms'.[54] He appears to be using 'associative field' to refer to the syntagmatic and paradigmatic relationships of the terms – he is not looking at associative fields. His method is to reduce most of the information in the psalm to kernal sentences with the *dramatis personae* YHWH, the righteous and the evil. The percentage of occurrence of each lexical item in each form is calculated. Botha then employs the semantic differential technique to produce a spatial representation of the field of Torah terms. He claims that this demonstrates the three words משפטים, דבר and אמרה are closely linked together and serve more often than not to define the relation

---

[51] Fox, 'Wisdom', 150.
[52] Fox, 'Wisdom', 151.
[53] P. Botha, 'The Measurement of Meaning', 4.
[54] Botha, 'Measurement', 5.

between YHWH and the righteous.[55] Such mathematical analysis produces compact graphs and diagrams representing the syntactic structures within which each lexical item appears.

In his study of the field of 'obligation' in the Dead Sea Scrolls, Kaddari makes the important point that 'in order to illustrate the structure of any given field, it is necessary to confine oneself to one section of that field, to describe it in full, and to send out feelers from its centre in different directions until the entire field is covered'.[56] He lists thirty-three nouns which belong to the 'Restricted Field of Obligation', by which he means words which denote obligation itself. But he does not explain where this list comes from. Kaddari declares that 'the principles of division into semantic fields are specific to each language examined, and they cannot be transferred from one language to the next, even when those languages are most akin'.[57] He means that the structure and content of a semantic field is language-specific, rather than that the method for discovering semantic fields is language-specific. The method demonstrated by Kaddari himself is one which should be followed.

A full description of each word taking into account the context revealed two principles of division: (1) the source of obligation, and (2) whether the word belonged to other semantic fields. This leads to the classification (a) words denoting divine obligation, (b) words which denote divine or human (sectarian) obligation, and (c) words denoting human (sectarian or private) obligation. It is questionable whether these distinctions represent lexical meanings or contextual meanings. Is there a difference in *sense* between divine obligation and human obligation? Each of these three classes is then subdivided into (i) those which do not share other semantic fields, and (ii) those which do. Within these subdivisions Kaddari argues that words can be distinguished according to their specific semantic values on the basis of the root from which lexical items are derived. Restricted syntactical environments and frequency of occurrence within the restricted semantic field can further distinguish cognates.[58]

In such a restricted corpus of vocabulary the author declares it reasonable to assume that a word appearing frequently is more important than one that appears only once or twice. The resultant

---

[55] Botha, 'Measurement', 17.
[56] M.Z. Kaddari, *Semantic Fields in the Language of the Dead Sea Scrolls*, ix.
[57] Kaddari, *Semantic Fields*, ix.
[58] Kaddari, *Semantic Fields*, x.

figures have to be correlated with the frequency of that word in the vocabulary at large. This further analysis reveals that keywords in the restricted field of obligation (those which appear more than might be expected according to figures for frequency of occurrence in the language at large) are not completely identical with the words appearing most frequently in the field. This very useful type of analysis should be repeated for other semantic fields. In the field of obligation it demonstrates that the keywords are חוק, ברית, תורה, דרך and מצוה.[59] Kaddari notes that the majority of words in the field are transparent in that the etymology of the root of each word explains its entry into the field of obligation. Thus he carefully combines both synchronic and diachronic analysis in his investigation of meaning.

In recent years several projects have begun to analyse BH and CH vocabulary according to semantic fields on a large scale. L.J. de Regt reports on the method of the *Hebrew-English Lexicon of the Old Testament Based on Semantic Domains*: Stage one involves going through the concordance and considering each and every occurrence of every word:

- to determine what the lexical meanings of that particular word might be.
- to formulate definitions of those meanings.
- to determine to which semantic field / domain they belong.[60]

The lexical meanings of a word are discovered through distributional analysis. 'Each lexical meaning has a specific semantic value which corresponds to its systematic, minimal, contribution to the interpretation of all the sentences in which the word with that lexical meaning occurs.'[61] It is recognized that different lexical meanings of a word usually belong to different semantic fields and the final arrangement of words according to semantic domains will express the meanings of words paradigmatically. However, the method for the identification and labelling of semantic domains is not discussed.

The Dictionary of Classical Hebrew edited by David Clines claims to have a theoretical base in modern linguistics: 'we subscribe to

---

[59] Kaddari, *Semantic Fields*, xiii.
[60] L.J. de Regt, 'Multiple Meaning and Semantic Domains in Some Biblical Hebrew Lexicographical Projects', 66.
[61] De Regt, 'Semantic Domains', 67.

the dictum that the meaning of a word is its use in the language'.[62] The focus therefore is on the patterns and combinations in which words are used; the record of syntagmatic and paradigmatic information is exhaustive: 'all the subjects and objects that are attested for every verb, and, for nouns, all the verbs and all the other nouns with which they are connected'.[63] Thus in theory this dictionary provides all the data necessary for a detailed semantic analysis of CH. Section 6 of each article comprises *Semantic Analysis*, where the 'meanings' or 'senses' that may be attributed to the word are analysed. The example given in the introduction is אֹהֶל with the senses (1) tent for human habitation, (2) tent of soldiers, (3) tent, tabernacle as divine habitation.[64] This raises the immediate question as to whether soldiers can be understood to be human. Surely, 'human' is a superordinate of 'soldier'. These three senses are contextual meanings of the term אֹהֶל not lexical senses. The entry for אֹהֶל in the main body of the dictionary records two senses (1) tent of human beings, (2) tent of sanctuary of YHWH, tabernacle.[65] But for linguists there is only one lexical sense regardless of who occupies אֹהֶל: this might be termed 'temporary habitation'.

The introduction readily acknowledges, 'It needs to be stressed that all such analyses have a large subjective element in them, and that our perception of sense is often dependent on the semantic structure of the English language. That is how it must, and should be, of course, in an interlingual dictionary.'[66] To a certain extent the influence of the linguist's native language is inevitable, but that is certainly not 'how it should be' in any dictionary. The semantic analysis of any language should be conducted from within that language and only subsequently should the results of such analysis be translated.

The syntagmatic and paradigmatic analysis, which records synonyms and antonyms, in sections 7 and 8 of each article, often appear to be generated automatically. The resultant lists of synonyms and antonyms do not always reflect semantic analysis: how might יְרִיעָה 'curtain' and כְּלִי 'vessel' be considered synonyms of אֹהֶל? What semantic features do they share? What are the sense relations between these three words? Once again there seems to

---

[62] 'Introduction', *Dictionary*, I:14.
[63] 'Introduction', I: 5.
[64] 'Introduction', I:19.
[65] Clines, *Dictionary*, I:143.
[66] 'Introduction', I:19.

be some lack of clarity in the distinction between lexical meaning, contextual meaning and collocation. Nonetheless, this dictionary provides an extremely useful database from which to begin the semantic analysis of CH.

The ESF Network 'The Semantics of Classical Hebrew' does not aim either to add a new kind of dictionary to the already existing ones, or to tackle a semantic study on the basis of a special method or methods. 'Its purpose is to prepare a tool which can be a useful inducement to further semantic methods.'[67] The work has been divided between various centres each of which concentrates on particular lexical fields, and the language of the project is English. Each lexical entry has seven sections: the root and comparative material, formal characteristics, syntagmatics, versions, lexical/semantic fields (including paradigmatics), exegesis and conclusion. Some articles have now been published.[68] The sections discussing lexical/semantic fields tend to list paradigmatic relationships, occurrences of parallelism and collocations without attempting a semantic differentiation between lexemes. The longer article on דֶּרֶךְ contains a list of other lexemes in the field (although no explanation of how they are known to be in the same field) and information on which words are employed in poetry and prose. There is also an attempt at distinguishing דֶּרֶךְ from חוּץ and אֹרַח.[69] This database is still in its early stages and there is much work to be done before it can provide the basis for a comprehensive semantic analysis of Hebrew lexical fields.

4. The Application of Lexical Semantics to Classical Hebrew

In attempting to apply lexical semantics, and in particular semantic field studies to CH, various factors have to be taken into consideration. The first and perhaps most important of these is the limited nature of the available corpus. Any analysis of semantic fields in CH is inevitably partial and provisional, with results being true of the corpus but not necessarily true of the language. Many gaps and questions will remain even about those semantic fields which

---

[67] J. Hoftijzer and G.I. Davies, 'A Database for the Study of Ancient Hebrew'.

[68] Muraoka, *Semantics*.

[69] J.K. Aitken, 'דֶּרֶךְ', 27–8.

evidence a rich vocabulary. The different types of material, the synchronic and diachronic strata, and literary genres contained therein, provide suitable data for comparing the senses of related lexemes in assorted linguistic contexts. However, to begin with too tight a restriction of the linguistic corpus defeats any study of lexical fields as there will be insufficient instances of vocabulary to investigate.

The second factor to be considered is that CH consists of written language, considered by linguists to be secondary to spoken data. Written language lacks the vitality of speech: mood, intonation, facial expressions and body language all add to the illocutionary force of an utterance. Most modern linguistic theories depend on being able to consult the intuition of contemporary native speakers to refine their model of the language system. Sawyer asserts that 'A knowledge of Hebrew implies that I can intuitively recognize words of related meaning.' But he also acknowledges that 'intuition is only a starting point for semantic analysis, and no more'.[70] There is no way of knowing whether modern scholars' reconstruction of semantic fields and sense relations in an ancient dead language are merely a reflection of their own intuition, or their own native language, or whether those fields existed in CH. Furthermore, there is no way of knowing whether the person who included a particular word in a text was aware of the alternatives available according to reconstructed semantic fields.

The meanings of many lexical items work at the level of designation as well as that of signification. This entails reference to the extra-linguistic world, and comprehension of such terms requires knowledge of situational context as well as linguistic context. Details about participants, relevant people and places, may be gained from the text itself, and analysis of sentences can indicate the verbal and non-verbal actions undertaken. Relevant objects and the effects of actions may also be available. All these factors assist with some comprehension of designation and provide a context for individual lexemes. Scholars are fortunate in the amount of archaeological and extra-biblical information relating to the culture of the Israelites and their neighbours. It is not always easy, however, to identify the particular referent of a lexeme, especially within semantic fields which concern household items such as cooking pots.[71] The application of lexical semantics to an ancient textual

---

[70] Sawyer, *Semantics*, 34.
[71] Cf. A.M. Honeyman, 'The Pottery Vessels of the Old Testament'.

corpus therefore has to be content with concentrating primarily on the level of signification. As Kaddari notes, 'We may learn the meaning of words, but not a knowledge of their intended content which must be derived from other, non-linguistic sources, or which there is no hope of recognizing at all.'[72]

In starting to study semantic fields in CH or BH the temptation is either to rely on one's own intuition or first to refer to lexicographic descriptions from interlingual reference works to determine which words belong to a particular field. But such study must be based on the language itself and not through recourse to translation of the literature. Fronzaroli suggests a useful method for delimiting the lexical field based on substitution: beginning with the hypothesis that lexeme *A* belongs to a particular field, and considering it an invariant, creates an inventory of class *B*. These are lexemes which occur in association with *A*:

A	white	*B*	horse, garment, flower

Then for each member of class *B*, extract the members of *A'* which can replace *A* in *A + B*:

B	horse	*A'*	black, bay, sorrel
B	garment	*A'*	black, yellow, green

The members of class *A'* occur in opposition to one another and in fact each member of *A'* can replace *A* in some specific utterances, but not all of them (partial synonymy). For each member of *A'* class *B* must be similarly extracted:

A + A'	white	*B*	horse, garment, flower
A + A'	black	*B*	horse, garment

The procedure ends when new extractions are no longer possible and the class *A'* of lexemes are shown to belong to the semantic field of *A*.[73] This method requires a lot of data for verification and therefore may not be widely applicable to CH.

Most of the studies of semantic fields in BH or CH have produced a lot of information about *la parole*, with detailed analysis of paradigmatic and syntagmatic relations. The most comprehensive studies, such as those by Fox and Kaddari, describe

---

[72] Kaddari, *Semantic Fields*, vii.
[73] Fronzaroli, 'Componential Analysis', 86–7.

the different uses of words within the same semantic field and elucidate subtle variations in meaning. However, such analysis may or
may not explain why a particular word, rather than another related
one, has been used on a specific occasion.

There is much more work to be done in the lexical semantics of
CH. Whereas such studies of the lexicon may not necessarily assist
in identifying the meaning of a particular word in a specific context,
they do provide a guide to the relations between words and serve to
further knowledge and sharpen the intuition of Hebrew scholars.

7

Text Linguistics

1. Introduction

This chapter explores what makes a text a text and investigates how linguists have sought to clarify how and why meanings are expressed through particular linguistic forms. Text linguistics or discourse analysis (terms which are practically equivalent) concerns both the forms of language used and the meanings those forms convey. Text linguistics is a procedural approach to language – it concerns language in use, how texts function in human interaction. There is no consensus on terminology; therefore this chapter begins with a critical survey of some text-linguistic theory to differentiate terminology. The survey includes a review of applications to BH texts. Section 3 analyses the textual structure of Judges 4, and the final part evaluates the usefulness of such applications for investigating meaning in CH. It must be acknowledged at this point that both text linguistics and rhetorical criticism are flourishing fields in biblical studies and the boundaries between the two are not always clear cut.

2. Text Linguistic Theory

2.1 What is a text?

According to Brown and Yule 'discourse' is language in use and 'a text' is the verbal record (spoken or written) of a communicative act.[1] Discourse is a process, an attempt at communication, and the resultant text is the record of that communication. A text according

---

[1] G. Brown and G. Yule, *Discourse Analysis*, 1, 6.

to this definition may be of any length and of any linguistic form. But it cannot be explained as a configuration of morphemes or sentences; rather the morphemes or sentences are said to function as operational units and patterns for signalling meanings and purposes during communication. According to Halliday and Hasan, a text is best regarded as a semantic unit which is realized by or encoded in sentences.[2]

Beaugrande and Dressler are more specific: 'a text' is 'a communicative occurrence which meets seven standards of textuality'.[3] The standards are as follows:

Standard 1: Cohesion
This concerns how components of the surface text are mutually connected within a sequence. Cohesion rests upon grammatical and lexical dependencies.[4]

Standard 2: Coherence
This concerns how components of the textual world, that is, the configuration of concepts and relations which underlie the surface text, are mutually accessible and relevant. 'Concept' is defined as a configuration of knowledge and 'relations' are links between concepts which appear together in the textual world. Coherence is illustrated particularly well by the group of relations subsumed under causality where 'cause' identifies the necessary conditions for something, 'enablement' the sufficient but not necessary conditions, 'reason' indicates rational response, and 'purpose' a planned event or situation. Another way of looking at events or situations is their arrangement in time.

A text does not make sense by itself, but by interaction of text-presented knowledge with people's stored knowledge of the world. Where 'meaning' refers to the potential of the language expression and 'sense' refers to knowledge actually conveyed by that expression in a text,[5] a text 'makes sense' because of the continuity of senses within it – its coherence. Beaugrande and Dressler use 'topic' to describe text-world concepts with the greatest density of linkage to other concepts. Unless topic concepts are activated, processing of the textual world is not feasible

---

[2] M.A.K. Halliday and R. Hasan, *Cohesion in English*, 2.
[3] R. de Beaugrande and W. Dressler, *Introduction to Text Linguistics*, 3.
[4] Cf. section 2.3.
[5] Beaugrande and Dressler, *Introduction*, 84.

because there are no control centres to show the main ideas.[6] Readers need to know what a text is about in order to understand it. Both cohesion and coherence are text centred, whereas standards 3–7 are user centred.

Standard 3: Intentionality

This concerns the attitude of producers of texts towards producing a cohesive and coherent text instrumental in fulfilling their intentions. Presumably authors want to communicate to readers and will do so to the best of their linguistic ability.

Standard 4: Acceptability

The receiver of the text expects it to be both cohesive and coherent and of some relevance. The psychological process of inferencing assists the receiver in making sense of the text. In everyday conversation much of the information conveyed from speaker to hearer is implied rather than asserted, and the act of communication depends heavily upon the hearer's ability to infer what is meant.

Standard 5: Informativity

This measures expected versus unexpected information and known versus unknown factors. The receiver expects to gain from a text and every text will inform to a certain extent. If the producer tries to convey too much unexpected information, the receiver will quickly tire. If the text conveys very little new information the receiver is likely to become bored and uninterested. Stretches of BH narrative can seem repetitive compared to modern narratives: in 2 Samuel 11:18–19 Joab tells the messenger precisely what to say to David; the narrative then records the messenger delivering those very words. How information is encoded in linguistic structures will be discussed further in section 4.

Standard 6: Situationality

Situationality concerns factors which make the text relevant to its situation of occurrence. It can affect the means of cohesion – a text that has to be read quickly by passing motorists will be expressed in the minimum way possible, expecting readers to infer the complete message. Biblical narratives may have been written to be heard in public rather than to be read at home. People have limited auditory memories; so important material needs to be reinforced if it is to be

---

[6] Beaugrande and Dressler, *Introduction*, 136.

remembered. When listening to stories, receivers cannot refer back to previous material to refresh memories, but when reading a book they can.

Standard 7: Intertextuality
This concerns what makes the utilization of one text dependent upon knowledge of one or more previously encountered texts. Intertextuality is responsible for the evolution of text types with typical patterns of characteristics. It is a phenomenon evident in the Hebrew Bible as exemplified by the refrain in Judges 'the Israelites again did evil in the eyes of the LORD'.

Other linguists, like Lyons, specify that a text must exhibit the properties of cohesion and coherence, and then collapse standards 3–7 into the broader realm of context.[7] Context is taken to be the determining factor in the meaning of an utterance. It is the context of communication which will determine how much knowledge is shared or conveyed among the participants, how participants are trying to monitor or manage the situation and how texts composing the discourse are related to each other.[8]

Standards 1–7 function as 'constitutive principles' (after Searle) of textual communication: they both define and create the text. Beaugrande and Dressler then add three 'regulative principles' which control textual communication rather than define it: the *efficiency* of a text depends on it communicating with a minimum of effort required on the part of all participants; *effectiveness* depends on the text leaving a strong impression and creating favourable conditions for attaining a goal; *appropriateness* is agreement between the text's setting and how the standards of textuality are upheld.[9]

A 'text-type' is defined as 'a set of heuristics for producing, predicting and processing textual occurrences and hence acts as a prominent determiner of efficiency, effectiveness and appropriateness'.[10] Narrative texts, for example, arrange actions and events in a particular sequential order. They frequently utilize relations of cause, reason, purpose, enablement and time proximity. The surface text reflects the density of subordinations.

---

[7] J. Lyons, *Linguistic Semantics*, 263.
[8] Lyons, *Linguistic Semantics*, 265.
[9] Beaugrande and Dressler, *Introduction*, 11.
[10] Beaugrande and Dressler, *Introduction*, 186.

The identification of appropriate text-type is important to the interpretation of a BH text. According to Dawson, text-type is one of the strongest motivating factors at macro-syntactic levels in the deployment of micro-syntactic constructions.[11] That is to say, text-type or genre determines the use of particular linguistic forms and constructions. Judges 4 and 5 provide an ideal comparison of how Hebrew poetry and prose convey the same story:

וַיֹּאמֶר אֵלֶיהָ הַשְׁקִינִי־נָא מְעַט־מַיִם כִּי צָמֵאתִי
וַתִּפְתַּח אֶת־נֹאוד הֶחָלָב וַתַּשְׁקֵהוּ וַתְּכַסֵּהוּ

He said to her, 'Please give me a little drink of water, for I am thirsty.'
And she opened the milk container and gave him a drink, and covered him. (Jdg. 4:19)

מַיִם שָׁאַל
חָלָב נָתָנָה
בְּסֵפֶל אַדִּירִים הִקְרִיבָה חֶמְאָה

Water he asked, milk she gave; in a princely bowl she offered curds. (Jdg. 5:25)[12]

An alternative scheme to Beaugrande and Dressler's three regulative principles would be Grice's five Maxims of Conversation. These are the Maxim of Co-operation (co-operate as required), the Maxim of Quantity (be as informative as necessary without providing any unnecessary information), the Maxim of Quality (be truthful), the Maxim of Relation (be relevant), and the Maxim of Manner (be perspicuous, avoid obscurity, avoid ambiguity, be brief and be orderly).[13] Presumably the producer of a text wanting to communicate to a receiver would be acting according to these five maxims.

2.2 *What is a Classical Hebrew text?*

The definition of a text as the record of a communicative act is applicable to practically any example of CH. A partially decipherable inscription remains the record of a communicative act whether or not it can be understood by modern scholars. The Hebrew Bible

---

[11] D.A. Dawson, *Text Linguistics and Biblical Hebrew*, 23.
[12] Cf. A. Berlin, *The Dynamics of Biblical Parallelism*, 12–13.
[13] H.P. Grice, 'Logic and Conversation', 41–2.

as a whole can be seen as a single text under this definition, as can an individual book or psalm. If linguists choose to take the biblical text as it is presented (the usual practice in modern linguistics), then each section may be considered an individual text. But is the Hebrew text as it stands today the true record of a communicative act or the record as previous interpreters would have it transmitted? When linguists talk about communicative acts they are usually referring to conversations between people, and the record is a tape-recording or written transcription. They are studying discourse in their native language and in a familiar and well-defined context. The majority of CH data is a literary composition with a history of transmission. When applying the insights of text linguistics to CH the scholar needs to clarify which form of the text is being analysed and what is known about its particular *Sitz im Leben*.

Beaugrande and Dressler's definition of a text as a communicative occurrence meeting seven standards of textuality proves to be more difficult with respect to CH. Findings from investigation of cohesion and coherence in a particular piece of Hebrew have often been used to argue for identification of a text: Berlin has demonstrated how a study of lexical cohesion can reveal more continuity in a passage than commentators might have previously thought.[14]

The user-centred standards of textuality are not so readily applicable to CH: intentionality presumes the producer wants to make their intention clear within the cohesion and coherence of the communication. There has been great debate among biblical scholars as to whether authorial intention can be derived from biblical texts. Again the history of the data complicates matters. Scholars need to specify which producer's intention they are seeking to comprehend and what is known about that particular producer. Acceptability is dependent largely upon the receiver's ability to infer correctly the intended message. Inference begins with shared world knowledge and experience, shared concepts and presuppositions. Scholars today are aware of various aspects of the culture and world of the producers of the Bible but are obviously not living in the same era; therefore today's receivers of such texts are at a disadvantage. What was inferentially obvious to members of the original culture because of shared knowledge may not be inferable to modern readers.[15] Nevertheless, life as human beings on this earth has some constant elements throughout history, and if the current reader can

---

[14] A. Berlin, 'Lexical Cohesion and Biblical Interpretation', 29–40.

[15] P.J. MacDonald, 'Discourse Analysis and Biblical Interpretation', 165.

identify the correct script for a text, then an appropriate sequence of inferences may be triggered for comprehension. Of course scripts or text-styles also differ across cultures and centuries. The failure to recognize genres and appropriate ways in which to interpret them leads to readers misunderstanding the Hebrew Bible, taking certain proverbs, for instance, as promises.

Concerning informativity, some scholars have begun studying the information structure of BH texts using Tagmemics.[16] The standard of situationality concerns what makes the text relevant to the discourse situation. In the case of CH, the question is 'Which situation?' It is debatable whether the original situation is recoverable. Intertextuality is evident within BH with repeated patterns and cross-references to other books. This factor can assist in providing the receiver with an appropriate script for understanding a new text.

To summarize, the two text-centred standards of cohesion and coherence are applicable to CH and useful in increasing understanding of such data. The other standards, which broadly concern context, cause problems for Hebrew scholars, for in practice they are trying to discover details about context from within texts rather than looking at how texts function pragmatically. Discourse analysts rarely need to ask, 'What does this text mean?' because they are studying their native language in a familiar context. They are more likely to ask, 'How does this text mean what it does?' Biblical scholars tend to be preoccupied with discovering what the text means. For the receiver who may not be the intended one, interpretation involves not only study of the linguistic properties of the text but also the pragmatic context of the original communicative act and the mental processes involved in its production. This fundamental difference in approach needs to be borne in mind when applying text linguistics to CH.

As a minimum requirement, a CH text can be defined as 'a record of a communicative act which is both linguistically cohesive and coherent in its expression'. Considering context to be the determining factor in comprehension of a text, it would be desirable to add something to the effect of 'appropriate to and consistent with its pragmatic context', but that criterion would be more difficult to assess with respect to the situation of the original author and intended receiver. The biblical text has been interpreted in different ways throughout history as the pragmatic context of the receiver

---

[16] Cf. section 2.4.

changed and the text was investigated from a different perspective: there is ongoing debate about whether the Bible can be fully understood only from within the community of faith.

2.3 Cohesion

Halliday and Hasan define cohesive relations as semantic relations between two or more elements in a text that are independent of structure: between the personal pronoun 'he' and antecedent proper noun 'John'. Cohesion is a semantic relation between an element in the text and some other element that is crucial to the interpretation of it. The pronoun 'he' could refer to any male; therefore further information is required to identify the intended referent. This other element may be found within the text, but its location in the text is not determined by the structure.[17] A semantic relation of this kind may be set up within a sentence or between sentences. The proper noun 'John' may have last appeared two or three paragraphs prior to the pronoun.

A tie is a single instance of cohesion, one occurrence of a pair of cohesively related items. A tie between two elements provides texture and when such a cohesive relation is set up between sentences, it makes them cohere. The stability or texture of a text is a function of the continuity of occurrences, the number of ties at the level of word, phrase, clause and sentence. In a text every sentence (except the first) exhibits some form of cohesion with the preceding sentence(s). A brief summary of various kinds of cohesive ties follows.

2.3.1 Reference

This is a relation between meanings. In most written language the reference will be textual rather than situational. Co-referentiality is a cohesive agency which works in two directions. Anaphoric reference is based on the previous mention of a person or thing. In English it is usually identified by the use of a pro-form after the co-referring expression, whereas in cataphora the pro-form is used before the co-referring expression, thus establishing reference within the same clause. Cataphoric reference is less usual, requires more processing by the receiver and therefore creates focus on a particular block of text. Anaphoric reference is the default form and appears

---

[17] Halliday and Hasan, *Cohesion*, vii, 6–7.

very frequently in written texts: in Judges 4:2 וַיִּמְכְּרֵם יְהוָה בְּיַד יָבִין 'The LORD sold them into the hand of Jabin', where the pronominal suffix 'them' refers back to the Israelites in verse 1 בְּנֵי יִשְׂרָאֵל. An example of cataphoric reference is Genesis 45:12 פִּי הַמְדַבֵּר 'It is my mouth that is speaking to you'.

Co-referentiality may be expressed through reiteration of lexical items, either through exact repetition of words, anaphoric use of a general word, or the use of a synonym or near-synonym. In Judges 4, Jabin is introduced: יָבִין מֶלֶךְ־כְּנַעַן אֲשֶׁר מָלַךְ in verse 17 he is referred to as יָבִין מֶלֶךְ־חָצוֹר and in verses 23–24 as יָבִין מֶלֶךְ־כְּנַעַן. Partial recurrence may also involve shifting of already used elements to different classes, for example, from noun to verb.

2.3.2 Substitution

This is a relation between linguistic items, that is between words or phrases. Substitution may be nominal, verbal or clausal. Basically, a different counter fills the slot. Whereas in ellipsis the slot is left empty and something is understood from a previous part of the text, parallelism repeats the structure but fills it with new elements. Judges 4:19 provides an example of ellipsis: the verb וַתְּכַסֵּהוּ omits the object employed in the previous verse: וַתְּכַסֵּהוּ בַּשְּׂמִיכָה. Parallelism is evident in abundance in the psalms and elsewhere in biblical texts.[18]

2.3.3 Collocation

Lexical collocation provides another example of cohesion between related forms. However, it must be remembered that there are degrees of proximity within the lexicon. Some words have a high probability of co-occurrence and therefore may function as cohesive elements. A lexical item that occurs with great frequency in the language as a whole will play a much smaller part in lexical cohesion.

2.3.4 Junction

A semantic connection between elements in a text, junction may take the relation of conjunction which links things with the same status and is the default option; disjunction – linking things with alternative status: true versus false; contrajunction which links things with the same status that appear incongruous or incompatible in the textual world; and subordination – linking things when the

---

[18] Cf. Berlin, *Biblical Parallelism*.

status of one depends on that of the other. Paraphrase repeats the content but conveys it in different expressions.

2.3.5 *The analysis of cohesion*

To undertake an analysis of cohesion, first identify cohesive relations within the text, including a note of those which remain unresolved. Then for each tie, specify the type of cohesion involved, with an account of whether it is immediate, mediated or remote and some indication of the number of intervening sentences. A count of cohesive ties in a text with a note of their distance will give an indication of overall texture.

Cohesion does not concern what a text means; it concerns how a text is constructed as a semantic edifice. Halliday and Hasan point out that analysis of cohesion, together with other aspects of texture, will not in general add anything new to the interpretation of a text. But it will show why the text is interpreted in a certain way, including why it is ambiguous in interpretation wherever it is so.[19] The analysis of cohesion is nevertheless very useful in investigating CH texts particularly with respect to recognizing the rich semantic structure of individual texts and the positive identification of ambiguities.

2.4 *Information structure*

This looks at why producers package messages in one particular linguistic form in preference to propositionally equivalent alternatives. Lambrecht writes, 'grammatical analysis at this level is concerned with the relationship between linguistic form and the mental states of speakers and hearers ... the linguist dealing with information structure must deal simultaneously with formal and communicative aspects of language'.[20] Certain formal properties of sentences cannot be fully understood without looking at the linguistic and extra-linguistic contexts in which sentences are embedded. Once again the primacy of context in interpretation is encountered.

Lambrecht defines 'Information Structure' as 'That component of sentence grammar in which propositions as conceptual representations of states of affairs are paired with lexicogrammatical structures in accordance with the mental states of interlocutors

---

[19] Halliday and Hasan, *Cohesion*, 328.
[20] K. Lambrecht, *Information Structure and Sentence Form*, 1.

who use and interpret these structures as units of information in given discourse contexts.[21] The student of information structure is not primarily concerned with the interpretation of words or sentences in given conversational contexts, but rather with the discourse circumstances under which given pieces of propositional information are expressed via one rather than another possible morpho-syntactic or prosodic form. In other words, situational context determines the choice of linguistic form.

It must be noted that Lambrecht is dealing with modern European languages and furthermore spoken data. This is vitally important because prosodic form is one of the main information carrying elements. Some considerations of information structure may nevertheless be applied to written CH texts. The investigator can ask why one particular sentence structure might have been used to convey content rather than another propositionally equivalent structure. Clues may be obtained from the surrounding text and theological or situational context.

Lambrecht identifies the three most important categories of information structure as: Presupposition and Assertion, Identifiability and Activation, and Topic and Focus.[22] Presupposition and Assertion concern the structuring of propositions into portions which the producer assumes that the receiver already knows or does not yet know. Sentences typically contain some lexical or grammatical indication of the information which is assumed to be already activated in the receiver's mind, as a basis or point of departure for the new information to be added. In the example sentence 'I finally met the woman who moved in downstairs' the assertion is 'I have met my new neighbour'. Presuppositions are revealed by use of the definite article 'the woman', assuming the receiver already knows that the new neighbour is female; and the restrictive clause 'who moved in downstairs', indicating the receiver knows that someone has moved in downstairs; and the adverb 'finally', demonstrating the expectation that the speaker would have met that individual before now.[23] A presupposed proposition is one of which speaker and hearer are presumed to have some shared knowledge or representation at the time of the utterance, whilst an asserted proposition is one of which only the speaker has a representation at the time of the utterance. It is new information to the hearer.

---

[21] Lambrecht, *Information Structure*, 5.
[22] Lambrecht, *Information Structure*, 6.
[23] Lambrecht, *Information Structure*, 52–3.

Identifiability and Activation concern the producer's assumptions about the statuses of mental representations of discourse referents in the receiver's mind at the time of the utterance. An identifiable referent is one for which a shared representation already exists in both speaker's and hearer's minds at the time of utterance, whilst an unidentifiable referent is one for which a representation exists only in the mind of the speaker. Definite noun phrases often (but not always) serve to indicate an identifiable referent ('the woman') and in cases of anaphoric reference the referent is identifiable because it has been mentioned earlier in the discourse. In order for correct comprehension, the referent must not only be identifiable but also active in the consciousness of the receiver. The cognitive category 'activeness' has grammatical correlates in prosody and morphology, an active referent being formally expressed pronominally, whilst an inactive referent receives full lexical coding ('the woman who moved in downstairs').[24]

Topic and Focus concern the producer's assessment of the relative predictability versus unpredictability of relations between propositions and elements in given discourse situations. Lambrecht defines the topic of a sentence as 'the thing which the proposition expressed by the sentence is about'.[25] He restricts his attention to sentence or clause topics; he is not concerned with 'topic' as Halliday and Hasan use it in connection with discourse. According to Lambrecht, a statement about a topic can only count as informative if it conveys information which is relevant to this topic. The syntactic structure of a sentence cannot always be relied upon to determine the topic; it is frequently necessary to know the context in order to identify the correct topic. Lambrecht makes the following distinction: 'While a topic expression always necessarily designates a topic reference, a referent which is topical in a discourse is not necessarily coded as a topic expression in a given sentence or clause.'[26] The focus of a sentence is the information conveyed about the topic. Every sentence has a focus, whether or not it makes explicit the topic.

Information structure is formally manifested in aspects of prosody, in special grammatical markers, in the form of syntactic (in particular nominal) constituents, in the position and ordering of such constituents in a sentence, in the form of complex grammatical

---

[24] Lambrecht, *Information Structure*, 77–8.
[25] Lambrecht, *Information Structure*, 118.
[26] Lambrecht, *Information Structure*, 130.

constructions, and in certain choices between related lexical items. Information structure analysis therefore focuses on the comparison of semantically equivalent but formally and pragmatically divergent sentence pairs such as active/passive or canonical/cleft constructions. Differences in information structure are then understood as contrasts between such allosentences.[27]

It is known that interpreters sometimes use semantic and pragmatic information in making judgements about the syntactic structure of a sentence. Lambrecht proposes that the most promising approach to grammatical analysis is one in which components of grammar are seen as interdependent forces competing with each other for the limited coding possibilities offered by the structure of the sentence.[28]

In English there are two assumptions about markedness in information structure: the pragmatically unmarked constituent order is subject–verb–object; and the pragmatically unmarked sentence accent position is clause final. The unmarked element of a pair of allosentences has greater distributional freedom and also greater overall frequency of occurrence. In English the unmarked information structure is topic focus with new information tending to be introduced by indefinite expressions. Given information may be indicated by lexical units mentioned for the second time, or by lexical units from within the same semantic field as previous material. Pronominal forms may be used anaphorically following a full lexical form or exophorically where the referent is present, and in English pro-verbal forms, typically from the verb 'to do', may be used. Some of the work on information structure in BH will be reviewed below.

While the meaning of a sentence is a function of the linguistic expressions it contains and therefore remains constant, the information value of the utterance of that sentence depends on the mental states of the producer and receiver. Even with marked sentence patterns there is often no one-to-one relationship between a syntactic form and a specific communicative function. Halliday has therefore developed the theory of Functional Grammar which analyses the function of linguistic elements rather than concentrating on their place in the linguistic system.

---

[27] Cf. F.I. Andersen, *The Sentence in Biblical Hebrew*, 186–7.
[28] Lambrecht, *Information Structure*, 12.

2.5 Functional grammar

Halliday's approach to discourse analysis interprets language as a system of meanings which are accompanied by forms through which the meanings can be realized.[29] In such a systemic theory meaning is considered to be a matter of choice, with the language interpreted as networks of interlocking options. This appears to correspond to Lambrecht's investigation of choice between allosentences. But his perspective, which views language as a structure of slots each with a choice of fillers some of which are unmarked and others marked, is syntagmatic in approach. Halliday's theory is paradigmatic in approach – it views the description of any feature as being its relationship to all the others, not its position in the overall structure.[30]

Below the level of the sentence the typical relationship between elements is constructional (syntagmatic), parts into a whole (the analysis of constituent structure), whilst above the level of the sentence non-constructional forms of organization take over. There is no grammar of text or discourse comparable to the constituent structure of a sentence. Halliday therefore labels elements according to both class and function. The purpose of functional labelling is to provide a means of interpreting the grammatical structure in such a way as to relate any given instance to the system of the language as a whole. In nearly all instances a constituent has more than one function at a time.

At the level of a text consisting of more than one sentence, semantic relations (revealed through cohesion and coherence) become more important to understanding the message conveyed than a straightforward syntactic analysis. Linguists are becoming increasingly aware that meaning cannot be treated as a separate component of language, but that every component of language should be analysed in relation to meaning.

Functional sentence perspective concerns the ordering of expressions to show the importance or newness of content. Halliday defines the theme of a sentence as what that sentence is about and the rheme as everything that follows, that is what the producer says about or in regard to the theme.[31] In English informativity tends to rise towards the end of a clause or sentence. The theme is usually

---

[29] M.A.K. Halliday, *An Introduction to Functional Grammar*, xiv.
[30] Cf. Halliday, *Functional Grammar*, xxvii.
[31] Halliday, *Functional Grammar*, 38.

the first major constituent of the sentence, and in most English sentences the subject is the first element, so theme and subject are usually identical. This sometimes leads to the assumption that theme (or topic) is automatically the first element in the sentence. In some languages the syntax for a sentence is often distinctive for sentences in which old topics are repeated and new topics are introduced.

Payne has identified two types of BH clause: 'verb' clause (non-copula): verb–subject, and 'noun' clause (+/– copula): subject –(verb)–copula or copula–(verb)–subject.[32] In narrative texts he concludes that where a fixed thematic ordering obtains, the verb–subject clause is used to:

1. Create the event-line (*waw*-consecutive).
2. To condense the event-line to express habitual action (*waw*-consec. perfect).

And the subject–verb clause is used to:

1. Side-step or interrupt the event-line to effect
   (a) anterior reference (perfect);
   (b) topic/character introduction / reintroduction (perfect / participle);
   (c) focus (perfect),
2. Describe a prevailing situation (participle).

A noun or relational clause provides the backdrop for the event-line by scene-setting, description and intermittent provision of information.

Payne makes a distinction between 'theme' and 'topic'. He reserves 'theme' for the first non-obligatory clause-element. 'Topic' is then used to refer to what the clause is about.[33] 'Theme' is a linguistic category whilst 'topic' is a conceptual category which may or may not be encoded linguistically. Brown and Yule observe that 'formal attempts to identify topics are doomed to failure'.[34] There is no objective way of identifying the topic of any particular sentence. The knowledgeable receiver seems to infer it intuitively from pragmatic context and the coherence of the discourse.

---

[32] G. Payne, 'Functional Sentence Perspective', 69.

[33] Payne, 'Functional Sentence Perspective', 67.

[34] Brown and Yule, *Discourse Analysis*, 68.

Scholars studying CH are in danger of observing changes in linguistic structure and attributing them to changes in topic. The above consideration of information structure demonstrates the need for careful distinctions between statements about linguistic structure and statements about presupposed mental representations and pragmatic context derived from observed linguistic structures. Today's scholars cannot know what was in the mind of the producer of a CH text and neither can they know what that producer presumed was in the mind of the intended receiver.

2.6 *Tagmemics*

This theory has been the one adopted by scholars studying the information structure of BH texts. Tagmemics aims to set language in the general context of human behaviour. It views language in terms of discrete entities (words, constituents), continuity and change (dynamic – looking at events along a continuum; for example, a string of words or sentences), and relatedness (a network of paradigms, conjugations and declensions).

Tagmemics offers four principles:

1. The viewpoints of observers affect how they formulate concepts of discourse.
2. Form cannot be divorced from meaning because language is structured and not random. Form-meaning composites are therefore the goal of analysis.
3. People process information in chunks; therefore units need to be organized in some way – language is hierarchical, so each form is embedded in a higher form.
4. Each unit has a place in the system (a slot), an indication of what may fill that slot (a class, or set) and how it relates to other slots (cohesion).[35]

A tagmeme has four parts: a slot (syntagmatic relation), a class (paradigmatic filler), a role (pragmatic relevance) and cohesion (agreement of items). It is discerned within the hierarchies of grammar, sound and the referential realm. Dawson prefers to work with simpler two-cell tagmemes using the slot and class elements, where a tagmeme is defined as a functional slot in a grammatical

---

[35] K.E. Lowery, 'The Theoretical Foundations of Hebrew Discourse Grammar', 114.

construction correlated with the lexical item / class of items which could be said to fulfil that function.[36] Tagmemics was developed for use in language surveys, data being collected through conversation with native speakers. Working with CH obviously does not provide the same sort of data or ease of reference to further clarification from context; hence the need to simplify tagmemes and concentrate on the formal linguistic elements.

Longacre has done most work in applying tagmemic theory to BH.[37] He has devised the concept of 'discourse genres' or 'discourse typologies' which are defined in grammatical terms. He uses two axes to divide types of discourse: how the text is oriented to time and the orientation of its agents. The result is four broad classes of text or discourse genre: narrative (+ agent, + temporal succession), procedural (– agent, + temporal succession), hortatory or behavioural (+ agent, – temporal succession), and expository (– agent, – temporal succession).[38] Each discourse type uses different syntactic structures according to whether the sentence concerned is carrying the storyline or providing background information: the main line of narrative text is advanced by *wayyiqtol* forms and that of hortatory text by strings of imperatives.

2.7 Foreground versus background in narrative texts

Hopper has proposed that the distinction between events on the main storyline 'foreground' and the supporting material 'background' is a linguistic universal of narrative discourse. This distinction may be indicated through tense-aspect morphology of the verb, word order, particles, or the use of active and passive voice. Whereas foregrounded events occur in narrative in the same order as in the real world, in the background they do not. Whereas in foregrounded clauses the subject tends to be highly propositional, in the background there is greater freedom for topic change and new information.[39] The insertion of background information into a narrative serves to arrest the reader's progress, either to highlight a particularly significant moment in the narration, or to provide a means of distinguishing one subsection of the narrative from what follows.

---

[36] Dawson, *Text Linguistics*, 85.
[37] Cf. R.E. Longacre, *The Grammar of Discourse* and *Joseph*.
[38] Cf. Longacre, *Grammar of Discourse*, 10.
[39] P. Hopper, 'Aspect and Foregrounding in Discourse', 213–14.

In Hebrew prose a linguistic distinction is made between main line (foreground) and subsidiary lines (background) of communication. Dawson follows Niccacci in asserting that main-line clause types are text-type specific, and that text-types can be identified by the predominant clause type.[40] The two constructions usually associated with the primary storyline are *wayyiqtol* and *weqatal*, and the two that mark background information are *we-X-qatal* and *we-X-yiqtol*. According to Niccacci, the main line of communication in narration is constituted by a chain of *wayyiqtol* forms,[41] as in Jeremiah 28:10–11:

וַיִּקַּח חֲנַנְיָה הַנָּבִיא אֶת־הַמּוֹטָה ... וַיִּשְׁבְּרֵהוּ :

וַיֹּאמֶר חֲנַנְיָה ... וַיֵּלֶךְ יִרְמְיָה הַנָּבִיא לְדַרְכּוֹ :

Hananiah, the prophet *then took* the yoke ... *and broke* it. *And* Hananiah *said* ... *and* Jeremiah the prophet *went* his way.

A *wayyiqtol* may also start an independent textual unit or introduce a main line of communication following a secondary line of subsidiary information, as in Genesis 2:5–7:

וְכֹל שִׂיחַ הַשָּׂדֶה טֶרֶם יִהְיֶה בָאָרֶץ וְכָל־עֵשֶׂב הַשָּׂדֶה טֶרֶם יִצְמָח כִּי לֹא הִמְטִיר

יְהוָה אֱלֹהִים עַל־הָאָרֶץ וְאָדָם אַיִן לַעֲבֹד אֶת־הָאֲדָמָה : וְאֵד יַעֲלֶה מִן־הָאָרֶץ וְהִשְׁקָה

אֶת־כָּל־פְּנֵי־הָאֲדָמָה : וַיִּיצֶר יְהוָה אֱלֹהִים אֶת־הָאָדָם עָפָר מִן־הָאֲדָמָה וּ

All the wild bush was not yet on the earth nor had any wild plant yet sprung up, for Yahweh God had not sent rain on the earth, nor was there any man to till the soil. However, a flood was rising from the earth and was watering all the surface of the soil. *Then* Yahweh God *fashioned* man of dust from the soil and ...[42]

The *weqatal* is considered to be main line form in procedural and predictive discourse.[43] It occurs in 1 Samuel 10:2–3 (predictive):

בְּלֶכְתְּךָ הַיּוֹם מֵעִמָּדִי וּמָצָאתָ

... וְאָמְרוּ אֵלֶיךָ ... וְחָלַפְתָּ מִשָּׁם ... וּבָאתָ עַד־אֵלוֹן תָּבוֹר וּמְצָאוּךָ

When you leave me now, you *will meet* ... *and* they *will say* to you ... *And* you *will go* from there ... *and* you *will come* to the Oak of Tabor *and* they *will meet* you ...

---

40 Dawson, *Text Linguistics*, 212.
41 Cf. A. Niccacci, *The Syntax of the Verb in Classical Hebrew Prose*.
42 Examples taken from C.H.J. van der Merwe, 'Discourse Linguistics and Biblical Hebrew Grammar'.
43 R.E. Longacre, 'Discourse Perspective on the Hebrew Verb', 181–3.

It also occurs in Leviticus 4:4–6a (procedural):

וְהֵבִיא אֶת־הַפָּר ... וְסָמַךְ אֶת־יָדוֹ ...

וְשָׁחַט ... וְלָקַח הַכֹּהֵן ... הַמָּשִׁיחַ ... וְהֵבִיא ... וְטָבַל הַכֹּהֵן

He *must bring* the bull ... *and* he *must lay* his hand ... *and immolate* ...
Then the anointed priest *must take* ... *and bring* it ... *Then* the priest
must dip ...

The structuring of clauses and texts in terms of new or given information also has implications for understanding principles of word
order. The expected or unmarked order of constituents provides
given information before new. BH is regarded as a verb–(subject)
–object language and marked word order occurs when the verbal
constituent or predicate is preceded by any other constituent. Only
in sentences where the verb is a participle is the unmarked word
order subject–verb (part.). The marked word order (X–verb) is a
construction often associated with the binary opposition foreground versus background. Van der Merwe concludes that in BH
X–verb word order is used as a general marker of discontinuity.[44]

Bandstra has observed that word orders where the subject is
made explicit typically occur at the beginning of a paragraph unit
and introduce a new subject or reintroduce a subject after a break.
He provides the following example:

וַיִּקַּח אַבְרָהָם אֶת־עֲצֵי הָעֹלָה

and Abraham took the wood of the sacrifice (Gen. 22:6a)

Non-verb-first clauses, as well as verbless clauses, are inform-
ationally marked, they typically signal informational discontinuity
or discourse transition from one unit to another:

וְהָאֱלֹהִים נִסָּה אֶת־אַבְרָהָם

and God tested Abraham (Gen. 22:1b)

בַּיּוֹם הַשְּׁלִישִׁי וַיִּשָּׂא אַבְרָהָם אֶת־עֵינָיו

on the third day raised Abraham his eyes. (Gen. 22:4a)

The introduction of Deborah in Judges 4:4 and Heber in Judges
4:11 provide further examples:

---

[44] Van der Merwe, 'Discourse Linguistics', 29–30.

וּדְבוֹרָה אִשָּׁה נְבִיאָה אֵשֶׁת לַפִּידוֹת הִיא שֹׁפְטָה

And Deborah, a woman, a prophetess, wife of Lappidoth, she was judging

וְחֶבֶר הַקֵּינִי נִפְרָד מִקַּיִן

And Heber the Kenite had separated from the Kenites.

Bandstra notes that forty-four of forty-seven narrative clauses in his text (Gen. 22:1–19) begin with a *waw*-prefix verb. When this is not so, this is primarily a sign of narrative discontinuity. He defines 'topicalization' as the process whereby a writer brings into prominence new information and puts it in the given information slot or topic position.[45] His study demonstrates the value of applying text linguistics to a familiar text in order to gain greater understanding of the significance of the structure of individual sentences.

De Regt has investigated the way participants are referred to in BH discourse. He noted two types of normal conventions: first, that explicit references with a proper name are normally associated with paragraph borders:

וַתָּשָׁב נָעֳמִי וְרוּת הַמּוֹאֲבִיָּה כַלָּתָהּ עִמָּהּ הַשָּׁבָה מִשְּׂדֵי מוֹאָב

This was how Naomi, she who returned from the country of Moab, came back with Ruth the Moabite, her daughter-in-law (Ruth 1:22).

And second, main character participants are referred to differently from others.[46] Marked ways of referring to participants include withholding of full reference (e.g., Gen. 18:1–13, where full reference to the LORD as participant appears only in v. 13) and developing the persona before finally assigning a name, repetition (e.g., Ruth 1, 2 where repetitive reference to 'Ruth the Moabite' serves to remind readers of her background) and the use of 'superfluous' pronouns with finite verbal forms that already include pronominal reference:

וַיַּכֵּר יוֹסֵף אֶת־אֶחָיו וְהֵם לֹא הִכִּרֻהוּ

Joseph recognized his brothers, but *they* did not recognize him (Gen. 42:8).

---

[45] B.L. Bandstra, 'Word Order and Emphasis in Biblical Hebrew Narrative', 109–123.

[46] Reported in van der Merwe, 'Discourse Linguistics', 34–35.

This study illustrates that contrast between the unmarked construction and the marked form can occur at any level of a language. Analysis needs to start with characterization of the unmarked forms of a text and then view deviation from the norm as significant to meaning. Points of deviation are identifiable by their special structures.

3. A Text Linguistic Analysis of Judges 4

This section looks at Judges 4 in the light of some of the above theoretical discussion of text linguistics. Discussion here concentrates on identification of the linguistic forms in the narrative which indicate foreground or background material, word order, and the cohesion created through reference. Although the poem in Judges 5 relates the same story, it will not be considered here, because structurally it is completely different. Examples which have already been cited within this chapter will not be repeated. As is usual in text linguistics, the analysis is based on observation of the *BHS* text.

3.1 *Analysis*

The main line of the story is carried by the narrative tense 1 + Qal imperfect and verb–subject word order. Variations from this structure serve to change the scene, introduce new characters or provide background information.

The opening sentence of Judges 4 echoes a recurrent theme in that book and serves to guide the reader towards the relevant script or presupposition pool for understanding the text. Structurally, this is expressed in an almost set phrase:

וַיֹּסִפוּ בְּנֵי יִשְׂרָאֵל לַעֲשׂוֹת הָרַע בְּעֵינֵי יְהוָה וְאֵהוּד מֵת

And again the sons of Israel did evil in the eyes of the LORD after Ehud died.

Comparable sentences introducing similar episodes are found in 2:11; 3:7; 3:12; 6:1; 10:6; and 13:1. Judges 3:12; 10:6; and 13:1 begin with the same sentence structure as 4:1, whereas verses 2:11; 3:7; and 6:1 begin with a slightly different structure:

וַיַּעֲשׂוּ בְנֵי־יִשְׂרָאֵל אֶת־הָרַע בְּעֵינֵי יְהוָה

And the sons of Israel did evil in the eyes of the LORD.

The first group uses infinitive construct + definite article following Hiphil imperfect of יסף, the second uses Qal imperfect of עשׂה with object marker את־, and definite article + noun. There is no obvious reason why one structure is chosen above the other in each instance. The repetition of this sentiment assists in providing coherence at the level of the book of Judges. The use of one of these phrases functions as the introduction to another episode in the life of the Israelites and to indicate the need for a new judge.

In what follows the opening statement, 4:1 is an exception to the norm with indication of temporal context 'after Ehud died'. The subject–verb word order indicates background information and the subject is surprising in that Shamgar, the most recently mentioned judge (3:31), appears to have been forgotten. There is no mention of the apostasy which was the usual way of doing evil in the eyes of the LORD as expressed in 2:11; 3:7 and 10:6 'And they served the Baals'. The recorded response of the LORD to such behaviour was to hand the Israelites over to a foreign power. In 3:12 'The LORD made Eglon king of Moab strong against Israel.' And the reason is repeated: 'Because they did evil in the eyes of the LORD.' In 6:1 'And the LORD gave them into the hand of Midian for seven years.' In 13:1 'And the LORD gave them into the hand of the Philistines for forty years.'

In three of the texts, the reader is also informed of the LORD's anger. In 2:14 'The anger of the LORD burned against Israel so he gave them into the hand of plunderers and they plundered them and he sold them into the hand of their surrounding enemies.' In 3:8 the Israelites are not given but sold: 'The anger of the LORD burned against Israel so he sold them into the hand of Cushan-Rishathaim King of Aram Naharaim and the sons of Israel served Cushan-Rishathaim for eight years.' In 10:7 'The anger of the LORD burned against Israel and he sold them into the hand of Philistines and into the hand of the sons of Ammon.' The opening phrase is identical in all three occurrences and is followed by the handing over or selling of Israel into oppression or slavery.

Readers aware of co-text at the level of the Hebrew Bible might notice echoes from Genesis (ch. 37 records Joseph being sold as a slave to Potiphar in Egypt) and Exodus (ch. 32 records the LORD's anger burning against the Israelites after they made the golden calf). That is not to say that the author(s) of Judges would have been aware of such texts. Text linguistics works on the text as it is presented: therefore the whole of the Hebrew Bible serves as potential background knowledge for today's readers of this passage, providing further echoes of the LORD's anger against the Israelites because of their idolatry and apostasy.

Returning to Judges 4:2, the LORD's response on that particular occasion was to sell the Israelites to Jabin, king of Canaan, who ruled in Hazor:

וַיִּמְכְּרֵם יְהֹוָה בְּיַד יָבִין מֶלֶךְ־כְּנַעַן אֲשֶׁר מָלַךְ בְּחָצוֹר

There is no mention here of anger. The opening two verses of chapter 4 are by far the shortest introduction to such an episode in Judges. They are nevertheless sufficient to set the scene for the reader. The appropriate presuppositions have been activated: Israel has done wrong, God in his anger has handed her over to an enemy, she will cry out to the LORD from her oppression and it is expected that he will provide a Judge to come to her rescue. By the end of the second verse the reader is subconsciously aware of the right frame or script for the correct interpretation of this text.

In v. 2 the enemy has been introduced: Jabin, king of Canaan, ruling from Hazor. Immediately, there follows the introduction of the commander of his forces, Sisera, who lived in Haroshet Hagoyyim. Jabin is mentioned twice more during the story and on each occasion only in a passing reference. Then, at the end of the episode, as he is defeated by the Israelites, he is named three times in the final two verses, each time being referred to as: יָבִין מֶלֶךְ־כְּנַעַן. The sons of Israel are similarly only mentioned at the beginning and end of the story (vv. 1, 3, 5, 23, 24). The main action focuses on four key human characters, in order of appearance they are Sisera, Deborah, Barak and Jael.

Sisera at first sight may appear to be the most active participant in the story, for he is mentioned by name twelve times in twenty-four verses, twice being identified as the commander of Jabin's forces (vv. 2, 7). Yet, he is the recipient of the action. Deborah, although only mentioned by name five times in the first fourteen verses, is in fact the active character. In verses 6–7, Deborah asks Barak whether God had said he would lure Sisera to the river Kishon where he would be given into Barak's hand; and in v. 9, Deborah predicts that the LORD will sell Sisera into the hand of a woman:

כִּי בְיַד־אִשָּׁה יִמְכֹּר יְהֹוָה אֶת־סִיסְרָא

The word order places an enhanced focus on the prepositional phrase and the vocabulary echoes that of verse 2, where the LORD sold Israel into the hand of Jabin and his commander Sisera. This serves to heighten the meaning of the defeat of Sisera, it reverses the fortunes of the Israelites. Note that it is the LORD, and not any of the human characters, who is said to be responsible for placing the Israelites under the power of Jabin and it will be the LORD who places Sisera under the power of a woman (neither a strong man nor a judge).

After twenty years of oppression, the sons of Israel cry out to the LORD as expected in verse 3. (In the co-text of Judges cf. 3:9; 3:15; 6:7; 10:10). And in verse 4 there is an abrupt shift from the narrative tense to nominal and participial sentences as the judge is introduced:

וּדְבוֹרָה אִשָּׁה נְבִיאָה אֵשֶׁת לַפִּידוֹת

Deborah, a woman, a prophetess, the wife of Lappidoth.

She is the only female judge and this is reiterated three times: 'a woman, a prophetess, wife of ...' In fact she is not called a judge, the narrative recounts that she, and no-one else (emphasized by use of the pronoun preceding the verb), was judging Israel at that time (v. 4). The scene is filled out a little here (circumstantial clause: ו + pronoun + Qal active participle): she used to sit under the Palm of Deborah, between Ramah and Bethel in the hills of Ephraim and the Israelites went up to her for judgement (v. 5).

The first thing Deborah is reported as doing in the current situation is to send for Barak, the third of the key human characters. Barak is identified as the son of Abinoam, from Kedesh in Naphtali (v. 6). He is referred to by name eleven times in the chapter, and as the son of Abinoam again in verse 12 (such repetition illustrates the tight cohesion in this text). He does not appear to act on his own initiative, but only in response to Deborah. She challenged him:

הֲלֹא צִוָּה יְהוָה אֱלֹהֵי־יִשְׂרָאֵל לֵךְ וּמָשַׁכְתָּ בְּהַר תָּבוֹר וְלָקַחְתָּ עִמְּךָ עֲשֶׂרֶת אֲלָפִים
אִישׁ מִבְּנֵי נַפְתָּלִי וּמִבְּנֵי זְבֻלוּן׃ וּמָשַׁכְתִּי אֵלֶיךָ אֶל־נַחַל קִישׁוֹן אֶת־סִיסְרָא שַׂר־צְבָא
יָבִין וְאֶת־רִכְבּוֹ וְאֶת־הֲמוֹנוֹ וּנְתַתִּיהוּ בְּיָדֶךָ

'Didn't the LORD God of Israel command you to gather at Mount Tabor and to take with you 10,000 men from the tribes of Naphtali and Zebulun? And didn't he say to you, "I will gather to you by the river Kishon Sisera, commander of the forces of Jabin, with his chariots and his troops and I will give them into your hand"?' (vv. 6, 7)

But Barak is unwilling to go without Deborah (v. 8). With the construction typical of reported speech in Hebrew narrative (ו + Qal imperf. 3rd pers. sing.), 'she said "I will surely go with you"', but the glory for any victory would not then go to Barak, but rather to a woman. Here again we have repetition of both lexical items and structures used earlier to indicate the concept of God selling someone into the hand of their enemy (cf. v. 2). Note, the woman is not named, but from now on the reader will be looking to identify her and will be wondering how she will be victorious over Sisera, for the usual strong-man tactics of the judges are no longer appropriate in this incident.

After this warning (v. 9), Deborah, who has not been mentioned by name since she was first introduced in verse 4, goes with Barak to Kedesh, his home (cf. v. 6). Anaphoric references keep the text tightly structured. Barak then called together Zebulun and Naphtali to Kedesh and 10,000 went up at his heels, and Deborah went too (v. 10).

Verse 11 appears to introduce a new topic as a completely new character is announced. The structure of the sentence (verbless clause expressing state) and use of a Niphal participle emphasize the novelty of the information. The storyline is placed on hold and the reader is held in suspense as clarification and familiarity are sought: Where does this person fit into the story?

וְחֶבֶר הַקֵּינִי נִפְרָד מִקַּיִן מִבְּנֵי חֹבָב חֹתֵן מֹשֶׁה
וַיֵּט אָהֳלוֹ עַד־אֵלוֹן בְּצַעֲנַנִּים אֲשֶׁר אֶת־קֶדֶשׁ

Heber the Kenite had separated from the Kenites, the descendants of Hobab, the father-in-law of Moses, and he had pitched his tent as far as the oak in Zaanannim which is near Kedesh (v. 11).

At the last word, the reader finally discovers a connection with the current story: 'Kedesh' (cf. v. 9), home of Barak and where he has now gathered 10,000 men, with Deborah. The mention of Moses, place names and an oak tree may trigger connections for the reader familiar with the co-text of the Hebrew Bible. The following verse reverts to the storyline, but meanwhile the reader has gained a piece of background information which will prove useful to interpretation later on in the story.

וַיַּגִּדוּ לְסִיסְרָא כִּי עָלָה בָּרָק בֶּן־אֲבִינֹעַם הַר־תָּבוֹר: וַיַּזְעֵק סִיסְרָא אֶת־כָּל־רִכְבּוֹ
תְּשַׁע מֵאוֹת רֶכֶב בַּרְזֶל וְאֶת־כָּל־הָעָם אֲשֶׁר אִתּוֹ מֵחֲרֹשֶׁת הַגּוֹיִם אֶל־נַחַל קִישׁוֹן:

When Sisera was told that Barak, son of Abinoam, had gone up to Mount Tabor, Sisera called together all his chariots, 900 chariots of iron, and all the people who were with him from Haroshet Hagoyyim, to the river Kishon (vv. 12, 13).

These two verses contain numerous anaphoric references: 'Barak, son of Abinoam' echoes his first appearance in verse 6; 'Mount Tabor' reminds the reader that God had commanded Barak to gather his people there (v. 6) (it also raises a question about the connection between Mount Tabor and Kedesh); the initial verb of verse 13 was used for Barak calling together his people in verse 10; and those 900 chariots of iron had been used to oppress the Israelites cruelly (v. 3); Haroshet Hagoyyim was Sisera's home town (v. 2) and the river Kishon was where God would hand Sisera along with all his chariots and all his troops into the hands of Barak (v. 7). The tension mounts as various predictions about Israel's deliverance are fulfilled. But still there remains the comment about Sisera being handed over to a woman and the loose end about Heber.

Deborah again tells Barak what to do: 'Get up for this is the day when the LORD will give Sisera into your hand' (v. 14). Earlier she had said that Sisera would be given into the hand of a woman (v. 9). With further assurance that God went before him, Barak led the men down from Mount Tabor. The LORD duly routs Sisera, all the chariots and the whole army לְפִי־חֶרֶב 'with the edge of the sword' before Barak. Sisera alights from his chariot and flees on foot. The same phrase בְּרַגְלָיו was used to describe Barak's men following at his heels in verse 10. Sisera no longer has any advantage of ironware, it is a level field, and all are on foot.

Meanwhile (circumstantial clause with subject–verb word order and change of character), in verse 16 Barak pursues the chariots and army as far as Haroshet Hagoyyim, Sisera's home town (cf. verses 2, 13). There falls all of Sisera's army (the third occurrence of הַמַּחֲנֶה in two verses). לְפִי־חֶרֶב provides another anaphoric reference to the previous verse. Such continual repetition keeps the text very tightly structured. לֹא נִשְׁאַר עַד־אֶחָד 'And not even one remained' emphasizes the utter defeat of Sisera's forces.

Meanwhile (circumstantial clause with subject–verb word order and change of character), Sisera has fled on foot (repetition of the end of v. 15) to the tent of Jael. The reader might well be asking, 'Where does she fit into the story?' Jael, the fourth main character, is finally introduced in verse 17 as the wife of Heber the Kenite. The reader is expected to recall the information presented in verse 11.

Where was Heber's tent? Near Kedesh. Sisera has fled towards Kedesh, the home of Barak. But he has good reason to head in that direction:

כִּי שָׁלוֹם בֵּין יָבִין מֶלֶךְ־חָצוֹר וּבֵין בֵּית חֶבֶר הַקֵּינִי

there was peace between Jabin king of Hazor and the house of Heber the Kenite ...

Sisera is the commander of Jabin's forces; therefore he might expect to be safe in Heber's home. Once again the writer has not just mentioned people by name but given new information about them to place them in context and raise to awareness earlier statements.

But, is he safe? The reader already knows that Sisera will be handed over to a woman. His army has been defeated and Barak is in hot pursuit. A new character, a woman, has just been introduced and Sisera is approaching her tent. The tension mounts. Jael decides to act. She approaches Sisera and invites him into her tent (v. 18). He is relieved and turns aside into her tent. There is much repetition in this verse:

וַתֵּצֵא יָעֵל לִקְרַאת סִיסְרָא וַתֹּאמֶר אֵלָיו סוּרָה אֲדֹנִי סוּרָה אֵלַי אַל־תִּירָא וַיָּסַר
אֵלֶיהָ הָאֹהֱלָה וַתְּכַסֵּהוּ בַּשְּׂמִיכָה

And Jael came out to meet Sisera and she said to him, 'Turn aside, my LORD, turn aside to me, do not be afraid'. And he turned aside to her, to her tent, and she covered him with a rug.

Sisera appears unaware of Deborah's prediction about his downfall. He allows Jael to cover him with a rug. Sisera like Barak allows a woman to dictate his actions. In the text he is not mentioned by name after Jael has called out to him. He is only referred to pronominally. He asks for a little water to drink for he is thirsty. Jael, being a good hostess, does not provide him with mere water; rather she opens a skin of milk, which he drinks and she covers him again (repetition of the end of the previous verse with ellipsis of 'the rug'). He proves to be quite submissive, allowing himself to be wrapped up comfortably after a filling drink, and content to leave this woman on watch, merely asking her not to tell anyone that he is there (v. 20). Jael is not recorded as responding to Sisera's orders; rather the narrative records that she takes matters into her own hands:

וַתִּקַּח יָעֵל אֵשֶׁת־חֶבֶר אֶת־יְתַד הָאֹהֶל וַתָּשֶׂם אֶת־הַמַּקֶּבֶת בְּיָדָהּ וַתָּבוֹא אֵלָיו בַּלָּאט
וַתִּתְקַע אֶת־הַיָּתֵד בְּרַקָּתוֹ וַתִּצְנַח בָּאָרֶץ וְהוּא־נִרְדָּם וַיָּעַף וַיָּמֹת

Jael wife of Heber took a tent peg and a hammer in her hand and she went to him softly and she drove the peg into his temple until it went down into the earth and he was fast asleep and he was faint and he died (v. 21).

Sisera, commander of the forces, fades away both in the story and in the vocabulary and syntax used to describe events. Jael is in command of the situation; Sisera falls into her hands; and, like many of the other judges, she performs a grotesque murder. The reader may well remember Ehud (ch. 3).

Verse 22 beginning with the clause וְהִנֵּה בָרָק רֹדֵף (subject–verb order) calls attention to an important development: Barak is still pursuing Sisera (cf. v. 16). But the hero has missed the action. Jael calls out to him, reminding the reader of how she called out to Sisera in verse 18, 'Come and I will show you the man you are seeking'. And Barak, like Sisera, goes to her, and he sees Sisera lying dead with a peg through his head. End of story.

The narrator concludes in verse 23:

וַיַּכְנַע אֱלֹהִים בַּיּוֹם הַהוּא אֵת יָבִין מֶלֶךְ־כְּנַעַן לִפְנֵי בְּנֵי יִשְׂרָאֵל׃

God subdued on that day Jabin king of Canaan before the sons of Israel.

אֱלֹהִים and not יְהֹוָה, Jabin and not Sisera, Israel and not Barak. The incident is placed in the wider context of the history of Israel. The death of Sisera, commander of Jabin's forces, and the routing of his army began Israel's defeat of the Canaanites. As the final verse of the chapter (v. 24) notes, 'the hand of the sons of Israel weighed heavier and heavier upon Jabin king of Canaan until they destroyed Jabin king of Canaan'.

3.2 *Conclusions*

Judges 4 is a very highly structured text with frequent repetition of both vocabulary and syntactic constructions. The numerous instances of anaphoric reference, both by explicit reiteration and by means of implicit repetition, ensure that the text is tightly tied together. The opening verses of the chapter point the informed reader to the correct script for interpreting the whole story. It follows a pattern familiar to any reader of the book of Judges, yet remains coherent to the reader who has only the current chapter available. Each time a new character is introduced, the writer provides sufficient information about them to carry the appropriate connotations for later reference.

The relationship between Deborah and Barak is opposite to what might have been expected: judges are usually men and men are the leaders of Israelite society. Yet Deborah acts as the judge and she brings God's word to Barak who will only venture out with her at his side. The woman Jael acts in accordance with usual expectations as a good hostess providing shelter, sustenance and a comfortable resting place for the weary warrior Sisera. Yet she also brings about the deliverance of Israel through as bloody and violent an action as any of the male judges. And Sisera is presented as being an unwary warrior: he is very grateful for the opportunity to turn aside and rest in Jael's tent.

The writer of this episode followed the conventional script for telling a story about a judge of Israel and the story does indeed come to the expected conclusion, but the means by which it gets there challenge many of the reader's presuppositions about the possible contents of the slots in the script: women as key characters take the leading roles.

4. The Application of Text Linguistics to Classical Hebrew

Text linguistics has much to offer the student of CH both in the approach's emphasis on texts recording communicative acts, which relates linguistic structure to its function in conveying meaning, and in the realization that much of the sense of a particular sentence is dependent upon its co-text and pragmatic context. The main feature of applications of text linguistics to BH to date has been that they are problem-oriented. The tendency has been to use available linguistic methods to assist in the comprehension of difficult texts. More recently, however, Longacre and others have sought to analyse large sections of BH in order to discover what constitutes a normal or unmarked sentence structure in each of the various identified text-types. The danger in this method is that text-types are defined according to the structures discovered within them, and then the structures are taken to indicate text-type.

The analysis of cohesion and coherence above the level of the sentence promises to yield fruit in the interpretation both of individual sentences and entire texts. But lack of knowledge about the author and situational context will inevitably limit the information obtained. The way that intended receivers arrived at the meaning of a text will most probably always be quite different from the way that later analysts can ever describe. When the structural needs of the text do not specify an element, analysts need to bear in mind the possibility that a certain word or construction has been chosen by the producer because of particular ideologies, attitudes or prejudices. These are not always recoverable from the text itself.

This chapter has looked at the theory of text linguistics and definitions of 'text'. It concludes that CH cannot be treated in exactly the same way as much of the data the theories were developed on. The approach of functional grammar, the analysis of cohesion and the application of tagmemics are nevertheless useful tools in furthering understanding of the significance of the construction of Hebrew texts.

Conclusion

1. Review

This thesis has produced a comprehensive survey of linguistic theories and methods used by scholars to investigate meaning in the Hebrew Bible. It has clarified terminology, identified presuppositions, surveyed some applications, and assessed the contribution of each approach towards gaining meaning from the Hebrew Bible.

The book began with the basic hermeneutical model

AUTHOR   –   TEXT   –   READER,

recognising that:

1. The reader may approach the text from any number of different perspectives.
2. Linguistic coding places certain limits on potential interpretations of the text.
3. The author of the text is responsible for producing the precise wording.

Knowledge of both the language and context of composition are therefore considered to be crucial to comprehension.

The study has been based on two key premises:

1. A word primarily gains its meaning from within its own language; therefore the text provides the most important clues to meaning.
2. Words mean in relation to the world, with language being used for communication; therefore pragmatic context is also highly significant.

It is recognized that biblical texts provide only partial witness to CH (the language in existence prior to the cessation of spoken Hebrew in 200 CE). Some of the theories are text-centred, while others concern the language in which the texts are written:

1.   Comparative philology concentrates on comparing cognate languages.
2.   The versions are obviously translations of the text.
3.   Lexical semantics investigates the structure of the lexicon of the language.
4.   Text linguistics examines how the text is structured as a semantic edifice.

From the two key premises it becomes evident that any investigation into the meaning of a word should begin with a complete analysis of the text within which it occurs: the application of text linguistics. This should be succeeded by a systematic study of the lexicon within which the word operates: the investigation of Hebrew lexical semantics. Once all the available Hebrew data have been exhausted, both within the current corpus and later material, then translations and interpretations of the text should be consulted: the versions. Subsequently, cognate languages should be appealed to for further clues as to the semantic identity of the word in question: comparative philology. At this stage it may be necessary to question the form of the text itself: textual criticism.

The preferential ordering in the application of linguistic theories to CH texts derives from the observation that each theory approaches the data from a slightly different perspective, thereby potentially illuminating different aspects of meaning:

1.   Comparative philology identifies cognate words in closely related languages. It then proposes that the Hebrew word in question may have the same or a similar meaning to that of the cognates. However, meaning may diverge considerably in cognate forms across two or more languages. The meaning discovered is inevitably a product of the philological process and ultimately that which seems most appropriate to the modern scholar. Due to the abstract nature of the results this method should be resorted to only after all available Hebrew data have been examined.
2.   The versions reveal how early translators read their Hebrew source text and how they chose to transmit that sacred scripture

in their own language. The hermeneutical model becomes: AUTHOR – TEXT1 – TRANSLATOR – TEXT2 – READER. The meaning obtained from modern scholars' back-translation is a product of their own observations about the translation techniques employed in the versions and the intentions of the translators. The study of the versions is valuable in itself but attempts to understand the meaning of a word through recourse to translations should follow only after a complete investigation of the text and its source language.

3. Lexical semantics provides valuable information on the relations between words in the Hebrew lexicon. It may therefore assist in the identification of potential alternatives to the current lexical item. The semantic fields of CH constructed by modern scholarship may or may not reflect those available to the consciousness of biblical authors. However, the careful investigation of many BH semantic fields has already increased awareness of the subtle semantic differences between lexical items.

4. Text linguistics provides clues to the comprehension of a particular word through analysis of the semantic structure of the text as a whole. The study of cohesion, coherence, text-types and information structure can assist in predicting the meaning of a lexical item or syntactic structure. Any meaning obtained thereby is a product of modern linguistic analysis, to a certain extent dependent on the interpretation of the reader. The subtle connotations derived from this method may or may not have been those intended by the author. Nevertheless, it respects the text as constructed by the author and seeks to discover as much meaning as possible from its linguistic form.

Of course, the identification of the text itself is sometimes debatable. There are multiple textual witnesses to both the Hebrew Bible and the versions, each with a history of transmission and potential for scribal error and deliberate exegesis. The choice of text for investigation must therefore be specified in each case, with acknowledgement of the implications for authorship and intended readership. It is recognized that criticism and even emendation of the Hebrew text may be necessary following reference to the versions and cognate languages.

Information about the author and context of composition of biblical texts tends to be ascertained from the text itself. When texts have been translated and transmitted they witness to layers of

authorship. Translators may have either deliberately or accidentally altered the meaning of their source in encoding the target text.
Scholars therefore need to know as much as possible about the
producer(s) of the text under investigation: their motives, theology,
linguistic ability and intended readership.

In modern linguistics information about the language system is
abstracted from observation of language use. In the case of CH,
written texts provide limited witness to the language system. In
practice, linguistic theories are always developed on restricted data
and then refined through reference to living informants. This
process of refinement is not possible with CH. Thus, although
linguistic forms can be abstracted with reasonable accuracy, the
meaning and significance of those forms cannot be confirmed
through reference to native speakers: there is no certitude that an attested form carried a particular meaning in CH.

Applications of linguistic theories to BH texts have tended to
be problem oriented and atomistic. The theories themselves have
usually been developed on plentiful data, hence the call for further
systematic study of Hebrew texts, CH, the versions and cognate
languages. Language functions as an organic whole and new data
always have implications for the current shape of theories and
systems; therefore every proposal of a new meaning for a Hebrew
form should be accorded careful consideration with a detailed
analysis of the consequences of adopting that proposal for the
language as a whole.

2. Towards an Integrated Approach

The above survey of linguistic theories and methods used to investigate meaning in the Hebrew Bible has demonstrated that each is of
value. Each one approaches the text from a different perspective and
illuminates different facets of its meaning. Therefore, in order to
gain as much meaning as possible from the text, it is suggested that
these various methods be combined into one integrated approach.

Such an approach is illustrated below with words taken from
Judges 4 which has provided much of the source material for this
book. The two lexemes identified for investigation are מכר and
בַּשְׂמִיכָה. The verb מכר occurs in verses 2 and 9 of this chapter and
is relatively common in the *BHS*, whereas בַּשְׂמִיכָה is a *hapax
legomenon*: it occurs only in Judges 4:18.

The first step in investigating the meaning of any BH word is to assess what is known about the text within which the word appears. Judges 4 is a self-contained narrative account of an incident in the life of the people of Israel. It follows a pattern which is repeated in the book of Judges. A detailed analysis of the text is provided in section 3 in Chapter 7 of this book. The observations contained within that section will not be repeated here.

Once the text has been isolated and its structure analysed, then the immediate linguistic cotext of the word under investigation is examined. מכר first occurs in verse 2 as part of the scene-setting for the story: וַיִּמְכְּרֵם יְהוָה בְּיַד יָבִין מֶלֶךְ־כְּנַעַן. The verb is in the narrative tense: *waw* consecutive + Qal imperf. third pers. masc. sing.. The subject is יְהוָה 'the LORD' and the third pers. masc. pl. suffix, indicating the direct object, refers back to בְּנֵי יִשְׂרָאֵל 'the sons of Israel' in the previous verse. The construction includes a preposition phrase בְּיַד יָבִין 'into the hand of Jabin', who is identified as the king of Canaan.

A search is made for further examples of this precise form and structure, initially within the book of Judges. Coincidentally, the three other cases all occur in Judges, with the LORD as subject (understood from cotext) and Israel as direct object (verbal suffix). In Judges 2:14 the indirect object is the 'surrounding enemies', in Judges 3:8 it is 'Cushan-Rishathaim', and in Judges 10:7 'the Philistines and the Ammonites'. In each case the construction appears as part of the editorial material.

It is vitally important to observe that Judges 2:14 also contains a parallel formula using the familiar verb נתן: וַיִּתְּנֵם בְּיַד־שֹׁסִים 'he [referring back to "the LORD"] gave them [suffix referring back to "the sons of Israel"] into the hand of raiders'. A similar construction is found in Judges 6:1 and 13:1 with verb + suffix (indicating direct object) + subject + בְּיַד + indirect object. Once again these examples occur within editorial material. Syntactically, they are highly stereotyped.[1]

The phrase נתן ביד is also employed twice in Judges 4, but in different forms. Deborah's challenge to Barak in verses 6–7, 'Didn't the LORD God of Israel command you ... And didn't he say to you ...' ends with the words וּנְתַתִּיהוּ בְיָדֶךְ 'I will give him into your hand.' The construction here is Qal perf. 1cs (referring back to 'the LORD, the God of Israel' in v. 6) + third masc. sing. suffix (referring

---

[1] Cf. D.F. Murray, 'Narrative Structure and Technique in the Deborah–Barak Story', 175.

back to Sisera) + בְּיַד + second pers. masc. sing. suffix (referring to
Barak). In verse 14, where Deborah declares to Barak that 'this is
the day on which the LORD will give Sisera into your hand', the
form is Qal perf. third pers. masc. sing. + subject + direct object
(with marker) + בְּיַד + second pers. masc. sing. suffix indicating
indirect object:

נָתַן יְהוָה אֶת־סִיסְרָא בְּיָדֶךְ.

This narrative is tightly structured. As noted in Chapter 7, the
content of verse 14 refers back to verse 9, which includes the other
occurrence of the verb under investigation: מכר. Here the construction is בְּיַד + indirect object 'a woman' + Qal imperf. third pers.
masc. sing. + subject 'the LORD' + direct object 'Sisera':

בְּיַד־אִשָּׁה יִמְכֹּר יְהוָה אֶת־סִיסְרָא

The word order is emphatic with the prepositional phrase placed
before the verb 'into the hand of *a woman*' (preposition–verb–subject–object). This precise construction exists only here in the Hebrew Bible. Furthermore, the irony of this statement is enhanced by
the fact that מכר ביד always elsewhere applies to a military force, as
in verse 14, never to an individual.[2] It should be noted that verses 7,
9 and 14 are not editorial material; they are all reported speech
within the narrative.

The investigation so far has revealed that, in the book of Judges
the construction מכר ביד is used in parallel with נתן ביד. It is therefore presumed that there is some semantic overlap between them.
מכר ביד is relatively rare in the Hebrew Bible – outside Judges it
appears only in 1 Samuel 12:9, Joel 4:8 and Ezekiel 30:12 (where
the land is the object). In the majority of instances the LORD is the
subject, Israel the object, and her enemies the indirect object. From
knowledge gathered about the immediate cotext and context of
each occurrence and familiarity with the more common parallel
phrase, it seems that מכר ביד means something like 'to give over', 'to
hand over', 'to put in the power of'.

Because no two phrases are completely synonymous, the next
step is to define the difference between מכר ביד and נתן ביד.
Considering that נתן is by far the more common verb in the *BHS*, it
may be presumed that the meaning of מכר is more specific. The root

---

[2] Lindars, *Judges*, 189.

מכר is productive and generative, existing in many forms within the biblical text.[3] It is therefore possible to inspect cases of the verb appearing without ביד. The search is initially restricted to occurrences of מכר with the LORD as subject and his people as object. This results in the following references: Deuteronomy 32:30, Isaiah 50:1; 52:3 and Psalm 44:13.

An examination of the immediate cotext and context in the latter two examples reveals the expectation that the subject should gain financially from his actions:

כִּי־כֹה אָמַר יְהוָה חִנָּם נִמְכַּרְתֶּם וְלֹא בְכֶסֶף תִּגָּאֵלוּ

'For thus says the LORD, "You were (handed over) for nothing and you shall be redeemed without money" ' (Is. 52:3).

תִּמְכֹּר־עַמְּךָ בְלֹא־הוֹן וְלֹא־רִבִּיתָ בִּמְחִירֵיהֶם

You (handed over) your people for no wealth and you gained not by their price (Ps. 44:13).

An analysis of all occurrences of מכר in the *BHS* demonstrates that the subject is always either God or people. The object of the verb can be people (e.g. Gen. 31:15; 37:27; 45:4; Ex. 21:7; Deut. 24:7) or commodities (e.g. land in Lev. 25:25; 27:20; Ezek. 48:14; Ru. 4:3; livestock in Ex. 21:35, 37; Zech. 11:5; oil in 2 Kgs. 4:7; food in Neh. 13:15–16; clothes in Prov. 31:24).[4] The use of the preposition ל sometimes indicates the indirect object as in לְכוּ וְנִמְכְּרֶנּוּ לַיִּשְׁמְעֵאלִים 'to the Ishmaelites' (Gen. 37:27, cf. Ex. 21:8; 27:20; Is. 50:1), on other occasions it indicates the result of the action: לְאָמָה 'as a slave girl', or 'to be a slave girl' (Ex. 21:7).

The phrase מכר בכסף 'to hand over for money' occurs in Deuteronomy 21:4 and Amos 2:6. Furthermore, in Genesis 37:28 Joseph is handed over to the Ishmaelites 'for twenty pieces of silver': וַיִּמְכְּרוּ אֶת־יוֹסֵף לַיִּשְׁמְעֵאלִים בְּעֶשְׂרִים כָּסֶף. A similar expectation of financial gain is found in 2 Kings 4:7, where the Shunamite widow is told to give the oil and pay her debts. In English the concept of giving something to someone in exchange for money would be termed 'to sell'.

---

[3] Cf. A. Even-Shoshan, *A New Concordance of the Old Testament Using the Hebrew and Aramaic Text*, 655–656; 569.

[4] Cf. Even-Shoshan, *Concordance*, 655–6; L. Koehler, W. Baumgartner and J.J. Stamm, *Hebräisches und Aramäisches Lexikon zum alten Testament*, 2:581.

Further investigation reveals that there are several occasions in the *BHS* where מכר occurs in parallel with קנה 'to buy'. One narrative example is:

אֲנַחְנוּ קָנִינוּ אֶת־אַחֵינוּ הַיְּהוּדִים הַנִּמְכָּרִים לַגּוֹיִם

we bought our brothers the Jews who were sold to the nations (Neh. 5:8).

Other occurrences can be found in Genesis 47:20–22 and Zechariah 11:5. Examples from the genre of poetry include:

כָּעֶבֶד כַּאדֹנָיו כַּשִּׁפְחָה כַּגְּבִרְתָּהּ כַּקּוֹנֶה כַּמּוֹכֵר

as with the slave so his master, as with the maid so her mistress, as with the buyer so the seller (Is. 24:2).   And:

הַקּוֹנֶה אַל־יִשְׂמָח וְהַמּוֹכֵר אַל־יִתְאַבָּל

let not the buyer rejoice and let not the seller grieve (Ezek. 7:12; cf. Prov. 23:23).

It can therefore be concluded that the verb מכר generally means 'to sell' in BH. In the particular construction מכר ביד which occurs in Judges 4:2 and 4:9 there is no expectation of financial gain so it does not seem appropriate to translate מכר as 'to sell'. In such contexts it might be more appropriate to render the verb 'to sell out' (which may be considered too colloquial in English) or 'to betray' rather than the more general 'to give' or 'to hand over', thereby distinguishing it from the phrase נתן ביד.

   In investigating the meaning of מכר as found in Judges 4 there has been no need to refer beyond the *BHS* at all. Sufficient detailed information about its possible meanings and connotations can be derived from within the biblical texts; therefore there has been no mention of either the versions or cognate languages.

   The case is clearly different with respect to בַּשְּׂמִיכָה because it only occurs once in the *BHS*. Nevertheless, investigation into its meaning still begins with a detailed examination of the immediate cotext and context. The end of Judges 4:18 according to the BHS reads:

וַיָּסַר אֵלֶיהָ הָאֹהֱלָה וַתְּכַסֵּהוּ בַּשְּׂמִיכָה

The sentence is in the narrative tense. Its first clause is parsed as *waw* consecutive + Qal imperf. third pers. masc. sing. + prep. + third pers. fem. sing. suffix + def. art. + noun masc. sing. + ה of direction, giving the meaning 'he turned aside to her into the tent'. The second clause is parsed as *waw*-consecutive Piel imperf. third pers. fem. sing. + third pers. masc. sing. suffix + prep. + def. art. + noun fem. sing., giving 'and she covered him with the [unknown]'. The end of verse 19 repeats the verb וַתְּכַסֵּהוּ with ellipsis of the preposition phrase. There are no further references to the article in question within the text.

The next step is to investigate the other elements in the syntagm. In the majority of its 156 appearances in the *BHS*, the verb כסה is formed according to the Piel. On more than a dozen occasions, as in Judges 4:18, the phrase כסה בְּ indicates 'to cover with' or 'to cover by means of'.[5] The three broad contexts in which it occurs concern 'clothing' to cover a person (e.g. כְּסוּת in Deut. 22:12; בֶּגֶד in 1 Sam. 19:13 and 1 Kgs. 1:1); people providing 'a covering' to protect the altar (e.g. מִכְסֶה in Num. 4:8, 11, 12); and the LORD producing elements such as clouds to cover the sky (עָב in Ps. 147:8; cf. עָנָן in Ezek. 32:7 and צַלְמָוֶת in Ps. 44:20).[6] The first of these comes closest to the context in Judges 4 therefore it is conceivable that either of the two nouns כְּסוּת or בֶּגֶד (which exist in a paradigmatic relationship to בַּשְּׂמִיכָה) could have been used in this case. However, כְּסוּת appears only eight times in the *BHS* and not at all in the book of Judges. בֶּגֶד on the other hand is far more common, occurring five times within Judges where it refers to garments or clothing in general.[7] It might therefore be assumed that the author of Judges was familiar with the noun בֶּגֶד but chose not to employ it in Judges 4:18. This suggests that the article used by Jael to cover Sisera was not a garment or item of clothing. Thus, a simple study of the syntagmatic and paradigmatic relations has provided some slight insight into the possible meaning of the *hapax legomenon*.

A more detailed examination of the context surrounding the use of בַּשְּׂמִיכָה is now required. The characters involved in the episode described in Judges 4 are Sisera the enemy, who is fleeing from Barak, and Jael the owner of the tent. Verse 17 has informed the reader that Sisera is heading for Jael's tent because there is peace between her husband, Heber, and Sisera's king, Jabin. The

---

[5] Genesis 38:14; Leviticus 17:13; Numbers 4:5, 8, 11, 12; Deuteronomy 22:12; 1 Samuel 19:13; 1 Kings 1:1; Job 15:27; Psalm 44:20; 147:8; Isaiah 6:2; Ezekiel 32:7.

[6] Cf. Even-Shoshan, *Concordance*, 553–4; Clines, *Dictionary*, 4:441–3; BDB, 491–2.

[7] Judges 8:26; 11:35; 17:10; 14:12, 13.

narrative makes it fairly obvious that the tent could be a safe place to hide. Jael explicitly invites Sisera inside (v. 18). He asks for a drink because he is thirsty. This Jael provides. Sisera then asks her to stand guard at the entrance of the tent, denying his existence to anyone who asks (v. 19). From the immediate cotext and context it seems reasonable to presume that בַּשְּׂמִיכָה refers to an article which would help to conceal the person it covered.[8]

The poem in Judges 5 which also recounts the adventures of Deborah and Barak has no mention of Jael covering Sisera with anything. Thus there are no further clues to the meaning of בַּשְּׂמִיכָה within the main text. The *Masorah Parva*, however, has the following note: י׳ כת ש ול בליש 'One of the ten words written with שׂ, and בַּשְּׂמִיכָה occurs nowhere else' (*Mm* 1411). The heading to this note further clarifies that the words were written שׂ but spoken ס, thus reflecting an earlier stage in the formation of the Hebrew text.[9] The critical apparatus of the *BHS* also records that two manuscripts have בסמיכה.

A noun סמיכה could in theory derive from the root סמך which appears as a verb forty-eight times in BH with two main uses. It is employed more than twenty times to indicate 'to lean' or 'to lay' as in to lay a hand on the head of a sacrificial animal (Ex. 29:10, 19; Lev. 1:4; 3:2, 8, 13). In the prophets and Psalms it tends to mean 'to sustain' or 'to uphold' frequently appearing in parallel with other verbs connoting help (Is. 59:16, 63:5; Ps. 112:8; 145:14).

The root appears only once (in the Niphal) in the book of Judges:

וַיִּלְפֹּת שִׁמְשׁוֹן אֶת־שְׁנֵי עַמּוּדֵי הַתָּוֶךְ אֲשֶׁר הַבַּיִת נָכוֹן עֲלֵיהֶם וַיִּסָּמֵךְ עֲלֵיהֶם

Then Samson grasped the two middle pillars on which the house was established and he leaned on them (Jud. 16:29).

It is important to observe that there is no evidence of a noun formed from this root within BH. The root is, however, found in post-biblical Hebrew with much the same meanings as discussed above and there is a post-biblical noun סְמִיכָה which refers to the laying on of hands as in ordination.[10] Unfortunately, such an interpretation does not fit the current context which, contra Burney, is of some significance in comprehending unknown words. Having

---

[8] This opposes the view taken by C.F. Burney, *The Book of Judges*, 92.
[9] Cf. P.H. Kelley, D.S. Mynatt and T.G. Crawford, *The Masorah of the Biblia Hebraica Stuttgartensia*, 183.
[10] Cf. M. Jastrow, *Dictionary*, 1000.

failed to gain sufficient understanding of the meaning of בַּשְּׂמִיכָה from BH and later Hebrew sources, it is necessary to consult the versions.

Following the usual practice, the LXX is referred to first. An overview of the nature of the translation techniques employed in the version is provided in section 2.3 in Chapter 5 and observations made in that section will not be repeated here. The LXX A text of Judges 4:18 ends with the phrase καὶ συνεκάλυψεν 'and she covered/concealed him with her δέρρις'. This phrase is also repeated exactly at the end of verse 20. The unusual technical term δέρρις is employed for the *hapax legomenon*. δέρρις is mostly used to translate יְרִיעָה especially in Exodus 26 where it refers to the curtain of goat skins hanging around the tabernacle. The only other occasions on which it is used it represents אַדֶּרֶת (Zech. 13:4), אֹהֶל (Ex. 26:11) and מֵיתָה (Jer. 10:20).

Moving on to look at the other elements in the syntagm, the verb καλύπτειν is one of a dozen used to render כסה in the Piel, yet it does not render any other Hebrew verb. Like כסה it carries the connotation 'to conceal' as well as 'to cover'. On the basis of the LXX A translation it has been suggested that Jael hid Sisera behind the curtain which separated the women's quarters in the tent.[11] This proposal, however, fails to take into account how Jael managed to approach her victim unnoticed in verse 21.

LXX B is more vague in its rendition: καὶ περιέβαλεν αὐτὸν ἐπιβολαίῳ 'she wrapped him up in a covering'. Theodotion has ἐν τῷ σάγῳ which indicates a cloak or perhaps a blanket and Symmachus ἐν κοιμήτρῳ suggesting 'bedclothes'. It becomes apparent that the translators of the versions also wrestled with בַּשְּׂמִיכָה. None of the others follow the LXX A text in using the technical term employed to refer to the curtains in the tabernacle; neither do they follow LXX B in using a bland word meaning 'covering'. If anything, they follow Theodotion. The quite literal translation found in the Peshitta has *baḥmīltā*, which implies 'with a rug' or 'with a cloak'; the fairly literal Targum Jonathan employs *begūnkā* which means 'with a hairy rug';[12] and the Vulgate has *pallio*, suggesting 'with a cloak'. It should be remembered that several of these translations are likely to be interdependent; therefore the renditions should be weighed and not simply counted. The evidence collected from the versions

---

[11] Soggin, *Judges*, 67.
[12] Cf. W.F. Smelik, *The Targum of Judges*, 389.

discussed here does seem to indicate that the traditional translation of the *hapax legomenon* בַּשְּׂמִיכָה as 'with a rug' remains the most appropriate.

It has not been necessary to refer to cognate languages on this occasion. Nor has it been necessary to resort to emendation of the text (except for the recognition that the word was most probably written בסמיכה in the earliest manuscripts). However, much to the chagrin of people like James Barr some scholars still insist on more serious emendation: Wilkinson justifies such action in her comment, 'Although the problems encountered in the traditional translations are minimal, it is still worthwhile to explore the possibility of another explanation.'[13] She then proceeds to introduce a new division of the words of the MT from *baśśᵉmîkâ* to *bōśem ykh* (from √*khh*). This results in a completely different translation: 'she overwhelmed him with *perfume*. He *grew faint* and said ...'[14] Wilkinson's ingenious article is contextually creative but her linguistic argument fails to convince.

Burney insists on translating the *hapax legomenon* as 'with a fly-net', which he claims is based on philological considerations and accords with the context. He makes the very plausible comment that a fly-net would be more comfortable for a hot and weary man than a rug. He also suggests that the noun שְׂמִיכָה is derived from an original biliteral root סך or שך, meaning 'interweave' or 'intertwine', which has been triliteralized by מ, thus producing the root √שׂמך.[15] Burney has discounted both the data from the versions and the contextual emphasis on concealment. Furthermore, his philological explanation is convoluted and in the circumstances unnecessary.

The above studies of מכר and בַּשְּׂמִיכָה as they appear in the *BHS* text of Judges 4 have illustrated an integrated approach to the investigation of meaning in the Hebrew Bible. Such an approach takes into account the insights gained from modern linguistic analysis as well as implementing the more traditional philological methods where necessary. It demonstrates the vital significance of a detailed preliminary analysis of the text within which the word occurs, along with a careful consideration of its context. This is the first step in any investigation of the meaning of a word.

Subsequent study searches for evidence of the word elsewhere in BH before expanding the corpus considered to CH and beyond. An

---

[13] E. Wilkinson, 'The *Hapax Legomenon* of Judges IV 18', 512.

[14] Wilkinson, '*Hapax Legomenon*', 512–13.

[15] Burney, *Judges*, 92.

exploration of the syntagmatic and paradigmatic relations within which the word operates provides further material for inspection. Not everything which is discovered is necessarily significant in the search for the meaning of a particular word in a specific context. The gathered evidence should be weighed rather than automatically counted. The current cotext and context of the lexical item in question are the determining factors in deciding what is relevant.

Once all available Hebrew material has been exhausted, then the investigator turns to the versions for guidance on how the early translators understood the Hebrew text before them. At this point it may also be appropriate to refer to cognate languages. Contrary to the impression given by traditional dictionaries of BH, cognate languages are not the first port of call; rather they are the last resort. After all avenues have been exhausted it may be necessary to amend the text and begin the whole process over again. Whatever the result of the investigation, scholars should be able to give a concise account of their linguistic analysis and above all a reasonable explanation of how the proposed meaning fits the lexical item's current cotext and context.

Translations

p. 9, quote from Knauf

'Not only is Biblical Hebrew not a language, there was not even an 'old Hebrew' language as presently understood. What there was, was a Judean language from the eighth to the sixth century before Christ with local and class-specific dialects, and there were at least two Israelite languages.' (my trans.)

p. 12, quote from Lemaire

'One can agree to include the Hebrew texts from Qumran and thus an extension to the beginning of the Roman era but then Classical Hebrew becomes a language in use for a good thousand years and, in this case, a purely synchronic approach appears unrealistic and fallacious.' (my trans.)

Bibliography

Adair, J.R., 'A Methodology for Using the Versions in the Textual Criticism of the Old Testament', *JNSL* 20 (1994), 111–42

——, ' "Literal" and "Free" Translations: A Proposal for a More Descriptive Terminology', *JNSL* 23 (1997), 181–209

Aejmelaeus, A., 'What Can We Know about the Hebrew *Vorlage* of the Septuagint?', *ZAW* 99 (1987), 58–89

Aitken, J.K., 'דֶּרֶךְ', in T. Muraoka (ed.), *Semantics of Ancient Hebrew*, AbrN Sup. 6, Louvain: Peeters, 1998, 11–37

Aitken, J.K. and G.I. Davies, 'The Semantics Database Project: Highways and Byways', Unpublished paper, Old Testament Seminar, Cambridge, 7 February 1996

Albrektson, B., 'Reflections on the Emergence of a Standard Text of the Hebrew Bible', *Congress Volume: Göttingen*, VTS 29, Leiden: Brill, 1978, 49–65

——, 'Difficilior Lectio Probabilior', in *Remembering All the Way* …, OTS 21, Leiden: Brill, 1981, 5–18

Albright, W.F., 'New Light on Early Canaanite Language and Literature', *BASOR* 46 (1932), 15–20

——, 'A Re-examination of the Lachish Letters', *BASOR* 73 (1939), 16–21

——, 'The Gezer Calendar', *BASOR* 92 (1943), 16–26

——, 'The Old Testament and Canaanite Language and Literature', *CBQ* 7 (1945), 5–31

——, 'New Light on Early Recensions of the Hebrew Bible', *BASOR* 140 (1955), 27–33

Alexander, P.S., 'Jewish Aramaic Translations of Hebrew Scriptures', in Mulder, *Mikra*, 1988, 217–53

Allen, W.S., 'Relationship in Comparative Linguistics', *TPSoc* (1953), 52–108

Alonso-Schökel, A., 'Hermeneutical Problems of a Literary Study of the Bible', *Congress Volume: Edinburgh*, VTS 28, Leiden: Brill, 1974, 1–15

——, *A Manual of Hermeneutics*, Biblical Seminar 54, Sheffield: SAP, 1998

Alter, R., *The Art of Biblical Poetry*, New York: Basic, 1985

Andersen, F.I., 'Review of J. Barr's *Comparative Philology and the Text of the Old Testament*', *JBL* 88 (1969), 345–6

——, *The Sentence in Biblical Hebrew*, New York: Mouton, 1974

Andersen, F.I. and A.D. Forbes, *Spelling in the Hebrew Bible*, Rome: Biblical Institute, 1986

——, *The Vocabulary of the Old Testament*, Rome: Biblical Institute, 1992

Anttila, R., *Historical and Comparative Linguistics*, CILT 6, Philadelphia: John Benjamins, 1989

Aronoff, M., 'Orthography and Linguistic Theory: The Syntactic Basis of Massoretic Hebrew Punctuation', *Lang* 61 (1985), 28–72

Avigad, N., 'Hebrew Epigraphic Sources', in A. Malamat and I. Eph'al (eds.), *The Age of the Monarchies: Political History*, WHJP, first series: Ancient Times, Jerusalem: Massada, 1979, 4:20–43

Bailey, C.J., 'The Garden Path That Historical Linguistics Went Astray On', *LangComm* 2 (1982), 151–60

Balentine, S.E., 'A Description of the Semantic Field of Hebrew Words for "Hide"', *VT* 30 (1980), 137–53

——, 'James Barr's Quest for Sound and Adequate Biblical Interpretation', in S.E. Balentine and J. Barton (eds.), *Language, Theology and the Bible: Essays in Honour of James Barr*, Oxford: Clarendon Press, 1994, 5–15

Bandstra, B.L., 'Word Order and Emphasis in Biblical Hebrew Narrative: Syntactic Observations on Genesis 22 from a Discourse Perspective', in Bodine, *Linguistics and Biblical Hebrew*, 1992, 109–23

Bar-Efrat, S., *Narrative Art in the Bible*, JSOTS 70, Sheffield: SAP, 1997

Barker, K.L., 'The Value of Ugaritic for Old Testament Studies', *BSac* 133 (1976), 119–29

Barr, J., *The Semantics of Biblical Language*, London: SCM Press, 1961

——, 'Hypostatization of Linguistic Phenomena in Modern Theological Interpretation', *JSS* 7 (1962), 85–94

——, 'St. Jerome's Appreciation of Hebrew', *BJRL* 49 (1966–7), 281–302

——, 'St. Jerome and the Sounds of Hebrew', *JSS* 12 (1967), 1–36

——, 'Vocalization and the Analysis of Hebrew among the Ancient Translators', *Hebräische Wortforschung*, VTS 16, Leiden: Brill, 1967, 1–11

——, 'The Ancient Semitic Languages: The Conflict between Philology and Linguistics', *TPSoc* (1968), 37–55

——, *Comparative Philology and the Text of the Old Testament*, Oxford: OUP, 1968; Winona Lake: Eisenbrauns, 1987

——, 'The Image of God in the Book of Genesis: A Study of Terminology', *BJRL* 51 (1968), 11–26

——, 'Seeing the Wood for the Trees? – An Enigmatic Ancient Translation', *JSS* 13 (1968), 11–20

——, *Biblical Words for Time*, SBT (first series) 33, London: SCM Press, 1969

——, 'Semantics and Biblical Theology: A Contribution to the Discussion', *Congress Volume: Uppsala*, VTS 22, Leiden: Brill, 1971, 11–19

——, 'Hebrew Lexicography', in P. Fronzaroli (ed.), *Studies on Semitic Lexicography*, QS 2, Florence: Università di Firenze, 1973, 103–26

——, 'After 5 Years: A Retrospect on Two Major Translations of the Bible', *HeyJ* 15 (1974), 381–405

——, 'Etymology and the Old Testament', in *Language and Meaning: Studies in Hebrew Language and Biblical Exegesis*, OTS 19, Leiden: Brill, 1974, 1–28

——, 'The Nature of Linguistic Evidence in the Text of the Bible', in H.H. Paper (ed.), *Languages and Texts: The Nature of Linguistic Evidence*, Ann Arbor: University of Michigan, 1975, 35–57

——, 'Review of E.Y. Kutscher's *The Language and Linguistic Background of the Isaiah Scroll*', *JJS* 21 (1976), 186–93

——, 'Semitic Philology and the Interpretation of the Old Testament', in G.W. Anderson (ed.), *Tradition and Interpretation*, Oxford: Clarendon Press, 1979, 31–64

——, 'The Typology of Literalism in Ancient Biblical Translations', *MSU* 15, *NAWG* I, Philologisch–Historische Klasse, 1979, 279–325

——, 'A New Look at Kethibh-Qere', in *Remembering All the Way ...*, OTS 21, Leiden: Brill, 1981, 19–37

——, 'Limitations of Etymology as a Lexicographical Instrument in Biblical Hebrew', *TPSoc* (1983), 41–65

——, 'Doubts about Homoeophony in the LXX', *Textus* 12 (1985), 1–77

——, *The Various Spellings of the Hebrew Bible*, Oxford: OUP, 1988

——, 'Hebrew Lexicography: Informal Thoughts', in Bodine, *Linguistics and Biblical Hebrew*, 1992, 137–51

——, 'Scope and Problems in the Semantics of Classical Hebrew', *ZAH* 6 (1993), 3–14

——, 'Three Interrelated Factors in the Semantic Study of Ancient Hebrew', *ZAH* 7 (1994), 33–44

——, 'The Synchronic, the Diachronic and the Historical: A Triangular Relationship?', in J.C. de Moor (ed.), *Synchronic or Diachronic? A Debate on Method in Old Testament Exegesis*, OTS 34, Leiden: Brill, 1995, 1–14

Beaugrande, R. de and W. Dressler, *Introduction to Text Linguistics*, London: Longman, 1992

Beeston, A.F.L., 'Hebrew Šibbolet and Šobel', *JSS* 24 (1979), 175–7

Ben-Hayyim, Z., 'Traditions in the Hebrew Language, with Special Reference to the Dead Sea Scrolls', *ScHier* 4 (1958), 200–14

Bennett, P.R., *Comparative Semitic Linguistics: A Manual*, Winona Lake: Eisenbrauns, 1998

Bergen, R.D., 'Text as a Guide to Authorial Intention: An Introduction to Discourse Criticism', *JETS* 30 (1987), 327–36

Bergey, R., 'Late Linguistic Features in Esther', *JQR* 75 (1984), 66–78

Bergsträsser, G., *Introduction to the Semitic Languages*, trans. T. Daniels, Winona Lake: Eisenbrauns, 1983, 1995

Berlin, A., 'On the Bible as Literature', *Proof* 2 (1982), 323–7

——, *The Dynamics of Biblical Parallelism*, Bloomington: Indiana University Press, 1985

——, 'Lexical Cohesion and Biblical Interpretation', *HS* 30 (1989), 29–40

——, 'A Search for a New Biblical Hermeneutics: Preliminary Observations', in J.S. Cooper and G.M. Schwartz (eds.), *The Study of the Ancient Near East in the Twenty-First Century*, Winona Lake: Eisenbrauns, 1996, 195–207

Billen, A.V., 'The Hexaplaric Element in the LXX Version of Judges', *JThS* 43 (1942), 12–19

Blau, J., 'Some Difficulties in the Reconstruction of "Proto-Hebrew" and "Proto-Canaanite"', in M. Black and G. Fohrer (eds.), *In Memoriam Paul Kahle*, BZAW 103, Berlin: Alfred Töpelmann, 1968, 29–43

——, 'Hebrew language – Biblical', *EncJud*, Jerusalem: Keter, 1972, 16:1568–1583

——, 'Hebrew and North-West Semitic', *HAR* 2 (1978), 21–44

——, 'The Historical Periods of the Hebrew Language', in Paper, *Jewish Languages*, 1978, 1–13

——, *On Polyphony in Biblical Hebrew*, PIASH 6.2, Jerusalem, 1982

Bloomfield, L., *Language*, London: Allen and Unwin, 1935

Bodine, W.R., *The Greek Text of Judges: Recensional Developments*, HSM 23, Chico: Scholars Press, 1980

——, 'Linguistics and Philology in the Study of Ancient Near East Languages', in D. Colomb and S. Hollis (eds.), *'Working with no data': Semitic and Egyptian Studies presented to Thomas O. Lambdin*, Winona Lake: Eisenbrauns, 1987, 39–54

——, 'How Linguists Study Syntax', in Bodine, *Linguistics and Biblical Hebrew*, 1992, 89–107

—— (ed.), *Linguistics and Biblical Hebrew*, Winona Lake: Eisenbrauns, 1992

—— (ed.), *Discourse Analysis of Hebrew Literature*, SBL, Atlanta: Scholars Press, 1995, 1–18

——, 'Discourse Analysis of Hebrew Literature: What It Is and What It Offers', in Bodine, *Discourse Analysis of Hebrew Literature*, 1995

Boling, R.G., Synonymous Parallelism in the Psalms', *JSS* 5 (1960), 221–55

——, *Judges: Introduction, Translation, and Commentary*, AB, New York: Doubleday, 1975

Bonfante, G., 'On Reconstruction and Linguistic Method', *Word* 1 (1945), 83–94, 132–61

Botha, P.J., 'The Measurement of Meaning: An Exercise in Field Semantics', *JSem* 1 (1989), 3–22

Boyce, R.N., *The Cry to God in the Old Testament*, SBLDS 103, Atlanta: Scholars Press, 1988

Brenner, A., *Colour Terms in the Old Testament*, JSOTS 21, Sheffield: SAP, 1983

——, 'On the Semantic Field of Humour, Laughter and the Comic in the Old Testament', in Y. Radday (ed.), *On Humour and the Comic in the Hebrew Bible*, JSOTS 92, Sheffield: SAP, 1990, 39–58

——, (ed.), *A Feminist Companion to Judges*, Sheffield: JSOT Press, 1993

——, 'A Triangle and a Rhombus in Narrative Structure: A Proposed Integrative Reading of Judges 4 and 5', in Brenner, *A Feminist Companion to Judges*, 1993, 89–109

Brock, S.P., 'Translating the Old Testament', in D.A. Carson and H.G.M. Williamson (eds.), *It Is Written: Scripture Citing Scripture: Essays in Honour of Barnabas Lindars*, Cambridge: CUP, 1988

——, 'To Revise or Not to Revise: Attitudes to Jewish Biblical Translators', in G.J. Brooke and B. Lindars (eds.), *Septuagint, Scrolls and Cognate Writings*, SBLSCS 33, Atlanta: Scholars Press, 1992, 301–38

Brock, S.P., C.T. Fritsch and S. Jellicoe, *A Classified Bibliography of the Septuagint*, Leiden: Brill, 1973

Brockington, L.H., *The Hebrew Text of the Old Testament: The Readings Adopted by the Translators of the New English Bible*, Oxford: OUP, 1973

Bronner, L.L., 'Valorized or Vilified? The Women of Judges in Midrashic Sources', in Brenner, *A Feminist Companion to Judges*, 1993, 72–95

Brooke, A.E. and N. McClean, *The Old Testament in Greek according to the Text of Codex Vaticanus, Supplemented from Other Uncial Manuscripts, with a Critical Apparatus Containing the Variants of the Chief Ancient Authorities for the Text of the Septuagint*, vol. I: Octateuch, pt. 4: Joshua, Judges and Ruth, London: CUP, 1917

Brotzman, E.R., *Old Testament Textual Criticism: A Practical Introduction*, Grand Rapids: Baker, 1994

Brovender, C., 'Hebrew Language: Pre-Biblical', *EncJud*, Jerusalem: Keter, 1972, 16:1560–1568

Brown, F., S.R. Driver and C.A. Briggs (eds.), *A Hebrew and English Lexicon of the OldTestament*, Oxford: Clarendon Press, 1953

Brown, G. and G. Yule, *Discourse Analysis*, CTbL, Cambridge: CUP, 1991

Brown, S., 'Biblical Philology, Linguistics and the Problem of Method', *HeyJ* 20 (1979), 295–8

Bruce, F.F., 'Biblical Literature and Its Critical Interpretation', *The New Encyclopaedia Britannica*, London: EncBrit, 1990, 14:848–9

Burney, C.F., *The Book of Judges with Introduction and Notes*, London: Rivingtons, 1918

Buth, R., 'Functional Grammar, Hebrew and Aramaic: An Integrated, Textlinguistic Approach to Syntax', in Bodine, *Discourse Analysis of Hebrew Literature*, 1995, 77–102

Bynon, J. and T. Bynon (eds.), *Hamito-Semitica*, JLSP 200, The Hague: Mouton, 1975

Cantineau, J., 'Essai d'une phonologie de l'hébreu biblique', *Bulletin de la Société de Linguistique [de Paris]* 46 (1950), 82–122

——, 'Le consonantisme du sémitique', *Sem* 4 (1951), 79–94

Chmiel, J., 'Semantics of the Resurrection', *StB* (1978), 59–64

Chrétien, C.D., 'Shared Innovations and Subgrouping', *IJAL* 29 (1963), 66–8

Clines, D.J.A., 'The Dictionary of Classical Hebrew', *ZAH* 3 (1990), 73–80

——, 'Was There an 'bl II "Be Dry" in Classical Hebrew?', *VT* 42 (1992), 1–10

—— (ed.), *The Dictionary of Classical Hebrew*, vol. 1–4, Sheffield: SAP, 1993–98

Cohen, C., 'The "Held Method" for Comparative Semitic Philology', *JANES* 19 (1989), 9–23

Cohen, H.R., *Biblical Hapax Legomena in the Light of Akkadian and Ugaritic*, SBLDS 37, Missoula: Scholars, 1978

Cohen, M.B., 'Masoretic Accents as a Biblical Commentary', *JANES* 4 (1972), 2–11

Cohen, M.S.R., *Essai Comparatif sur le vocabulaire et la phonétique du chamito-sémitique*, Bibliothèque de l'école des Hautes Études 291, Paris: Libraire Ancienne Honoré Champion, 1947

Coogan, M.D., 'A Structural and Literary Analysis of the Song of Deborah', *CBQ* 40 (1978), 143–66

Cook, J., 'Were the Persons Responsible for the Septuagint Translators and/or Scribes and/or Editors?' *JNSL* 21 (1995), 45–58

——, 'Aspects of the Translation Technique Followed by the Translator of LXX Proverbs', *JNSL* 22 (1996), 143–53

——, 'Following the Septuagint Translators', *JNSL* 22 (1996), 181–90

——, 'The Septuagint between Judaism and Christianity', *OTE* 10 (1997), 213–25

Cooke, G.A., *A Text-Book of North-Semitic Inscriptions*, Oxford: Clarendon Press, 1903

Cotterell, P., 'Linguistics, Meaning, Semantics, and Discourse Analysis', *NIDOTTE*, vol 1, 134–60

Cotterell, P. and M. Turner, *Linguistics and Biblical Interpretation*, London: SPCK, 1989

Cross, F.M., 'The History of the Biblical Text in the Light of Discoveries in the Judean Desert', *HTR* 57 (1964), 281–99

——, 'The Evolution of a Theory of Local Texts', in F.M. Cross and S. Talmon (eds.), *Qumran and the History of the Biblical Text*, London: Harvard University Press, 1975, 306–20

Cross, F.M. and D.N. Freedman, *Early Hebrew Orthography*, AOS 36, New Haven: AOS, 1952

——, 'Some Observations on Early Hebrew', *Bib* 53 (1972), 413–20

Cruse, D.A., *Lexical Semantics*, Cambridge: CUP, 1986

Crystal, D., *The Cambridge Encyclopedia of Language*, Cambridge: CUP, 1991

Dahood, M., 'Hebrew and Ugaritic', *Bib* 39 (1958), 67–9

——, 'The Value of Ugaritic for Textual Criticism', *Bib* 40 (1959), 160–70

——, 'Hebrew-Ugaritic Lexicography iv', *Bib* 47 (1966), 403–19

——, 'Hebrew-Ugaritic Lexicography v', *Bib* 48 (1967), 421–38

——, 'Ugaritic and the Old Testament', *ETL* 44 (1968), 35–54

——, 'Comparative Philology Yesterday and Today', *Bib* 50 (1969), 70–9

——, 'Hebrew-Ugaritic Lexicography vii', *Bib* 50 (1969), 337–56

——, 'Hebrew-Ugaritic Lexicography xi', *Bib* 54 (1973), 537–8

——, 'Northwest Semitic Texts and Textual Criticism of the Hebrew Bible', in C. Brekelmans (ed.), *Questions Disputées D'Ancien Testament: Méthode et Théologie*, BETL 33, 1989, 11–37

Davies, G.I., *Ancient Hebrew Inscriptions: Corpus and Concordance*, Cambridge: CUP, 1991

——, 'Draft Entry for TFP"L' <http://www.sable.ox.ac.uk/~dreimer/SAHD>, 1994

Davies, P.R., *In Search of Ancient Israel*, JSOTS 148, Sheffield: SAP, 1995

Dawson, D.A., *Text-Linguistics and Biblical Hebrew*, JSOTS 177, Sheffield: SAP, 1994

Deist, F.E., *Witnesses to the Old Testament: Introduction to Old Testament Textual Criticism*, Literature of the Old Testament vol. 5, Pretoria: Nederduitse Gereformeerde Kerk Boekhandel, 1988

Dever, W.G., 'Iron Age Epigraphic Material from the Area of Khirbet El-Kôm', *HUCA* 40–1 (1969–70), 139–204

Diakonov, I.M., 'On Root Structure in Proto-Semitic', in Bynon and Bynon, *Hamito-Semitica*, 1975, 133–53

Dijk-Hemmes, Fokkelien van, 'Mothers and a Mediator in the Song of Deborah', in Brenner, *A Feminist Companion to Judges*, 1993, 110–114

Diringer, D. and S. Brock, 'Words and Meanings in Early Hebrew Inscriptions', in P.R. Ackroyd and B. Lindars (eds.), *Words and Meanings: Essays Presented to David Winton Thomas*, Cambridge: CUP, 1968, 39–46

Dirksen, P.B., 'The Old Testament Peshitta', in Mulder, *Mikra*, 1988, 255–97

Donald, T., 'The Semantic Field of "Folly" in Proverbs, Job, Psalms, and Ecclesiastes', *VT* 13 (1963), 285–92

——, 'The Semantic Field of Rich and Poor in the Wisdom Literature of Hebrew and Akkadian', *OrAnt* 3 (1964), 27–41

Dotan, A., 'Masorah', in *EncJud*, Jerusalem: Keter, 1972, 16: 1402–82

Driver, G.R., *A Treatise on the Use of the Tenses in Hebrew*, Oxford: Clarendon Press, 1892

——, *Notes on the Hebrew Text and the Topography of the Books of Samuel with an Introduction on Hebrew Palaeography and the Ancient Versions*, Oxford: Clarendon Press, 1913

——, 'Studies in the Vocabulary of the Old Testament v', *JThS* 34 (1933), 33–44

——, 'Suggestions and Objections', *ZAW* 55 (1937), 68–71

——, 'Hebrew Notes on Prophets and Proverbs', *JThS* 41 (1940), 162–75

——, 'Hebrew Scrolls', *JThS* 2 (1951), 17–30

——, 'Hebrew Homonyms', *Hebräische Wortforschung*, VTS 16, Leiden: Brill, 1967, 50–64

Dyen, I., 'Lexicostatistics in Comparative Linguistics', *Ling* 13 (1965), 230–9

Ehrensvärd, M., 'Once Again: The Problem of Dating Biblical Hebrew', *SJOT* 11 (1997), 29–40

Eitan, I., 'A Contribution to Isaiah Exegesis', *HUCA* 12/13 (1937–8), 55–88

Ellenbogen, M., 'Linguistic Archeology, Semantic Integration, and the Recovery of Lost Meanings', in A. Shinan (ed.), *Proc. 6th WCJS*, 1, Jerusalem: Jerusalem Academic Press, 1977, 93–5

Elwert, W.T. (ed.), *Probleme der Semantik*, Zeitschrift für Französische Sprache und Literatur Beiheft, neue Folge 1, Wiesbaden: Franz Steiner, 1968

Elwolde, J.F., 'The Use of Arabic in Hebrew Lexicography: Whence? Whither? and Why?', in W. Johnstone (ed.), *William*

Robertson Smith: Essays in Reassessment, JSOTS 189, Sheffield: SAP, 1995, 368–75

Emerton, J.A., 'Review of Holladay, *A Concise Hebrew and Aramaic Lexicon of the Old Testament Based upon the Lexical Work of Ludwig Koehler and Walter Baumgartner*', *VT* 22 (1972), 511–12

——, 'Review of Koehler and Baumgartner, *Hebräisches und aramäisches Lexikon zum Alten Testament, Third Edition*', *VT* 22 (1972), 502–11

——, 'The Problem of Vernacular Hebrew in the First Century AD and the Language of Jesus', *JThS* 24 (1973), 1–23

——, 'Comparative Semitic Philology and Hebrew Lexicography', in J.A. Emerton (ed.), *Congress Volume: Cambridge 1995*, Leiden: Brill, 1997, 1–24

Erickson, R.J., 'Linguistics and Biblical Language: A Wide Open Field', *JETS* 26 (1983), 257–63

Even-Shoshan, A. (ed.), *A New Concordance of the Old Testament Using the Hebrew and Aramaic Text*, Jerusalem: Kiryat Sefer, 1993

Exter Blockland, A.F. den, *In Search of Text Syntax: Towards a Syntactic Text Segmentation Model for Biblical Hebrew*, Amsterdam: Vrije Universiteit Uitgeverij, 1995

Fellman, J., 'The Linguistic Status of Mishnaic Hebrew', *JNSL* 5 (1977), 21–2

——, 'Sociolinguistic Notes on the History of the Hebrew Language', *JNSL* 6 (1978), 5–7

Ferguson, C.A., 'Diglossia', *Word* 15 (1959), 325–40

Fishbane, M., *Biblical Interpretation in Ancient Israel*, Oxford: Clarendon Press, 1985

Fitzgerald, A., 'The Technology of Isaiah 40:19–20 and 41:6–7', *CBQ* 51 (1989), 426–46

Fitzmyer, J.A., 'The Languages of Palestine in the First Century AD', *CBQ* 32 (1970), 501–31

Fornberg, T., 'Textual Criticism and Canon: Some Problems', *StTh* 40 (1986), 45–53

Fox, M.V., 'Words for Wisdom', *ZAH* 6 (1993), 149–65

——, 'Words for Folly', *ZAH* 10 (1997), 4–15

Fredericks, D.C., 'A North Israelite Dialect in the Hebrew Bible? Questions of Methodology', *HS* 37 (1996), 7–20

Freedman, D.N., 'Archaic Forms in Early Hebrew Poetry', *ZAW* 72 (1960), 101–7

——, 'The Masoretic Text and the Qumran Scrolls: A Study in Orthography', *Textus* 2 (1962), 87–102

Fronzaroli, P., 'Sulla struttura dei colori in ebraico biblico', in Various, *Studi Linguistici in onore di Vittore Pisani*, Brescia: Paideia Editrice, 1969, 377–89

——, 'On the Common Semitic Lexicon and Its Ecological and Cultural Background', in Bynon and Bynon, *Hamito-Semitica*, 1975, 43–53

——, 'Componential Analysis', *ZAH* 6 (1993), 79–91

Gadamer, Hans-Georg, *Truth and Method*, London: Sheed & Ward, 1975

Garr, W.R., *Dialect Geography of Syria-Palestine, 1000–586 BCE*, Philadelphia: University of Pennsylvania, 1985

Gervitz, S., 'Of Syntax and Style in the "Late Biblical Hebrew" – "Old Canaanite" Connection', *JANES* 18 (1986), 25–9

Gibson, A., *Biblical Semantic Logic*, Oxford: Basil Blackwell, 1981

Gibson, J.C.L., *Textbook of Syrian Semitic Inscriptions. 1. Hebrew and Moabite Inscriptions*, Oxford: Clarendon Press, 1971

——, 'The Massoretes as Linguists', in *Language and Meaning: Studies in Hebrew Language and Biblical Exegesis*, OTS 19, Leiden: Brill, 1974, 86–96

——, 'Hebrew Language and Linguistics', *ExpTim* 104 (1993), 105–9

——, 'Review of D.J.A. Clines (ed.), *The Dictionary of Classical Hebrew: vol. 1*', *JThS* 46 (1995), 569–72

Gillingham, S.E., 'Review of D.J.A. Clines (ed.), *The Dictionary of Classical Hebrew: vol. 1* and L. Koehler, W. Baumgartner and M.E.J. Richardson (eds.), *The Hebrew and Aramaic Lexicon of the Old Testament, vol. 1*', *Anvil* 12 (1995), 256–8

——, *One Bible, Many Voices: Different Approaches to Biblical Studies*, London: SPCK, 1998

Ginsburg, C.D., *Introduction to the Massoretico-Critical Edition of the Hebrew Bible: With a Prolegomenon by H.M. Orlinsky*, New York: Ktav, 1966

Ginsburg, H.L., 'The Original Hebrew of Ben Sira 12:10–14', *JBL* 74 (1955), 93–5

——, 'The Northwest Semitic Languages', in B. Mazar (ed.), *Patriarchs*, WHJP, first series: Ancient Times, vol. II, London: W.H. Allen, 1970, 102–124, 270, 293

Gleason, H.A., 'Linguistics and Philology', in M. Black and W. Smalley (eds.), *On Language, Culture, and Religion: In Honor of E.A. Nida*, The Hague: Mouton, 1974, 199–212

Goetze, A., 'Is Ugaritic a Canaanite Dialect?' *Lang* 17 (1941), 127–38

Goldin, J., 'Not By Means of an Angel', in J. Neusner (ed.), *Religions in Antiquity: Essays in Memory of Erwin Ramsdell Goodenough*, Studies in the History of Religions 14, Leiden: Brill, 1968, 412–24

Goldingay, J., *Models for Scripture*, Grand Rapids: Eerdmans, 1994

——, *Models for Interpretation of Scripture*, Grand Rapids: Eerdmans, 1995

——, 'The Ongoing Story of Biblical Interpretation', *Churchman* 112 (1998), 6–16

Gooding, D.W., 'An Appeal for a Stricter Terminology in the Textual Criticism of the Old Testament', *JSS* 21 (1976), 15–25

Gordis, R., 'On Methodology in Biblical Exegesis', *JQR* 61 (1970–1), 93–118

——, *The Biblical Text in the Making: A Study in the Kethib–Qere*, New York: Ktav, 1971

Gordon, C.H., 'Northern Israelite Influence on Post-exilic Hebrew', *IEJ* 5 (1955), 85–8

Goshen-Gottstein, M.H., 'The History of the Bible-Text and Comparative Semitics: A Methodological Problem', *VT* 7 (1957), 195–201

——, 'Theory and Practice of Textual Criticism: The Text-Critical Use of the Septuagint', *Textus* 3 (1963), 130–58

——, 'Hebrew Biblical Manuscripts: Their History and Their Place in HUBP Edition', *Bib* 48 (1967), 243–90

——, 'Comparative Semitics: A Premature Obituary', in A.I. Katsh and L. Nemoy (eds.), *Essays on the Occasion of the Seventieth Anniversary of the Dropsie University*, Philadelphia: The Dropsie University, 1979, 141–50

——, 'The Textual Criticism of the Old Testament: Rise, Decline, Rebirth', *JBL* 102 (1983), 365–99

——, 'The Present State of Comparative Semitic Linguistics', in Kaye, *Semitic Studies*, 1991, 558–69

——, 'The Development of the Hebrew Text of the Bible: Theories and Practice of Textual Criticism', *VT* 42 (1992), 204–13

Grabbe, L., *Comparative Philology and the Text of Job: A Study of Method*, SBLDS, Missoula: Scholars Press, 1977

Gragg, G., 'Linguistics, Method, and Extinct Languages: The Case of Sumerian', *OrNS* 42 (1973), 78–96

Gray, L.H., *Introduction to Semitic Comparative Linguistics*, New York: Ithaca, 1934

Greenberg, J.H., 'The Patterning of Root-Morphemes in Semitic', *Word* 6 (1950), 162–81

——, 'The Afro–Asiatic (Hamito–Semitic) Present', *JAOS* 72 (1952), 1–9

Greenberg, M., 'The Use of the Ancient Versions for Interpreting the Hebrew Text', *Congress Volume: Göttingen*, VTS 29, Leiden: Brill, 1978, 131–48

Greenfield, J.C., 'The Lexical Status of Mishnaic Hebrew', PhD dissertation, Yale University, 1956

——, 'Etymological Semantics', *ZAH* 6 (1993), 26–37

Greenfield, J.E., 'Lexicographical Notes', *HUCA* 29 (1958), 202–28

Greenspahn, F.E., *Hapax Legomena in Biblical Hebrew: A Study of the Phenomenon and Its Treatment since Antiquity with Special Reference to Verbal Forms*, SBLDS 74, Chico: Scholars Press, 1984

Grice, H. Paul, 'Logic and Conversation', in P. Cole and J.L. Morgan (eds.), *Syntax and Semantics, 3: Speech Acts*, London: Academic Press, 1975, 41–58

Grossfeld, B., 'Ancient Versions: Aramaic: The Targumim', *EncJud*, Jerusalem: Keter, 1978, 4:841–51

Gunn D.M. and D.N. Fewell, *Narrative in the Hebrew Bible*, Oxford: OUP, 1993

Gutman, D., 'Phonology of Massoretic Hebrew', *HCompL* 7 (1973), 1–52

Haas, M.R., 'Historical Linguistics and the Genetic Relationship of Languages', in T.A. Sebeok (ed.), *CTL* 3, The Hague: Mouton, 1966, 113–53

Hackett, J.A., 'The Dialect of the Plaster Text from Deir 'Alla', *OrNS* 53 (1984), 57–65

Halliday, M.A.K., *An Introduction to Functional Grammar*, second edition, London: Edward Arnold, 1992

Halliday, M.A.K. and R. Hasan, *Cohesion in English*, English Language Series 9, London: Longman, 1976

Hamlin, E.J., *Judges: At Risk in the Promised Land*, ITC, Grand Rapids: Eerdmans, 1990

Handy, L.K., 'One Problem Involved in Translating to Meaning: An Example of Acknowledging Time and Tradition', *SJOT* 10 (1996), 16–27

Hanson, A., 'The Treatment in the LXX of the Theme of Seeing God', in G.J. Brooke and B. Lindars (eds.), *Septuagint, Scrolls and Cognate Writings*, SBLSCS 33, Atlanta: Scholars Press, 1992, 557–68

Harrington, D.J., 'The Prophecy of Deborah: Interpretative Homiletics in Targum Jonathan of Judges 5', *CBQ* 48 (1986), 432–42

Harrington, D.J. and A.J. Saldarini, *Targum Jonathan of the Former Prophets: Introduction, Translation and Notes*, Aramaic Bible vol. 10, Edinburgh: T. & T. Clark, 1987

Harris, Z.S., *The Development of the Canaanite Dialects: An Investigation into Linguistic history*, AOS vol. 10, New Haven: AOS, 1939

——, 'Linguistic Structure of Hebrew', *JAOS* 61 (1941), 143–67, 15–20

Hayon, Y., 'Response', in Paper, *Jewish Languages*, 1978, 15–20

Hetzron, R., 'La division les langues sémitiques', in A. Caquot and D. Cohen (eds.), *Actes du premier Congrès International de Linguistique Sémitique et Chamito-Sémitique, Paris 16–19 Juillet 1969*, JLSP 159, The Hague: Mouton, 1974, 181–94

——, 'Two Principles of Genetic Reconstruction', *Ling* 38 (1976), 89–108

——, 'Semitic Languages', in B. Comrie (ed.), *The Worlds Major Languages*, New York: OUP, 1987, 654–63

Hirsch, E.D., *Validity in Interpretation*, London: Yale University Press, 1967

——, *The Aims of Interpretation*, London: Chicago University Press, 1976

Hoenigswald, H.M., 'On the History of the Comparative Method', *AnLing* 5 (1963), 1–11

——, 'Criteria for the Subgrouping of Languages', in H. Birnbaum and J. Puhvel (eds.), *Ancient Indo-European Dialects*, Proc. Conference on Indo-European Linguistics, University of California, 25–7 April, 1963, Berkeley: University of California, 1966, 1–12

——, 'The Comparative Method', in T.A. Sebeok (ed.), *CTL* 11, The Hague: Mouton, 1973, 51–62

Hoffman, Y., *A Blemished Perfection: The Book of Job in Context*, JSOTS 213, Sheffield: SAP, 1996

Hoftijzer, J., 'The Semantics of Classical Hebrew', *Communications, JESF* 25 (1991), 6–7

——, 'Rules for Co-workers', unpublished paper, Leiden, 1994

——, 'The Structure of the Framework for the Database', unpublished paper, Leiden, 1994

——, 'The History of the Data-base Project', in Muraoka, *Studies in Ancient Hebrew Semantics*, 1995, 65–85

Hoftijzer, J. and G.I. Davies, 'A Database for the Study of Ancient Hebrew: Project Description', <http://www.sable.ox.ac.uk/~dreimer /SAHD>, 1994

Holladay, W.L. (ed.), *A Concise Hebrew and Aramaic Lexicon of the Old Testament*, Leiden: Brill, 1971

Honeyman, A.M., 'The Pottery Vessels in the Old Testament', *PEQ* 71 (1939), 76–90

Hopper, P., 'Aspect and Foregrounding in Discourse', in T. Givon (ed.), *Discourse and Syntax*, Syntax and Semantics 12, New York: Academic Press, 1979, 213–41

Horn, S.H., 'The Amman Citadel Inscription', *BASOR* 193 (1969), 2–13

Hospers, J.H., 'A Hundred Years of Semitic Comparative Linguistics', in *Studia Biblica et Semitica: Theodoro Christiano Vriezen qui munere professoris theologiae per XXV annos functus est, ab amicis, collegis, discipulis dedicata*, Wageningren: H. Veenman en Zonen, 1966, 138–51

——, 'Polysemy and Homonymy', *ZAH* 6 (1993), 114–23

Houston, W.J., 'Murder and midrash: The Prose Appropriation of Poetic Material in the Hebrew Bible (part I)', *ZAW* 109 (1997), 342–355

——, 'Murder and Midrash: The Prose Appropriation of Poetic Material in the Hebrew Bible (part II)', *ZAW* 109 (1997), 534–48

Huehnergard, J., 'Remarks on the Classification of the Northwest Semitic Languages' in J. Hoftijzer and G. van der Kooij (eds.), *The Balaam Text from Deir 'Alla Re-Evaluated*, Leiden: Brill, 1991, 282–93

Hummel, H.D., 'Enclitic Mem in Early Northwest Semitic, Especially Hebrew', *JBL* 76 (1957), 85–107

Hurvitz, A., 'The Chronological Significance of "Aramaisms" in Biblical Hebrew', *IEJ* 18 (1968), 234–41

——, 'Linguistic Criteria for Dating Problematic Biblical Texts', *HAb* 14 (1973), 74–9

——, 'The Evidence of Language in Dating the Priestly Code: A Linguistic Study in Technical Idioms and Terminology', *RB* 81 (1974), 24–56

——, *Linguistic Study of the Relationship between the Priestly Source and the Book of Ezekiel: A New Approach to an Old Problem*, CahRB 20, Paris: Gabalda, 1982

——, 'Dating the Priestly Source in Light of the Historical Study of Biblical Hebrew a Century after Wellhausen', *ZAW* 100 (1988), 88–100

——, 'Review of D.C. Frederick's *Qoheleth's Language: Re-evaluating its Nature and Date*', *HS* 31 (1990), 144–54

——, 'Continuity and Innovation in Biblical Hebrew: The Case of "Semantic Change" in Post-exilic Writings', in Muraoka, *Studies in Ancient Hebrew Semantics*, 1995, 1–10

Jastrow, M., *Dictionary of the Targumim, Talmud Bibli Yerushalmi and Midrashic Literature*, New York: The Judaica Press, 1992

Jellicoe, S., *The Septuagint and Modern Study*, Oxford: OUP, 1968

Jespersen, O., *Language, Its Nature, Development and Origin*, London: Allen and Unwin, 1922

Joüon, P. and T. Muraoka, *A Grammar of Biblical Hebrew*, 2 vols., Rome: Biblical Institute, 1991

Juhl, P.D., *Interpretation: An Essay in the Philosophy of Literary Criticism*, Princeton: Princeton University Press, 1980

Kaddari, M.Z., *Semantic Fields in the Language of the Dead Sea Scrolls*, Jerusalem: Shrine of the Book Fund, 1968

Kahle, P., *The Cairo Genizah*, Oxford: OUP, 1959

Kaltner, J., *The Use of Arabic in Biblical Hebrew Lexicography*, CBQMS 28, Washington: CBQ, 1996

Kaufman, S.A., 'The Classification of the North West Semitic Dialects of the Biblical Period and Some Implications Thereof', in *Proc. Ninth WCJS (Panel Sessions: Hebrew and Aramaic Languages)*, Jerusalem: Magnes, 1988, 41–57

——, 'Paragogic Nun in Biblical Hebrew: Hypercorrection as a Clue to a Lost Scribal Practice', in Zevit, Gitin and Sokoloff, *Solving Riddles and Untying Knots*, 1995, 95–9

Kautzsch, E., *Gesenius' Hebrew Grammar*, trans. A.E. Cowley, Oxford: Clarendon Press, 1910

Kaye, A.S. (ed.), *Semitic Studies: In Honor of Wolf Leslau on the Occasion of his 85th Birthday*, 2 vols., Wiesbaden: Harrassowitz, 1991

Kedar, B., *Biblische Semantik: Eine Einführung*, Stuttgart: Kohlhammer, 1981

——, 'The Latin Translations', in Mulder, *Mikra*, 1988, 299–338

Kedar-Kopfstein, B., 'Semantic Aspects of the Pattern Qôtel', *HAR* 1 (1977), 155–76

——, 'On the Decoding of Polysemantic Lexemes in Biblical Hebrew', *ZAH* 7 (1994), 17–25

——, 'Review of *Biblical Hebrew and Discourse Linguistics*, Robert D. Bergen (ed.), Winona Lake: Eisenbrauns, 1994', *HS* 37 (1996), 136–8

Kelley, P.H., D.S. Mynatt and T.G. Crawford, *The Masorah of Biblia Hebraica Stuttgartensia*, Grand Rapids: Eerdmans, 1998

Kennedy, C.A., 'The Semantic Field of the Term "Idolatry" ', in L.M. Hopfe (ed.), *Uncovering Ancient Stones: Essays in Memory of H. Neil Richardson*, Winona Lake: Eisenbrauns, 1994, 193–204

Khan, G., *Studies in Semitic Syntax*, LOS 38, Oxford: OUP, 1988

——, 'The Tiberian Pronunciation Tradition of Biblical Hebrew', *ZAH* 9 (1996), 1–23

——, 'The Masoretic Hebrew Bible and Its Background', unpublished manuscript, 1998

Kieffer, R., 'Die Bedeutung der modernen Linguistik für die Auslegung biblischer Texte', *TZ* 30 (1974), 223–33

Klein, L.R., *The Triumph of Irony in the Book of Judges*, Sheffield: Almond, 1988

Klein, M.L., 'Converse Translation: A Targumic Technique', *Bib* 57 (1976), 515–37

——, 'The Preposition qdm ('Before'): A Pseudo-Anti-Anthropomorphism in the Targums', *JThS* 30 (1979), 502–7

——, 'The Translation of Anthropomorphisms and Anthropopathisms in the Targumim', in *Congress Volume: Vienna 1980*, VTS 32, Leiden: Brill, 1981, 162–77

Klein, R.W., *Textual Criticism of the Old Testament: The Septuagint after Qumran*, GBS, OT Series 4, Philadelphia: Fortress Press, 1974

Knauf, E.A., 'War Biblisch-Hebräisch eine Sprache?', *ZAH* 3 (1990), 11–23

Koehler, L., 'Problems in the Study of the Language of the Old Testament', *JSS* 1 (1956), 3–24

Koehler, L., W. Baumgartner and J.J. Stamm, *Hebräisches und Aramäisches Lexikon zum alten Testament*, 4 vols, Leiden: Brill, 1994–1999

Kooij, A. van der, 'On Male and Female Views in Judges 4 and 5', in B. Becking and M. Dijkstra (eds.), *On Reading Prophetic Texts: Gender-Specific and Related Studies in Memory of Fokkelien van Dijk-Hemmes*, BInt 18, Leiden: Brill, 1996, 135–52

Kopf, L., 'Das arabische Wörterbuch als Hilfsmittel für die Hebräische Lexikographie', *VT* 6 (1956), 286–302

Kroeze, J.H., 'Semantic Relations in Construct Phrases of Biblical Hebrew', *ZAH* 10 (1997), 27–41

Kurylowicz, J., 'The Notion of Morphophoneme', in W.P. Lehmann and Y. Malkiel (eds.), *Directions for Historical Linguistics: A Symposium*, Austin: University of Texas, 1968, 67–81

Kutler, L., 'A Structural Semantic Approach to Israelite Communal Terminology', *JANES* 14 (1982), 69–77

Kutscher, E.Y., 'Mittelhebräisch und Jüdisch-Aramäisch im neuen Köhler-Baumgartner', *Hebräische Wortforschung*, VTS 16, Leiden: Brill, 1967, 158–75

——, 'Hebrew Language – Dead Sea Scrolls, Mishnaic Hebrew', *EncJud*, Jerusalem: Keter, 1972, 16:1584–607

——, *The Language and Linguistic Background of the Isaiah Scroll (1QIsa)*, Leiden: Brill, 1974

——, *A History of the Hebrew Language*, Leiden: Brill, 1982

Lambrecht, K., *Information Structure and Sentence Form: Topic, Focus and the Mental Representations of Discourse Referents*, CSL 71, Cambridge: CUP, 1996

LaSor, W.S., 'Proto-Semitic: Is the Concept No Longer Valid?', *Maarav* 5–6 (1990), 189–205

Leech, G.N., *Semantics*, Harmondsworth: Penguin, 1974

Lehmann, W.P., *Historical Linguistics: An Introduction*, New York: Holt, Rinehart and Winston, 1973

Lemaire, A., 'Réponse à J.H. Hospers', *ZAH* 6 (1993), 124–7

Levine, B.A., 'The Semantics of Loss: Two Exercises in Biblical Hebrew Lexicography', in Zevit, Gitin and Sokolofff, *Solving Riddles and Untying Knots*, 1995, 137–58

Levine, E., 'The Biography of the Aramaic Bible', *ZAW* 94 (1982), 353–79

——, *The Aramaic Version of the Bible: Contents and Context*, BZAW 174, New York: Walter de Gruyter, 1988

Levinson, S.C., *Pragmatics*, CTbL, Cambridge: CUP, 1985

Lieberman, S.J., 'Response' in Paper, *Jewish Languages*, 1978, 21–8

Lindars, B., 'Some Septuagint Readings in Judges', *JThS* NS 22 (1971), 1–13

——, 'Deborah's Song: Women in the Old Testament', *BJRL* 65 (1983), 158–75

——, 'A Commentary on the Greek Judges?', in C.E. Cox (ed.), *International Organisation for Septuagint and Cognate Studies Congress VI Volume, Jerusalem 1986*, SBLSCS 23, Atlanta: Scholars Press, 1987, 167–200

——, *Judges 1–5: A New Translation and Commentary*, Edinburgh: T&T. Clark, 1995

Lipinski, E., 'Kinship Terminology in 1 Sam. 25:40–42', *ZAH* 7(1994), 12–16

Liverani, M., 'Semites', in G.W. Bromiley *et al.* (eds.), *International Standard Bible Encyclopaedia*, Grand Rapids: Zondervan, 1988, 4:388–92

Lode, L., 'A Discourse Perspective on the Significance of the Masoretic Accents', in R.D. Bergen (ed.), *Biblical Hebrew and Discourse Linguistics*, Summer Institute of Linguistics, Winona Lake: Eisenbrauns, 1994, 155–72

Longacre, R.E., *Joseph: A Story of Divine Providence: A Text Theoretical and Text Linguistic Analysis of Genesis 37 and 39–48*, Winona Lake: Eisenbrauns, 1989

——, 'Discourse Perspective on the Hebrew Verb: Affirmation and Restatement', in Bodine, *Linguistics and Biblical Hebrew*, 1992, 177–89

——, *The Grammar of Discourse, Topics in Language and Linguistics*, New York: Plenum, 1996

Longman, Tremper, III, 'Literary Approaches and Interpretations', in VanGemeren, *NIDOTTE*, vol. 1, 103–124

Louw, J.P., *Semantics of New Testament Greek,* Philadelphia: Fortress Press, 1982

——, 'A Semantic Domain Approach to Lexicography', in Louw, *Lexicography and Translation*, 1985, 157–97

—— (ed.), *Lexicography and Translation: With Special Reference to Bible Translation*, Cape Town: Bible Society of South Africa, 1985

——, 'What Dictionaries Are Like', in Louw, *Lexicography and Translation*, 1985, 53–81

——, 'How Do Words Mean: If They Do?', *FilolNeo* 4 (1991), 125–42

——, 'The Analysis of Meaning in Lexicography', *FilolNeo* 6 (1993), 139–48

Lowery, K.E., 'The Theoretical Foundations of Hebrew Discourse Grammar', in Bodine, *Discourse Analysis of Hebrew Literature*, 1995, 103–30

Lübbe, J., 'Old Testament Sample Studies', in Louw, *Lexicography and Translation,* 1985, 118–37

——, 'Hebrew Lexicography: A New Approach', *JSem* 2 (1990), 1–15

——, 'Methodological Implications in Early Signs of a New Dictionary of Classical Hebrew', *ZAH* 4 (1991), 135–43

——, 'The Use of Syntactic Data in Dictionaries of Classical Hebrew', *JSem* 5 (1993), 89–96

——, 'Old Testament Translation and Lexicographical Practice', *JSem* 6 (1994), 170–9

——, 'An Old Testament Dictionary of Semantic Domains', *ZAH* 9 (1996), 52–7

Lyons, J., *Semantics*, 2 vols, Cambridge: CUP, 1977

——, *Linguistic Semantics: An Introduction*, Cambridge: CUP, 1995

McCarthy, C., *The Tiqqune Sopherim and Other Theological Corrections in the Masoretic Text of the Old Testament*, OBO 36, Göttingen: Vandenhoeck and Ruprecht, 1981

McNamara, M., 'Targums', in K. Crim *et al.* (eds.), *IDB Supplement*, Nashville: Abingdon, 1976, 856–61

MacDonald, P.J., 'Discourse Analysis and Biblical Interpretation', in Bodine, *Linguistics and Biblical Hebrew*, 1992, 153–75

Maisler, B., 'Two Hebrew Ostraca from Tell Qasîle', *JNES* 10 (1951), 265–7

Malone, J.L., 'Textually Deviant Forms as Evidence for Phonological Analysis: A Service of Philology to Linguistics', *JANES* 11 (1979), 71–9

Mansoor, M., 'Some Linguistic Aspects of the Qumran Texts', *JSS* 3 (1958), 40–54

Margain, J., 'Sémantique hébraque: l'apport des Targums', in Muraoka, *Studies in Ancient Hebrew Semantics*, 1995, 11–17

Margolis, M.L., 'Complete Induction for the Identification of the Vocabulary in the Greek Versions of the Old Testament with Its Semitic Equivalents: Its Necessity and the Means of Obtaining It', *JAOS* 30 (1910), 301–12

——, 'The Scope and Methodology of Biblical Philology', *JQR* 1 (1910–11), 5–41

Marlowe, W.C., 'A Summary Evaluation of Old Testament Hebrew Lexica, Translations, and Philology in Light of Developments in Hebrew Lexicographic and Semitic Linguistic History', *GTJ* 12 (1992), 3–20

Mendenhall, G.E., 'Review of J. Barr's *Comparative Philology and the Text of the Old Testament*', *Int* 25 (1971), 358–62

Millard, A.R., ' "Scriptio Continua" in Early Hebrew: Ancient Practice or Modern Surmise?', *JSS* 15 (1970), 2–15

Mitchell, C., 'The Use of Lexicons and Word Studies in Exegesis', *CJ* 11 (1985), 128–33

Morag, S., 'On the Historical Validity of the Vocalization of the Hebrew Bible', *JAOS* 94 (1974), 307–15

——, 'Qumran Hebrew: Some Typological Observations', *VT* 38 (1988), 148–64

Moran, W.L., 'The Hebrew Language in Its North West Semitic Background', in G.E. Wright (ed.), *The Bible and the Ancient Near East*, London: Routledge & Kegan Paul, 1961, 54–72

——, 'Review of J. Barr's *Comparative Philology and the Text of the Old Testament*', *CBQ* 31 (1969), 238–43

Moscati, S. (ed.), *An Introduction to the Comparative Grammar of the Semitic Languages: Phonology and Morphology*, PLO New Series 6, Wiesbaden: Otto Harrassowitz, 1969

Mulder, M.J., 'The Transmission of the Biblical Text', in Mulder, *Mikra*, 1988, 87–135

—— (ed.), *Mikra: Text, Translation, Reading and Interpretation of the Hebrew Bible in Ancient Judaism and Early Christianity*, Philadelphia: Fortress Press, 1988

Muraoka, T., 'On Septuagint Lexicography and Patristics', *JThS* 35 (1984), 441–8

——, 'Towards a Septuagint Lexicon', in C.E. Cox, (ed.), *IOSCS Congress VI Volume, Jerusalem, 1986*, SBLSCS 23, Atlanta: Scholars Press, 1987, 255–276

——, 'Hebrew Hapax Legomena and Septuagint Lexicography', in C.E. Cox (ed.), *IOSCS Congress VII Volume, Leuven 1989*, SBLSBS 31, Atlanta: Scholars, 1991, 205–22

——, 'A New Dictionary of Classical Hebrew', in Muraoka, *Studies in Ancient Hebrew Semantics*, 1995, 87–101

——, 'The Semantics of the LXX and Its Role in Clarifying Ancient Hebrew Semantics', in Muraoka, *Studies in Ancient Hebrew Semantics*, 1995, 19–32

—— (ed.), *Studies in Ancient Hebrew Semantics*, AbrN Sup. 4, Louvain: Peeters, 1995

—— (ed.), *Semantics of Ancient Hebrew*, AbrN Sup. 6, Louvain: Peeters, 1998

Murray, D.F., 'Narrative Structure and Technique in the Deborah–Barak Story (Judges IV 4–22)', in J.A. Emerton (ed.), *Studies in the Historical Books of the Old Testament*, VTS 30, Leiden: Brill, 1979, 155–89

Murtonen, A., 'The Semitic Sibilants', *JSS* 11 (1966), 135–50

——, *Hebrew in Its West Semitic Setting Vol. 1: A Comparative Lexicon*, Leiden: Brill, 1986

——, 'On Proto-Semitic Reconstructions', in Kaye, *Semitic Studies*, 1991, 1119–30

Naveh, J., 'Word Division in West-Semitic Writing', *IEJ* 23 (1973), 206–8

Niccacci, A., *The Syntax of the Verb in Classical Hebrew Prose*, Sheffield: JSOT Press, 1990

Nida, E.A., 'Implications of Contemporary Linguistics for Biblical Scholarship', *JBL* 91 (1972), 73–89

——, *Componential Analysis of Meaning*, The Hague: Mouton, 1975

O'Connell, R.H., *The Rhetoric of the Book of Judges*, VTS 63, Leiden: Brill, 1996

Olofsson, S., *God Is My Rock: A Study of Translation Technique and Theological Exegesis in the Septuagint*, CB OTS 31, Stockholm: Almqvist & Wiksell, 1990

——, *The LXX Version: A Guide to the Translation Technique of the Septuagint*, CB OTS 30, Stockholm: Almqvist and Wiksell, 1990

——, 'The Septuagint and Earlier Jewish Interpretative Tradition – Especially as Reflected in the Targums', *SJOT* 10 (1996), 197–216

Orlinsky, H.M., 'On the Present State of Proto-Septuagint Studies', *JAOS* 61 (1941), 81–91

——, 'The Septuagint: Its Use in Textual Criticism', *BA* 9 (1946), 21–34

——, 'The Origin of the Kethib–Qere System: A New Approach', *Congress Volume: Oxford*, VTS 7, Leiden: Brill, 1959, 184–92

——, 'The Masoretic Text: A Critical Evaluation', Prolegemenon to C.D. Ginsberg, *Introduction to the Masoretico-Critical Edition of the Hebrew Bible*, 1987, New York: Ktav, 1966

Paper, H.H. (ed.), *Jewish Languages: Themes and Variations*, Cambridge, MA: Association for Jewish Studies, 1978

Pardee, D., 'The Linguistic Classification of the Deir 'Alla Text written on Plaster', in J. Hoftijzer and G. van der Kooij (eds.), *The Balaam Text from Deir 'Alla Re-Evaluated*, Leiden: Brill, 1991, 100–5

Payne, D.F., 'Old Testament Exegesis and the Problem of Ambiguity', *ASTI* 5 (1966–7), 48–68

——, 'Old Testament Textual Criticism: Its Principles and Practice', *TynBul* 25 (1974), 99–112

Payne, G., 'Functional Sentence Perspective: Theme in Biblical Hebrew', *SJOT* 1 (1991), 62–82

Peckham, B., 'Tense and Mood in Biblical Hebrew', *ZAH* 10 (1997), 139–68

Petöfi, J.S., 'Logical Semantics: An Overview from a Textological Point of View', *ZAH* 6 (1993), 92–108

Polzin, R., *Late Biblical Hebrew: Towards an Historical Typology of Biblical Hebrew Prose*, HSM 12, Missoula: Scholars Press, 1976

Poythress, V.S., 'Analysing a Biblical Text: Some Important Linguistic Distinctions', *SJT* 32 (1979), 113–37

Pulgram, E., 'Family Tree, Wave Theory and Dialectology', *Orbis* 2 (1953), 67–72

——, 'The Nature and Use of Proto-languages', *Ling* 10 (1961), 18–37

Qimron, E., *The Hebrew of the Dead Sea Scrolls*, Atlanta: Scholars Press, 1986

——, 'Observations on the History of Early Hebrew (1000 BCE–200 CE), in the Light of the Dead Sea Documents', in D. Dimant and U. Rappaport (eds.), *The Dead Sea Scrolls: Forty Years of Research, Studies on the Texts of the Desert of Judah X*, Leiden: Brill, 1992, 349–61

Rabin, C., 'The Historical Background of Qumran Hebrew', *ScHier* 4 (1958), 144–61

——, 'The Origin of the Subdivisions of Semitic', in D.W. Thomas and W.D. McHardy (eds.), *Hebrew and Semitic Studies Presented to Godfrey Rolles Driver in Celebration of His Seventieth Birthday 20 August 1962,* Oxford: Clarendon Press, 1963, 104–15

——, 'Towards a Descriptive Semantics of Biblical Hebrew', *Proc. 26th ICO 1964*, New Delhi: ICO, 1968, 2:51–2

——, 'The Translation Process and the Character of the Septuagint', *Textus* 6 (1968), 1–26

——, 'Hebrew', in T.A. Sebeok *et al.* (eds.), *CTL* 6: Linguistics in South West Asia and North Africa, The Hague: Mouton, 1970, 304–46

——, 'Semitic Languages', *EncJud*, Jerusalem: Keter, 1972, 14: 1149–56

——, 'On Enlarging the Basis of Hebrew Etymology', *HAb* 15 (1974), 25–8

——, 'Lexicostatistics and the Internal Divisions of Semitic', in Bynon and Bynon, *Hamito-Semitica*, 1975, 85–102

——, 'The Emergence of Classical Hebrew', in A. Malamat (ed.), *The Age of the Monarchies: Culture and Society,* WHJP 4.2, Jerusalem: Massada, 1979, 71–8, 293–5

——, 'Israeli Research on Biblical Hebrew Linguistics', *Immanuel* 14 (1982), 26–33

——, 'Lexical Emendation in Biblical Research', in Y.L. Arbeitman (ed.), *FUCUS: A Semitic/Afrasian Gathering in Remembrance of Albert Ehrman,* CILT 58, Philadelphia: John Benjamins, 1988, 379–417

Rahlfs, A., 'History of the Septuagint Text', in *Septuaginta,* Stuttgart: Deutsche Bibelgesellschaft, 1997, lvi–lxv

Rainey, A.F., 'Semantic Parallels to the Samaria Ostraca', *PEQ* 102 (1970), 45–51

Rebera, B.A., 'Lexical Cohesion in Ruth', in E. Conrad and E. Newing (eds.), *Perspectives on Language and Text: Essays and Poems in Honor of Francis I Andersen's Sixtieth Birthday,* Winona Lake: Eisenbrauns, 1987, 123–49

Regt, L.J. de, 'Multiple Meaning and Semantic Domains in Some Hebrew Lexicographical Projects: The Description of *zera''*, *ZAH* 10 (1997), 63–75

Reid, T.B.W., 'Linguistics, Structuralism and Philology', *ArLing* 8 (1956), 28–37

Rendsburg, G.A., 'Late Biblical Hebrew and the Date of "P"', *JANES* 12 (1980), 65–80

——, 'Bilingual Wordplay in the Bible', *VT* 38 (1988), 354–7

——, *Diglossia in Ancient Hebrew,* AOS 72, New Haven: AOS, 1990

——, *Linguistic Evidence for the Northern Origin of Selected Psalms,* SBLMS 43, Atlanta: Scholars Press, 1990

——, 'The Strata of Biblical Hebrew', *JNSL* 17 (1991), 81–99

——, 'Morphological Evidence for Regional Dialects in Ancient Hebrew', in Bodine, *Linguistics and Biblical Hebrew,* 1992, 65–88

Roberts, B.J., *The Old Testament Text and Versions: The Hebrew Text in Transmission and the History of the Ancient Versions,* Cardiff: University of Wales, 1951

Robertson, D.A., *Linguistic Evidence in Dating Early Hebrew Poetry,* SBLDS 3, Missoula: Scholars Press, 1972

Rooker, M.F., 'The Diachronic Study of Biblical Hebrew', *JNSL* 15 (1988), 199–213

——, *Biblical Hebrew in Transition: The Language of the Book of Ezekiel,* JSOTS 90, Sheffield: SAP, 1990

——, 'Diachronic Analysis and the Features of Late Biblical Hebrew', *BBR* 4 (1994), 135–44

Rosen, H.B., 'A Marginal Note on Biblical Hebrew Phonology', *JNES* 20 (1961), 124–6

Ryken, L., 'The Bible as Literature', *BSac* 147 (1990), 3–15; 131–42, 259–69, 387–98

Sáenz-Badillos, A., *A History of the Hebrew Language*, trans. J. Elwolde, Cambridge: CUP, 1993

Sarfatti, G.B., 'Hebrew Inscriptions of the First Temple Period: A Survey and Some Linguistic Comments', *Maarav* 3.1 (1982), 55–83

——, 'Mishnaic Vocabulary and Mishnaic Literature as Tools for the Study of Biblical Semantics', in Muraoka, *Studies in Ancient Hebrew Semantics*, 1995, 33–48

Satterthwaite, P.E., 'Narrative Criticism: The Theological Implications of Narrative Techniques', *NIDOTTE*, vol. 1, 125–33

Saussure, F. de, *Course in General Linguistics*, trans. W. Baskin, London: Fontana, 1974

Sawyer, J.F.A., 'Root-Meanings in Hebrew', *JSS* 12 (1967), 37–50

——, *Semantics in Biblical Research: New Methods of Defining Hebrew Words for Salvation*, SBT (second series), 24, London: SCM Press, 1972

——, 'Hebrew Words for the Resurrection of the Dead', *VT* 23 (1973), 218–34

——, 'The Meaning of בְּצֶלֶם אֱלֹהִים, in Genesis I–XI', *JThS* 25 (1974), 420–6

——, 'The "Original Meaning of the Text" and Other Legitimate Subjects for Semantic Description', in C. Brekelmans (ed.), *Questions Disputées D'Ancien Testament: Méthode et Théologie*, BETL 23, 1974, 63–70

——, 'A Historical Description of the Hebrew Root YŠʻ in Bynon and Bynon, *Hamito-Semitica*, 1975, 75–84

——, 'The Teaching of Classical Hebrew: Options and Priorities', in J.H. Hospers (ed.), *General Linguistics and the Teaching of Dead Hamito-Semitic Languages*, SSLL 9, Leiden: Brill, 1978, 37–50

——, 'Review of D.J.A. Clines (ed.), *The Dictionary of Classical Hebrew*', *Society for Old Testament Study BookList* (1994), 159–60

——, *Sacred Languages and Sacred Texts*, London: Routledge, 1999

Scanlin, H.P., 'What Is the Canonical Shape of the Old Testament Text We Translate?', in P.C. Stine (ed.), *Issues in Bible Translation*, UBS Monograph Series 3, London: UBS, 1988, 207–20

——, 'The Study of Semantics in General Linguistics', in Bodine, *Linguistics and Biblical Hebrew*, 1992, 125–36

Schlerath, B., 'On the Reality and Status of a Reconstructed Language', *JIES* 15 (1987), 41–6

Schreiner, J., 'Zum B-Text des griechischen Canticum Deborae', *Bib* 42 (1961), 333–58

Seeligman, I.L., 'Problems and Perspectives in Modern Septuagint Research', *Textus* 15 (1990), 169–232

Segal, M.H., 'Mishnaic Hebrew and Its Relation to Biblical Hebrew and Aramaic', *JQR* 20 (1908), 647–737

——, *A Grammar of Mishnaic Hebrew*, Oxford: Clarendon Press, 1978

Segert, S., 'Considerations on Semitic Comparative Lexicography', *ArOr* 28 (1960), 470–87

——, 'Hebrew Bible and Semitic Comparative Lexicography', *Congress Volume: Rome*, VTS 17, Leiden: Brill, 1969, 204–11

——, 'The Use of Comparative Semitic Material in Hebrew Lexicography', in Kaye, *Semitic Studies*, 1991, 1426–34

Sekine, M., 'The Subdivisions of the North-West Semitic Languages', *JSS* 18 (1973), 205–21

Seow, C.L., *A Grammar of Biblical Hebrew*, Nashville: Parthenon, 1987

Siertsema, B., 'Language and World View (Semantics for Theologians)', *BTrans* 20 (1969), 3–21

Silva, M., 'Review of A. Vivian's *I campi lessicali della "separazione" nell' ebraico biblico, di Qumran e della Mishna: ouvero, applicabilità della teoria dei campi lessicali all'ebraico*', *WTJ* 43 (1980–1), 329–95

——, *Biblical Words and Their Meaning: An Introduction to Lexical Semantics*, Grand Rapids: Zondervan, 1994

Smelik, W.F., *The Targum of Judges*, OTS 36, Leiden: Brill, 1995

Smolar, L. and M. Aberbach, *Studies in Targum Jonathan to the Prophets*, Library of Biblical Studies, New York: Ktav, 1983

Soggin, J.A., *Judges, Old Testament Library*, London: SCM Press, 1987

Southworth, F.C., 'Family-Tree Diagrams', *Lang* 40 (1964), 557–65

Sperber, A., *A Historical Grammar of Biblical Hebrew: A Presentation of Problems with Suggestions to Their Solution*, Leiden: Brill, 1966

——, *The Bible in Aramaic Based on Old Manuscripts and Printed Texts. Vol. 4B: The Targum and the Hebrew Bible*, Leiden: Brill, 1973

Swadesh, M., 'Towards Greater Accuracy in Lexicostatistic Dating', *IJAL* 21 (1955), 121–37

Swart, I., 'The Hebrew Vocabulary of Oppression: The State of Semantic Description', *JNSL* 16 (1990), 179–97

——, 'In search of the Meaning of *hamas*: Studying an Old Testament Word in Context', *JSem* 3 (1991), 156–66

Swiggers, P., 'The Meaning of the Root LHM "Food" in the Semitic Languages', *UF* 13 (1981), 307–8

——, 'Recent Developments in Linguistic Semantics and Their Application to Biblical Hebrew', *ZAH* 6 (1993), 21–5

——, 'Paradigmatical Semantics', *ZAH* 6 (1993), 44–54

Talmon, S., 'The Old Testament Text', in P.R. Ackroyd and C.F. Evans (eds.), *The Cambridge History of the Bible, Vol. 1: From the Beginnings to Jerome*, Cambridge: CUP, 1970, 159–99

——, 'The Textual Study of the Bible: A New Outlook', in F.M. Cross and S. Talmon (eds.), *Qumran and the History of the Biblical Text*, London: Harvard University Press, 1975, 321–400

Tångberg, K.A., 'Linguistics and Theology: An Attempt to Analyze and Evaluate James Barr's Argumentation in *The Semantics of Biblical Language and Biblical Words for Time*', *BTrans* 24 (1973), 301–10

Taylor, J.R., *Linguistic Categorization: Prototypes in Linguistic Theory*, Oxford: Clarendon Press, 1995

Tene, D. and J. Barr, 'Hebrew Linguistic Literature', *EncJud*, Jerusalem: Keter, 1972, 16:1352–1401

Thiselton, A.C., 'The Semantics of Biblical Language as an Aspect of Hermeneutics', *FT* 103 (1976), 108–20

——, 'Semantics and New Testament Interpretation', in I.H. Marshall, *New Testament Interpretation*, Exeter: Paternoster, 1977, 75–104

Tov, E., 'Lucian and Proto-Lucian: Toward a New Solution of the Problem', *RB* 79 (1972), 101–13

——, 'Three Dimensions of LXX Words', *RB* 83 (1976), 529–44

——, 'Compound Words in the LXX Representing Two or More Hebrew Words', *Bib* 58 (1977), 189–212

——, 'The Textual History of the Song of Deborah in the Text of the LXX', *VT* 28 (1978), 224–32

——, 'Loan-words, Homophony and Transliterations in the LXX', *Bib* 60 (1979), 216–36

——, 'Did the Septuagint Translators Always Understand Their Hebrew Text?', in A. Pietersma and C. Cox (eds.), *De*

Septuaginta: Studies in Honour of John William Wevers on His Sixty-Fifth Birthday, Ontario: Benten, 1984, 53–70

——, 'Hebrew Biblical Manuscripts from the Judean Desert: Their Contribution to Textual Criticism', *JJS* 39 (1988), 5–37

——, 'The Original Shape of the Biblical Text', *Congress Volume: Leuven*, VTS 43, Leiden: Brill, 1991, 345–59

——, *Textual Criticism of the Hebrew Bible*, Minneapolis: Fortress Press, 1992

——, *The Text-Critical Use of the Septuagint in Biblical Research*, Jerusalem Biblical Series 8, Jerusalem: Simor, 1997

Tov, E. and B.G. Wright, 'Computer-Assisted Study of the Criteria for Assessing the Literalness of Translation Units in the LXX', *Textus* 12 (1985), 149–87

Trier, J., *Der Deutsche Wortschatz im Sinnbezirk des Verstandes*, Heidelberg: Winter, 1931

Trudinger, P., 'To Whom Then Will You Liken God?', *VT* 17 (1967), 220–25

Tyloch, W., 'The Evidence of the Proto-Lexicon for the Cultural Background of the Semitic Peoples', in Bynon and Bynon, *Hamito-Semitica*, 1975, 55–61

Ullendorff, E., 'What Is a Semitic Language?' *OrNS* 28 (1958), 66–75

——, 'Comparative Semitics', in G. Levi della Vida (ed.), *Linguistica Semitica: Presente e futuro*, SS 4, Rome: Universit^ di Roma, 1961, 13–32

——, 'Review of J. Barr's *Comparative Philology and the Text of the Old Testament*', *BSOAS* 32 (1969), 143–8

——, 'Comparative Semitics', in T.A. Sebeok *et al.* (eds.), *CTL* 6: Linguistics in South West Asia and North Africa, The Hague: Mouton, 1970, 261–73

——, *Is Biblical Hebrew a Language? Studies in Semitic Languages and Civilizations*, Wiesbaden: Harrassowitz, 1977

——, 'Review of A. Saenz-Badillos, *A History of the Hebrew Language*', *JJS* 46 (1995), 283–92

Ullmann, S., *Principles of Semantics*, Oxford: Basil Blackwell, 1959

——, *Semantics*, Oxford: Basil Blackwell, 1962

Ulrich, E., 'The Canonical Process, Textual Criticism, and Latter Stages in the Composition of the Bible', in M. Fishbane and E. Tov (eds.), *'Sha'arei Talmon': Studies in the Bible, Qumran, and the Ancient Near East Presented to Shemaryahu Talmon*, Winona Lake: Eisenbrauns, 1992, 267–91

van der Merwe, C.H.J., 'Recent Trends in the Linguistic Description of Old Hebrew', *JNSL* 15 (1989), 217–41

——, 'The Vague Term "Emphasis"', *JSem* 1 (1989), 118–32

——, 'An Adequate Linguistic Framework for an Old Hebrew Linguistic Database: An Attempt to Formulate Some Criteria', *JSem* 2 (1990), 72–89

——, 'Discourse Linguistics and Biblical Hebrew Grammar', in R.D. Bergen (ed.), *Biblical Hebrew and Discourse Linguistics*, SIL, Winona Lake: Eisenbrauns, 1994, 13–49

——, 'Reconsidering Biblical Hebrew Temporal Expressions', *ZAH* 10 (1997), 42–62

van Wolde, E.J., 'A Text-Semantic Study of the Hebrew Bible, Illustrated with Noah and Job', *JBL* 113 (1994), 19–35

——, 'Telling and Retelling: The Words of the Servant in Gen. 24', in J.C. de Moor (ed.), *Synchronic or Diachronic? A Debate on Method in Old Testament Exegesis*, OTS 34, Leiden: Brill, 1995, 227–44

Vanhoozer, K., 'Language, Literature, Hermeneutics and Biblical Theology: What's Theological about a Theological Dictionary?', *NIDOTTE*, vol. 1, 15–50

Vivian, A., *I campi lessicali della 'separazione' nell' ebraico biblico, di Qumran e della Mishna ...*, QS 4, Università di Firenze, 1978

Voigt, R.M., 'The Classification of Central Semitic', *JSS* 32 (1987), 1–21

Von Soden, W., 'Nachwort zu G.R. Drivers "Objections"', *ZAW* 55 (1937), 71–2

Vööbus, A., 'Syriac Versions', in K. Crim *et al.* (eds.), *IDB Supplement*, Nashville: Abingdon, 1976, 848–54

Waard, J. de, 'Homophony in the LXX', *Bib* 62 (1981), 551–61

Waldman, N.M., *The Recent Study of Hebrew: A Survey of Literature with Selected Bibliography*, Winona Lake: Eisenbrauns, 1989

Walters, S.D., 'Review of J. Barr's *Comparative Philology and the Text of the Old Testament*', *JAOS* 89 (1969), 777–81

Waltke, B.K., 'The Aims of Old Testament Textual Criticism', *WTJ* 51 (1989), 93–108

——, 'Textual Criticism of the Old Testament and Its Relation to Exegesis and Theology', *NIDOTTE*, vol. 1, 51–67

Waltke, B.K. and M. O'Connor, *An Introduction to Biblical Hebrew Syntax*, Winona Lake: Eisenbrauns, 1990

Walton, J.H., 'Principles for Productive Word Study' in Van-Gemeren, *NIDOTTE*, vol. 1, 161–71

Washburn, D.L., 'Chomsky's Separation of Syntax and Semantics', *HS* 35 (1994), 27–46

Watson, W.G.E., 'Shared Consonants in NorthWest Semitic', *Bib* 50 (1969), 525–33

Webb, B.G., *The Book of Judges: An Integrated Reading*, JSOTS 46, Sheffield: SAP, 1987

Weinberg, J.P., 'The Word *ndb* in the Bible: A Study in Historical Semantics and Biblical Thought', in Zevit, Gitin and Sokoloff, *Solving Riddles and Untying Knots*, 1995, 365–75

Weinberg, W., 'Language Consciousness in the Old Testament', *ZAW* 92 (1980), 185–204

Weinreich, U., 'Is a Structural Dialectology Possible?', *Word* 10 (1954), 388–400

Weinstock, L.I., 'Sound and Meaning in Biblical Hebrew', *JSS* 28 (1983), 49–62

Weitzman, M., 'From Judaism to Christianity: The Syriac Version of the Hebrew Bible', in J. Lieu, J. North and T. Rajak (eds.), *The Jews among Pagans and Christians in the Roman Empire*, London: Routledge, 1994, 147–73

Wendland, E. and E.A. Nida, 'Lexicography and Bible Translating', in Louw, *Lexicography and Translation*, 1985, 1–52

Wernberg-Moller, P., 'Review of J. Barr's *Comparative Philology and the Text of the Old Testament*', *JThS* 20 (1969), 558–62

——, 'Review of J.F.A. Sawyer's *Semantics in Biblical Research: New Methods of Defining Hebrew Words for Salvation*', *JThS* 24 (1973), 215–17

Whitley, C.F., 'The Positive Force of the Hebrew Particle BL', *ZAW* 84 (1972), 213–19

Wilkinson, E., 'The *Hapax Legomenon* of Judges IV 18', *VT* 33 (1983), 512–13

Woude, A.S. van der, 'Some Remarks on Literary Critical Source Analysis of the Old Testament and Hebrew Semantics', in Muraoka, *Studies in Ancient Hebrew Semantics*, 1995, 49–54

Wright, W., *Lectures on Comparative Grammar of the Semitic Languages*, Cambridge: CUP, 1890

Wyk, W.C. van, 'The Present State of OT Lexicography', in Louw, *Lexicography and Translation*, 1985, 82–96

Yeivin, I., *Introduction to the Tiberian Masorah*, SBLMS 5, Missoula: Scholars Press, 1980

Young, I., 'The Style of the Gezer Calendar and Some "Archaic Biblical Hebrew" Passages', *VT* 42 (1992), 362–75

——, *Diversity in Pre-Exilic Hebrew*, FAT 5, Tübingen: Mohr, 1993

——, 'The "Northernisms" of the Israelite Narratives in Kings', *ZAH* 8:1 (1995), 63–70

Younger, K.L., 'Heads! Tails! Or the Whole Coin?! Contextual Method and Intertextual Analysis: Judges 4 and 5', in K.L. Younger, W.W. Hallo and B.F. Balto (eds.), *The Biblical Canon in Comparative Perspective: Scripture in Context IV*, ANE Texts and Studies, Lampeter: Edwin Mellen, 1991, 11:109–46

Zatelli, I., *Il campo lessicale degli aggettivi di purita in ebraico biblico*, QS 7, Florence: Università di Firenze, 1978

——, 'Pragmalinguistics and Speech-Act Theory as Applied to Classical Hebrew', *ZAH* 6 (1993), 60–74

——, 'Analysis of Lexemes from a Conversational Prose Text: *hnh* as Signal of a Performative Utterance in 1 Sam. 25:41', *ZAH* 7 (1994), 5–11

——, 'Functional Languages and Their Importance to the Semantics of Ancient Hebrew', in Muraoka, *Studies in Ancient Hebrew Semantics*, 1995, 55–64

Zevit, Z., 'Converging Lines of Evidence Bearing on the Date of P', *ZAW* 94 (1982), 481–511

Zevit, Z., S. Gitin and M. Sokoloff (eds.), *Solving Riddles and Untying Knots: Biblical, Epigraphic, and Semitic Studies in Honor of Jonas C. Greenfield*, Winona Lake: Eisenbrauns, 1995